Expert Advice From The Home Depot®

Wiring 1-2-3®

Meredith® **BOOKS**

Wiring 1-2-3®

Writer: Steve Cory
Copy Chief: Terri Fredrickson
Publishing Operations Manager: Karen Schirm
Senior Editor, Asset and Information Manager: Phillip Morgan
Edit and Design Coordinator: Mary Lee Gavin
Editorial and Design Assistant: Renee E. McAtee
Book Production Managers: Pam Kvitne, Marjorie J. Schenkelberg, Rick von Holdt, Mark Weaver
Contributing Proofreaders: Jane Carlson, David Craft, Sue Fetters, David Krause, Cheri Madison, Joel Marvin
Indexer: Donald Glassman

Additional Editorial and Design contributions from Abramowitz Creative Studios

Publishing Director/Designer: Tim Abramowitz
Graphic Designer: Joel Wires
Photography: Image Studios
    Account Executive: Lisa Egan
    Photographers: Bill Rein, John von Dorn
    Assistants: Rob Resnick, Scott Verber
    Technical Advisor: Rick Nadke
Additional Photography: Doug Hetherington
Illustration: Jim Swanson, Performance Marketing

Meredith® Books

Executive Director, Editorial: Gregory H. Kayko
Executive Director, Design: Matt Strelecki
Managing Editor: Amy Tincher-Durik
Executive Editor/Group Manager: Benjamin W. Allen
Senior Associate Design Director: Tom Wegner
Marketing Product Manager: Isaac Petersen

Publisher and Editor in Chief: James D. Blume
Editorial Director: Linda Raglan Cunningham
Executive Director, New Business Development: Todd M. Davis
Director, Sales-Home Depot: Robb Morris
Executive Director, Sales: Ken Zagor
Director, Operations: George A. Susral
Director, Production: Douglas M. Johnston
Director, Marketing: Amy Nichols
Business Director: Jim Leonard

Vice President and General Manager: Douglas J. Guendel

Meredith Publishing Group

President: Jack Griffin
Senior Vice President: Bob Mate

Meredith Corporation

Chairman and Chief Executive Officer: William T. Kerr
President and Chief Operating Officer: Stephen M. Lacy

In Memoriam: E.T. Meredith III (1933-2003)

The Home Depot®

Marketing Manager: Tom Sattler
© Copyright 2005 by Homer TLC, Inc. Second Edition.
All rights reserved. Printed in the United States of America.
Library of Congress Control Number: 2005928791
ISBN: 0-696-22812-2
The Home Depot® and **1-2-3®** are registered trademarks of Homer TLC, Inc.

Distributed by Meredith Corporation.
Meredith Corporation is not affiliated with The Home Depot®.

We are dedicated to providing accurate and helpful do-it-yourself information. We welcome your comments about improving this book and ideas for other books we might offer to home improvement enthusiasts. Contact us by any of these methods:
Leave a voice message at: 800/678-2093
Write to: Meredith Books, Home Depot Books
    1716 Locust St.
    Des Moines, IA 50309–3023
Send e-mail to: hi123@mdp.com.

How to use this book

Wiring *1-2-3* is filled with practical home wiring projects you can do! Professional electricians from The Home Depot stores across the United States and Canada provided projects that people like you want to do. And they have checked the book for accuracy—an important consideration when dealing with electricity. They helped make sure the book has all the steps for you to successfully complete each project.

Start by reading **Safety first.** It walks you through basic rules for working with electricity. Throughout the book, pay close attention to **bold red type** and safety tips marked with stop signs.

If you're new to wiring projects or just need to brush up on the facts concerning home wiring, check out **Understanding wiring**. It provides you with knowledge of what you're working with before you start a project.

Basic tools and skills will help you prepare for most of the projects in this book. Any special skill required in the more difficult projects are usually covered with the project.

To discover what electrical upgrades you may need in your home, turn to the chapter on **Inspecting your home**.

Good lighting does more than illuminate. Turn to **Planning lighting** for help using lights to create indoor and outdoor areas with style and function.

Switches and receptacles and **Ceiling lights and fixtures** show you how to replace existing devices and fixtures with new ones. Projects like this usually do not require an inspection, and are usually simple tasks that involve detaching old wires and attaching new wires. Projects include installing special-duty switches, GFCI receptacles, track lighting, a ceiling fan, and grounding receptacles.

Once you've completed some easy upgrades, you'll have the skills to move on to **Planning for new services**.

Learn what tools you need and how to draw plans. Now you should be ready to tackle **Running new cable** and **Installing new services**.

Running new cable provides directions for installing lines, not only in new framing but also in a home that has finished walls. Turn to **Installing new services** when you're ready to run new cable to install a new electrical device or fixture. This type of work is more complicated than simply replacing existing devices or fixtures, and you will need to work with an inspector and conform to local codes.

Exhaust fans and vents shows how to install the major types of vent fans, to make your home more comfortable. **Outdoor wiring projects** describes the special techniques and materials used when running both low-voltage and standard-voltage wiring to your yard.

Home networking covers both new high-tech setups and the more mundane tasks of running phone lines.

Major projects covers installations that involve adding new circuits. Work through the projects in this chapter only after you've successfully completed projects throughout the book. If your local codes don't allow homeowners to add new circuits, this chapter will provide you with information to understand the project you're hiring an electrician to complete.

Electrical repairs shows how to fix lamps, plugs, wiring in boxes, and chimes.

If you prefer to hire a pro, you will still find this book valuable because it will provide you with the knowledge to make the right choice and help you judge the work that's done.

For the do-it-yourselfer, *Wiring 1-2-3* provides step-by-step directions, tips from the pros, lighting design ideas, and safety information to help you safely, easily, and accurately complete your home wiring projects and stylishly light your home.

Wiring 1-2-3®
Table of contents

Chapter 1
UNDERSTANDING WIRING   7

Chapter 2
BASIC TOOLS AND SKILLS   25

Chapter 3
INSPECTING YOUR HOME   36

Chapter 4
PLANNING LIGHTING   51

Chapter 5
SWITCHES AND RECEPTACLES   65

Chapter 6
CEILING LIGHTS AND FIXTURES   83

Chapter 7
PLANNING FOR NEW SERVICES   105

Safety first

Electricians and others who have worked with electricity for years know they always have to follow safety precautions. They've heard hair-raising stories about what happens to people who ignore safe work habits. This book is loaded with safety reminders to help you stay safe while you work. Follow them.

Electricity deserves your respect. Consider how household current can affect the human body. If your feet are dry and you are wearing rubber-soled shoes, receiving a shock from a 120-volt circuit will definitely hurt, but it will probably not cause you serious harm. However, if conditions are wet or your feet are not protected with rubber-soled shoes and you are standing on the ground or on a metal ladder, 120 volts can cause the muscles in your hands to contract so that you grasp the source of current involuntarily. The current will cause your heart to beat wildly, very likely to the point of heart failure. Expect the same consequence if you touch both live wires of a 240-volt circuit, even if your feet are dry and protected. Children are in even greater danger.

The wiring in a modern home should have safety features, such as grounding, ground fault circuit interruption and arc fault circuit interruption. (See pages 38–46 for how to inspect your home for these and other safety considerations.) All reduce the possibility of dangerous shock, but they don't offer complete protection to a person working on exposed wires and devices. This is why professional electricians work carefully. So should you.

Here are a few basic rules for safe electrical work. Follow them at all times, even when you are doing "just a little" electrical job.

POST A SIGN ON THE PANEL
Take steps to make absolutely certain that no one will turn the power back on while you are working. If possible, lock the service panel.

USE RUBBER-GRIPPED TOOLS
Don't use tools with plastic or wood handles unless they also have rubber sleeves to provide extra protection against electrical shock.

USE OF ELECTRICIAN'S TAPE
Electrician's tape can provides extra protection against dangerous ground faults and shorts. However, many inspectors prefer that it not be used so they can see your work. Besides, if tape is what is holding the wire nut on, you haven't installed the wire nut properly.

BE PROTECTED FROM THE GROUND UP
Always keep your feet protected with rubber soles, to lessen the effects of a possible shock. In damp areas stand on dry boards.

Shut off the power
If there is no electrical power, you cannot receive a shock. **Always shut off power to the circuit you are working on.** Do this by flipping a circuit breaker or completely unscrewing a fuse. Then test for the presence of power (see pages 30–31).

Test for power
Be aware that more than one circuit may be running in a box. **Test all the wires in an open box for power, not just the wires you will be working on. Test everything twice.**

Regularly test your tester to make sure it will indeed tell you when power is present. Touch it to a live circuit and see that it glows just before every test. Many a war story tells of someone turning off the power, only to have a family member or co-worker turn it back on while work is in progress. Post a sign telling people not to restore power.

Stay focused
Most electrical mishaps occur because of small mental mistakes. Remove all distractions. Keep people, especially children, well out of the way. Turn the radio off. **Even after turning off the power, work as if the wires are live.** Work methodically, and double-check all connections before restoring power.

Use protective tools and clothing
Rubber grips offer more protection than plastic or wood handles, so always **use rubber-gripped tools when wiring.** Get in the habit of using them correctly: Grab by the handle, not the metal shaft. Make sure your pliers and cutting tools have rubber grips that are long enough so you will not be tempted to touch the metal while working. Replace a tool when the rubber is damaged.

Wear rubber-soled shoes, such as athletic shoes, and perhaps rubber gloves, so that electrical current will not travel easily through you and into the ground. Never work with wet feet or while standing on a wet surface. **Do not wear jewelry or a watch**—anything that could possibly get snagged on wires. **Use a fiberglass or wood ladder;** an aluminum ladder conducts electricity.

Ask questions
Electricians consult with each other all the time, even when they are 99 percent sure they already understand. **Never proceed with an installation or repair unless you are completely sure you know what you are doing.** Don't hesitate to ask "stupid" questions of electrical experts in a Home Depot or an electrical supply store.

Understanding wiring

Chapter 1 highlights

Wiring contributes to the convenience of life. Flip a switch or turn a knob, and electricity instantly goes to work. Occasionally, however, a lamp flickers or a receptacle goes dead. Many electrical procedures are well within the range of most homeowners, but because electricity can be dangerous to work with, it may be tempting to call a professional electrician.

This chapter equips you with the basic knowledge you need to safely work on your home's wiring. It introduces you to the purpose and function of every wire and every device in your home. Take the time to become knowledgeable about how your home circuits work. Familiarize yourself with standard safeguards against electrical shocks and fire. For many projects you may decide to call in a pro, but this chapter will prepare you to understand what makes a job safe and reliable—useful information whether you do it yourself or hire someone to do the work.

How power gets distributed

If you need to plug in a lamp, you find an outlet, right? Well, almost. Technically, an electrical outlet is anyplace where electricity leaves the wires to perform a service—such as at a light fixture. A receptacle is a type of outlet; it is where electricity exits the system through, say, a toaster plug. A device is something that carries, but does not use, electricity itself; receptacles and switches are devices. A fixture is an electrical outlet that is permanently fixed in place, and an appliance is a user of electricity that can be moved. Thus an overhead light is a fixture, and a microwave oven is an appliance.

Electricity is the flow of electrons through a conductor—copper or aluminum wires in household construction. Electricity must travel in a loop, called a circuit. In most cases power travels out to a fixture or device through a hot wire—usually coated with black or red insulation—and back through a neutral wire, which has white insulation. When the circuit is broken at any point, power ceases to flow.

Newer homes are grounded. Grounding connects all outlets to the earth and is an essential safety feature (pages 11 and 17-18). Ungrounded outlets can give a serious shock if there is a short circuit because of a damaged wire or device. Ground wires are either bare copper or have green insulation. Polarization is an additional safety feature found in both older and newer homes (page 11).

Voltage and amps

Voltage is the electrical pressure exerted by the power source. Most household fixtures use 120 volts. Large items such as ranges and central air-conditioners require 240 volts. On the packaging of electrical devices or in manufacturer's instructions, you may see voltage figures, such as 115, 125, 220, or even 250 volts. These numbers reflect the fact that voltage can vary; a 115-volt receptacle is interchangeable with a receptacle rated at 125 volts. Here we'll refer to 120-volt and 240-volt circuits.

The pressure on all wires is approximately 120 or 240 volts, but the amount of electricity used by each fixture or appliance varies. This is because wires, fixtures, and appliances have different resistance to the voltage. Simply put, the thicker the wire, the more electricity travels through it. The terms amperes (or amps) and watts refer to the amount of electrical current and power that specific elements of a system use (pages 112-113).

From utility to home

Electrical power flows into neighborhoods through overhead (or underground) high-voltage wires. Transformers reduce the voltage so that the wires entering homes carry a relatively safe 120 volts per wire. Through a service head these wires enter a meter. The meter records for billing purposes how much power residents in a home use. The wires then enter the home's service panel, which divides the power into branch circuits (see opposite page).

Most homes have three wires—two "hot" wires to carry power into the house and one neutral wire to carry power back to complete the circuit. Having two hot wires means that a home can run 120-volt circuits and 240-volt circuits (for large appliances). Older homes with only two wires entering the home—a hot and a neutral—can run only 120-volt outlets. Some appliances, such as electric water heaters, are hardwired to the circuit (wires are attached directly to the unit without the use of a plug or receptacle).

Underground electrical service to homes is usually provided by three wires—two black and one white—that travel through a pipe called conduit. On occasion you may fine a black, red and white wire. Overhead service is usually provided by three wires, one of which may be bare. They all connect to the house at a service head. These wires must not be damaged. If an overhead wire rubs against a tree or if an underground line seems exposed, call your utility company. For tips on inspecting a service entrance, see page 43.

Know your limits

You can perform most repairs and installations on wires, devices, and fixtures in the home, but do not touch anything outside the home. Never touch wires leading to the service panel or wires upstream from the main shutoff (page 43). If you have questions about the wires entering your house or leading from the meter to the service panel, call your utility company. These wires are usually their legal responsibility.

From service head to receptacle

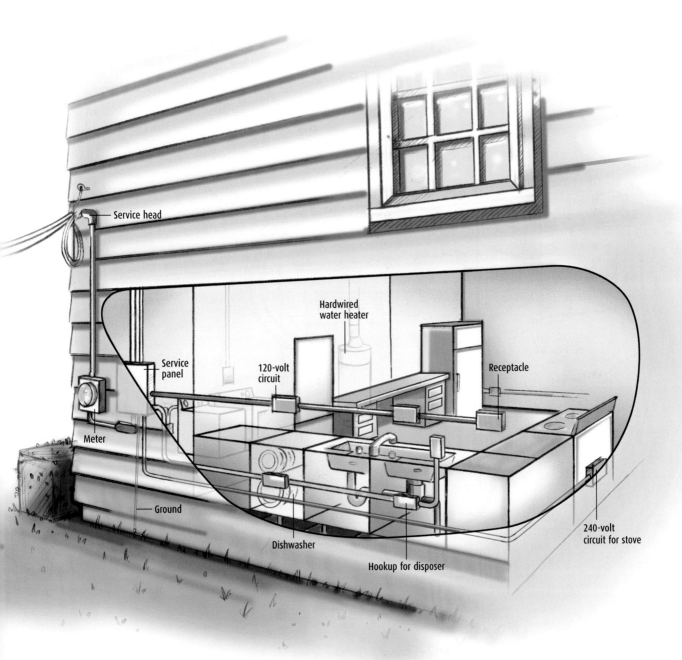

Service head

Hardwired
water heater

Service
panel

120-volt
circuit

Receptacle

Meter

Ground

Dishwasher

Hookup for disposer

240-volt
circuit for stove

How a circuit works

Service panels, whether they have breakers or fuses, divide household current into several circuits. Each circuit carries power from the service panel via hot (usually black or red) wires to various outlets in the house, and then back to the service panel via a neutral (usually white) wire.

Types of circuits

Most household circuits carry 120 volts. There also may be several 240-volt circuits. Circuits are rated according to amps. If the outlets on a circuit draw too many amps, the circuit overloads. When this happens, a fuse will blow or a breaker will trip (pages 26-27), preventing an unsafe condition.

A 120-volt circuit usually serves a number of outlets. For instance, it may supply power to a series of lights, a series of receptacles, or some of each. Heavy-use items, such as dishwashers and refrigerators, may have their own dedicated circuits. A 240-volt circuit is always dedicated to one outlet. A standard 120-volt 15-amp circuit uses #14 wire; a 20-amp circuit uses thicker #12 wire. Until recently 240-volt circuits used three wires—two hot and one neutral. Recent codes require four wires, as shown below; the added wire is for grounding.

Circuits provide convenience as well as safety. If a repair or new installation is under way, you can shut off power to an individual circuit instead of the entire house.

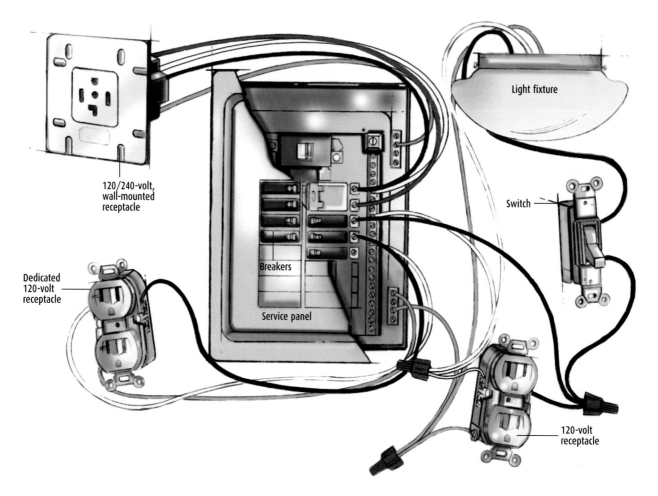

120/240-volt, wall-mounted receptacle

Dedicated 120-volt receptacle

Breakers

Service panel

Light fixture

Switch

120-volt receptacle

A SERVICE PANEL HAS 120- AND 240-VOLT CIRCUITS
Your service panel distributes power according to the needs of a circuit. For example, a 240-volt circuit is designed to supply electricity to a heavy-duty user of power, such as an electric range or a dryer. The single receptacle on a dedicated 120-volt circuit might feed a refrigerator or a large

microwave, while another 120-volt circuit feeds a series of receptacles and switched overhead light fixtures. Depending on local code and the manufacturer, some switches may not have a grounding wire.

Grounding and polarization

Normally, electricity travels in insulated wires and exits through a light fixture into a bulb, for example. If a wire comes loose or if a device cracks, a short circuit (ground fault) results, energizing something you don't want to be energized. A short can occur if a loose wire inside a dryer touches the dryer's frame or if cracked insulation allows bare wire to touch a metal electrical box. If you touch energized metal, you'll get a dangerous shock. Grounding and polarization protect against this. Here's how they work:

Grounding

Grounding minimizes the possibility that a short circuit will cause a shock. A grounded device, fixture, or appliance is usually connected to a grounding wire—either bare or green—which leads to the neutral bar in the service panel. This bar is connected to the earth by one or a combination of these:

- cold-water pipe
- grounding rods driven deep in the ground
- metal plate sunk in a footing or in undisturbed soil.

When a ground fault occurs, the ground path carries the power to the service panel. This extra path lowers resistance, causing a great deal of power to flow back to the panel. This in turn trips a circuit breaker or blows a fuse. At the same time, power is directed harmlessly into the earth.

Whether your system uses grounding wires or conduit as the ground path, it must be unbroken in order to operate safely. A single disconnected ground wire or a loose connection in the sheathing or conduit can make the grounding system useless. To check whether a receptacle is grounded, plug in a receptacle analyzer (page 30).

Polarization

Polarization is a way of making sure that electricity goes where you want it to go. Because a polarized plug has one prong wider than the other, there is only one way that the plug can be inserted into a polarized receptacle. If the receptacle is wired correctly and an appliance plug is polarized, the hot wire, and not the neutral wire, will always be controlled by the appliance switch. If the receptacle or plug isn't polarized, the neutral wire might be connected to the appliance switch instead, and power would be present in the appliance even when it is switched off. For extra protection against shock, install GFCI protection (page 74).

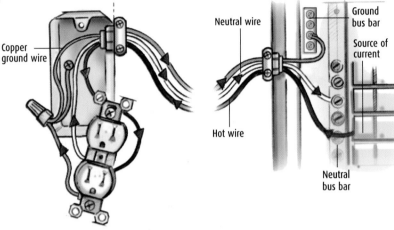

HOW A GROUNDED RECEPTACLE WORKS
To ground a receptacle, a ground wire (either bare or green) is attached to the receptacle (and to the box, if it is metal) and leads to the neutral bus bar in the service panel. The panel itself is grounded (pages 19-21). This receptacle is also polarized.

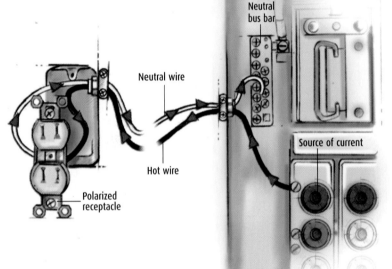

HOW A POLARIZED RECEPTACLE WORKS
The black wire is connected to the receptacle's brass terminal at one end and to the circuit breaker or fuse at the other end. The white wire runs from the silver terminal screw to the service panel's neutral bus bar.

Wires and cables

 REAL WORLD

While remodeling my old house, I pulled off the plaster and found cable running through the walls. It seemed in pretty good shape and had a ground wire, so I left it. Bad move. Electrical cable doesn't last forever. Even though the insulation wasn't cracked, it's possible that it will deteriorate within the next 20 years. I blew the chance to replace it easily.

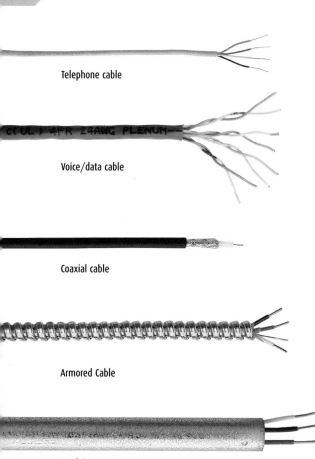

Telephone cable

Voice/data cable

Coaxial cable

Armored Cable

Conduit

Use the right wire and cable to avoid creating a dangerous situation that you'll have to tear out and redo. Here are the basics:

Wires

Wire is usually made of a single, solid strand of metal encased in insulation. For flexibility and ease of pulling, some wire is stranded. Wire is sized according to American Wire Gauge (AWG) categories. Size determines how much amperage the wire will carry. Common household wires and their ratings are:

- #14 wire (also called 14-gauge) carries 15 amps
- #12 wire carries 20 amps
- #10 wire carries 30 amps

If a wire carries more amperage than it is rated for, it will dangerously overheat. Older wires have rubber insulation, which lasts about 30 years. New wires have longer-lasting polyvinyl insulation. Insulation color often tells the function of wire. Black, red, or other colors indicate hot wire. White or off-white generally is neutral. Green or bare wire is ground.

Types of electrical cable

Cable is two or more wires wrapped together in plastic or metal sheathing. Nonmetallic (NM) cable is permitted inside wall, ceiling, and floor cavities. Special metal plates must be added to the framing to protect the cable from puncture (page 126). Printing on cable tells you what is inside: 12/3 means there are three #12 wires, not counting the ground wire. "G" means that there is a ground wire. For underground installations and in damp areas, use NMWU cable (also called underground-feed (UF) cable). NMWU cable encases the wires in solid plastic. Telephone cable is being supplanted by Cat 5e cable, suitable for telephones, modems, and computer networking. Coaxial cable carries television signals. Armored cable (pages 120–121) has a flexible metal sheathing but no ground wire—the sheathing is used for grounding. Conduit is a solid pipe through which individual wires are run (pages 122–123). Metal conduit is often required in commercial installations. Most building departments require it only where the wiring is exposed. Regardless of which types of cable are available you should contact your local building department or electrical inspector to find out which types of cable are allowable by your local codes.

Types of NM cable

In addition to the older type of NM cable shown on the opposite page, there are several other variations you may encounter. Cable with no printing, or printing that just reads "NM," is rated safe at temperatures up to 60 degrees C. NM-B is rated safe at 90 degrees C, making it safer in places exposed to the sun, or during a fire. NM-C cable has the same heat rating, but it has a tougher sheathing. Use NMD for most household wiring, and NM-C when the cable may be exposed to abuse (as when it runs exposed in a basement or garage), or when you need to embed the cable in concrete or mortar.

Older types of cable

In an older home you may encounter cables and wires that don't look like those on page 12. Don't panic; old wiring can remain durable and safe for decades if left undisturbed. However, it is possible the wiring could pose a hazard, so take the time to evaluate your wiring.

Fabric-sheathed nonmetallic (NM) cable has a rubberized fabric that encases the individual wires. Inside the sheathing there is paper wrapping around the plastic-insulated wires. Some old NM has only hot and neutral wires, with no grounding wire, which means that your system is not grounded (see page 11).

Knob-and-tube wiring uses two separate wires that run through porcelain knobs (which are nailed onto wood framing members) or tubes (which run through framing members). One wire is hot and the other is neutral, but it is often difficult to tell which is which once the wires get dirty. There is no ground wire, so the system is not grounded.

Older BX cable has a heavy sheathing and wires that are covered with fabric insulation. Like metal conduit that has no ground wire running through it, this wiring is grounded using the sheathing, rather than a separate wire. Don't use the thin metal "bonding wire" for a ground wire; it is there only to solidify the bond between the sheathing and the electrical box's clamp.

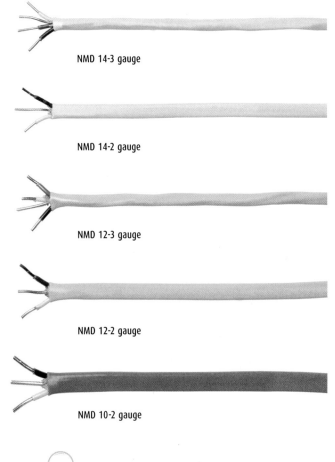

NMD 14-3 gauge

NMD 14-2 gauge

NMD 12-3 gauge

NMD 12-2 gauge

NMD 10-2 gauge

CLOSER LOOK

COMMON PROBLEMS WITH OLD WIRING

Replace old wiring whenever you get a chance—for example, when you are remodeling, or where wiring is exposed in a basement or garage. In many cases it is alright to leave old wiring where it is, as long as it is not exposed to damage.

If the wires in a box have brittle or cracked insulation, that does not necessarily mean that the wires running through your walls are in the same shape. Wires that are encased in sheathing are not exposed to the air, so their insulation stays flexible and strong much longer than wiring that is exposed. (Of course this does not apply to knob-and-tube wiring, which is exposed everywhere it runs.)

Old wiring gets dirty, so you often cannot tell a white neutral wire from a black hot wire. As a result many replacement switches or light fixtures get wrongly wired: The neutral, rather than the hot, wire is put on the switch (see pages 22–24 for ways to wire a switch). A neutral-switched light will switch on and off, but power will be present in the box even after the switch is off—a somewhat dangerous situation. To determine the wire color, shut off the power and wash the insulation by gently rubbing it with an alcohol-soaked rag.

Wire nuts and tape

W ire nuts, sometimes referred to as marettes, must cap all wire splices. These nuts come in several sizes, identified by color. On the package you will find a chart telling how many wires of a given size the nut can handle.

In older homes you may find spliced wire ends wrapped with rubberized tape that is covered with cloth friction tape. Electricians often wrapped these well, so you may find them difficult to unwrap. (Slice with a utility knife before unwinding.)

Small, colored wire nuts are often included with light fixtures. If they are all plastic (with no metal threads inside) or if it is a challenge to get them to twist on because they are too small, use orange nuts instead. Use yellow connectors for splices as small as two #14s or as large as three #12s. Orange nuts handle combinations ranging from two #16 wires up to two #14s. Use green wire nuts for ground wires only. The hole in the top allows you to make an instant pigtail, with one wire poking out. Red wire nuts will grab splices as small as two #12s and as large as four #12s.

BUYER'S GUIDE

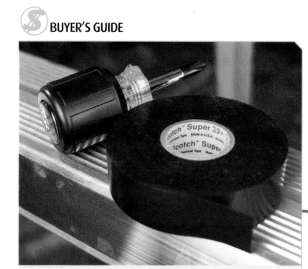

GET THE GOOD TAPE

The inexpensive tape often found in large bins at a home center will do the job, but many electricians prefer to use professional-quality tape. It's thicker and has better adhesive.

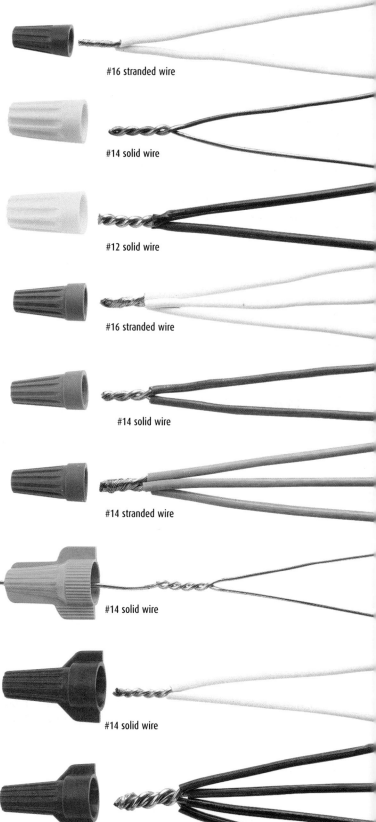

#16 stranded wire

#14 solid wire

#12 solid wire

#16 stranded wire

#14 solid wire

#14 stranded wire

#14 solid wire

#14 solid wire

#12 solid wire

Receptacles and switches

Switches and receptacles usually provide trouble-free operation for decades. However, they are not indestructible. If one of yours is cracked, singed, or seems too loose, replace it (pages 66-73).

Wires and amps

Most circuits comprise three elements—switches and/or receptacles, a circuit breaker, and the wire that connects them. Each must be compatible with the others.

Most switches and receptacles in a home are designed to carry 15 amps. Any 15-amp device should be connected to #14 wire (opposite page), which should lead to a 15-amp fuse or circuit breaker in the service panel. Twenty-amp circuits require a 20-amp switch or receptacle, #12 wire, and a 20-amp breaker. Other combinations can be dangerous: Overloading a circuit can lead to overheating, which can cause a fire. For example, if a 15-amp receptacle is connected to a fuse or breaker that is 20-amp or greater, the receptacle could be dangerously overloaded before the breaker trips.

Fifteen-amp GFCI receptacles (page 74) required in bathrooms and kitchens are the exception to this rule. They are rated for what is referred to as 20-amp pass-through because the motors in many appliances require more electricity at start-up (called power surge), but once they are running need only 15 amps to operate properly.

Be sure that the amperage of a 240-volt receptacle is rated no lower than that of the appliance. If you are not sure which receptacle to use, check with your local building department or ask an electrician.

Ground hole up or down?

Some electricians install receptacles with the ground holes down (when the receptacles are vertical) or to the right (when they're horizontal). Others do ground up or to the left.

Ground down and to the right is most common, but choose one way and then install them the same way throughout your house.

Choosing a 120-volt receptacle

Neutral slot

Ground hole

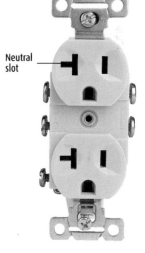

Neutral slot

UNGROUNDED 120-VOLT RECEPTACLE
This type of receptacle has two slots, with no hole for a grounding prong. This one is polarized (page 11), with one slot longer than the other so that a polarized plug can be inserted only one way.

GROUNDED 15-AMP, 120-VOLT RECEPTACLE
This receptacle is the most common household electrical device. It will serve most lamps and appliances and will overload if you plug in two heavy-use items that total more than 15 amps.

20-AMP, 120-VOLT RECEPTACLE
This receptacle has a neutral slot shaped like a sideways T so you can confidently plug in large appliances or heavy-use tools. It should connect to #12 wires that lead to a 20-amp circuit or fuse in the service panel.

Choosing a 240-volt receptacle

WALL-MOUNTED 120-VOLT 50 AMP STOVE RECEPTACLE

Appliances using more power have different plug designs so they can't be plugged into the wrong receptacle. To be safe check the information plate on the appliance to confirm that the amperage matches that of the receptacle.

SURFACE-MOUNTED 120/240-VOLT 50 AMP RECEPTACLE

Some heavy-duty appliances require receptacles with both standard voltage and high voltage. For example, a range commonly uses 240 volts for its burners and 120 volts for the light and the clock. A 120/240-volt receptacle provides both levels of power.

WALL-MOUNTED 120/240-VOLT 30 AMP RECEPTACLE

This wall-mounted receptacle is typically used with a dryer. Install it in an electrical box specifically designed for this receptacle. Like the stove receptacle to the left, this receptacle has a unique design so only appropriate appliances can be plugged into it.

Choosing a switch

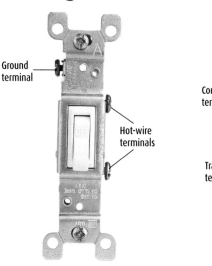

Ground terminal

Hot-wire terminals

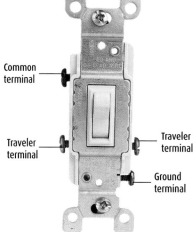

Common terminal

Traveler terminal

Traveler terminal

Ground terminal

SAFETY ALERT

THREE OR FOUR?

At one time it was common to wire high-voltage receptacles with three wires—two hot and one neutral for a 120/240 receptacle; two hot and one ground wire for a 240-volt receptacle. Current codes, however, often require a fourth wire so that the receptacle has both a ground and a neutral for added protection. See page 80 for the most common application—rewiring a dryer with a three-prong plug so it fits into a four-hole plug.

You are probably not required to upgrade existing three-wire receptacles. However, when remodeling, you may need to make the change; check local codes.

SINGLE-POLE SWITCH

This is the workhorse switch in your home. It has two terminals for hot wires and may also have a green terminal for a ground wire. The toggle is labeled ON and OFF and should be connected to two #14 wires. These wires should be two black wires or a black wire and a white wire that has been marked (pages 66–67). Check local codes.

THREE-WAY SWITCH

Three-ways are always installed in pairs—both switches control the same light(s). There are no ON and OFF markings on the toggle. The common terminal is where you attach the wire bearing power from the source or to the fixture. (See page 68 for how to wire a three-way switch.) Some three way switches have a ground terminal but others may not.

Grounding methods

Before you begin any electrical work, find out how your system is grounded. First plug a receptacle analyzer (page 30) into every receptacle to make sure it is grounded. Then check your service panel to make sure it's grounded—there should be a thick wire running from the neutral bus bar and firmly clamped onto a pipe or to grounding rods. Finally, look at the wiring of your receptacles or fixtures to see how they're grounded (opposite page).

If you have an older home without grounding, you should ground any new circuits you install. It is also possible to ground individual receptacles (page 81). A GFCI that is ungrounded can offer substantial protection for individual circuits (page 74).

Jumper cable

Water meter

JUMP A WATER METER

Grounding can be provided by attaching wires to a water pipe. However, there must be an unbroken path for a ground that uses a water pipe. A water meter, for instance, breaks the path. Make sure that the ground wire is connected on the upstream side of the meter (toward the street, not the house) or that there is a jumper cable, as shown. Local codes may require the jumper wire, as shown above, to run back to the panel to attach to neutral.

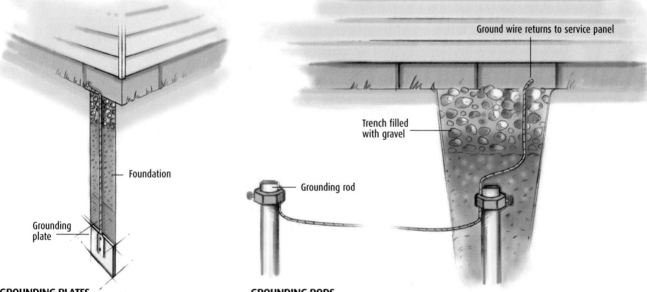

Foundation

Grounding plate

Ground wire returns to service panel

Trench filled with gravel

Grounding rod

GROUNDING PLATES

A house's ground wire may be attached to a grounding plate embedded in the concrete of a footing or foundation. Sometimes local codes allow you to use a grounding plate buried two feet deep in a horizontal position. Check your local codes to determine your options for grounding.

GROUNDING RODS

Usually, a standard grounding rod provides the best connection into the earth. Many systems use a single rod, but some codes require two connected rods, spaced at least 10 feet apart. A rod must be at least 10 feet long. Damp soil provides better grounding conditions than dry soil. If you have dry soil, add another rod or two to improve the connection. The grounding wire must be connected firmly to the rod, either with a special clamp or by welding. Local codes specify how deep the top of the rod should be buried.

How receptacles are grounded

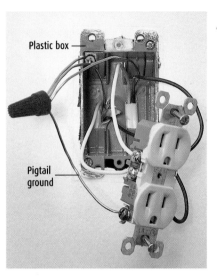

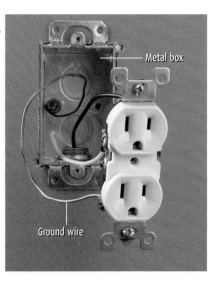

GROUND 'EM FIRST!

Always connect the ground wires first. Once you are sure all the ground connections are firm, connect the neutral wire, then the hot wire. To ensure a solid connection between the receptacle and the box, remove the cardboard washer from the receptacle's screws.

If you forget to ground a device, you may not detect the resulting danger because the ungrounded device or fixture will work just fine. Always test receptacles using a receptacle analyzer (page 30).

CABLES IN A PLASTIC BOX

Because plastic boxes do not conduct electricity, the receptacle must be grounded by attaching it to the bare ground wire in the cable. Check that bare copper grounding wires are spliced together and are attached to the grounding screw of the receptacle with a pigtail ground wire.

CONDUIT IN A METAL BOX

If conduit enters the box, it's likely it acts as the ground for the receptacle. To ground the receptacle, connect copper wire to the back of the box and the ground screw on the receptacle. Check the receptacle with an analyzer (pages 30–31) to make sure it is grounded.

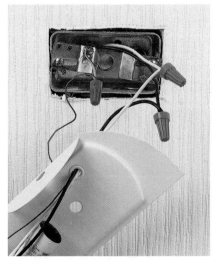

CABLE IN A METAL BOX

If one cable enters the box, you can ground the receptacle simply by attaching the ground wire directly to the ground screw on the receptacle and the box. This saves room in the box because you do not need to use a wire nut. Some local codes and inspectors insist on the grounding method as shown above. Check your codes before you do the work so you are not made to do it over.

TWO CABLES IN A METAL BOX

If cable enters a metal box, it's likely the metal box is NOT grounded. Ground the receptacle the way you would a plastic box with cables coming into it. Use a wire nut to connect the two bare ground wires to a third wire that is attached to the receptacle's ground screw and to the box. If there is not enough room in the box replace it with a deeper box sized to accommodate the receptacle, cables, and wire nuts.

GROUNDING LIGHT FIXTURES

Your light fixtures should be grounded. Whether a light fixture box is metal or plastic, a grounding wire should be connected to the fixture. The ground connection may be made to a fixture's thin ground wire or to a screw on the mounting strap. If the box is metal, it should also be connected to a ground wire.

Know your service panel

Find your home's service panel and learn how it works before you start wiring inspections, repairs, or installations. It's where you'll turn off power to circuits that you are working on and where you will run to when a circuit blows.

How a service panel works

A service panel is the nerve center of your household's electrical system. It routes power to the circuits in your home and shuts down any circuit that gets overloaded. Every adult in your house should know how to safely reach the service panel to turn off or restore electricity.

Power from the utility company enters the panel through three thick main wires—two hots and one neutral. The main neutral wire connects to a neutral bus bar, and the two hot mains connect to the main power shutoff—either a large circuit breaker or a pull-out fuse. Some panels use fuses (below left); some use breakers (below right).

Some very old homes have only two main wires, one hot and one neutral. Such a system is usually considered adequate if left alone, but if you add service to it you will be violating code. However, it will likely be inadequate for the electrical appliances in the average household. If this describes your home, get an electrician to install new service.

From the main shutoff two hot bus bars (also called legs) run most of the length down the panel. Each bar carries 120 volts. Circuit breakers or fuses connect to these bars. (This is easier to see in a breaker box than in a fuse box.) Fuses and breakers rated at 120 volts are attached to a single hot bar; 240-volt breakers or fuses are attached to both hot bars.

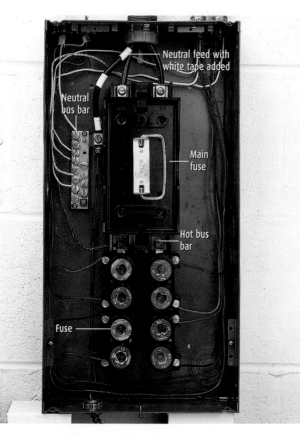

A 100-AMP FUSE BOX
A large fuse box with a capacity of 100 amps provides adequate electrical service for most medium-size homes. While breaker boxes (as shown on the right) are preferred for use, fuse boxes in good shape will also do the job. However, if you are thinking of modifying an existing fuse box in any way, it's better to replace it with a breaker box.

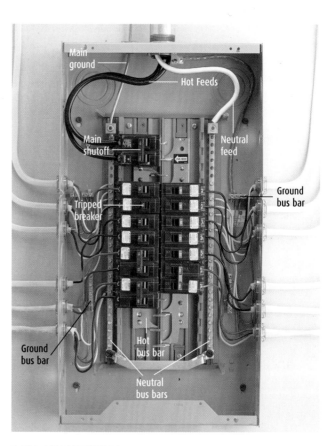

A 100-AMP BREAKER BOX
You can see the two hot bus bars more clearly on a breaker box. This 100-amp box has ample room for the wires, which are carefully laid out so you easily can see the path for each one.

Each 120-volt circuit has a black or color wire connected to a circuit breaker or fuse, and a white wire connected to a neutral bus bar. For each circuit ground wires lead to a separate ground bar. Neutral bars (usually two) connect to a system ground wire.

Power runs through each fuse or breaker and then out of the panel via a hot wire to whatever receptacles, lights, or appliances are on the circuit. White neutral wires bring power back to a neutral bus bar in the service panel, completing the loop.

When circuits overload

If a circuit becomes overloaded and is in danger of overheating, the circuit breaker will trip or the fuse will blow, disconnecting power to the entire circuit. The same thing happens during a ground fault (page 11) or a short circuit, when a hot wire accidentally touches a neutral wire. If a circuit shuts down frequently, you have a faulty appliance, device, or, most likely, an overloaded circuit (pages 48–49).

When to upgrade a panel

If your panel seems cramped or confusing, have an electrician make sure it is safe. Some panels are too small for the number of circuits they serve, crowding the wires. Others have the neutral bars too near the hot bus bars so that hot and neutral wires are dangerously close to each other. Others have the neutral bar too far away, so neutral wires have to travel around the panel.

If you plan to significantly increase your home's power capacity, have an inspector or an electrician evaluate your needs to see if you need to upgrade your basic service. For instance, you may need to replace a 100-amp panel with one that pulls 200 amps. Upping your basic power may or may not mean changing the wires that lead from the power company to your home.

⊘ SAFETY ALERT

RESPECT YOUR SERVICE PANEL

Even seasoned electricians are very careful when working on service panels. If you have reservations about working on your service panel yourself, hire help. If you decide to inspect or work on the panel yourself, follow these safety tips.

■ Always know what's hot. A shutoff device—a switch, a breaker, or a fuse—turns off power only to the wires beyond the device. The wires entering the shutoff device are hot at all times. Be sure you know which wires are upstream of the shutoff (prior to the device and therefore not controlled by it) and which are downstream (after it, and therefore controlled by it). If you turn off the main breaker or remove the main fuse, the whole house will go dead and all the circuits will be de-energized, but not all of the service panel will be safe. Unless the utility company turns them off, the thick wires entering the panel are always hot.

■ Keep your hands off the bus bar. When you turn off a breaker or remove a fuse, the wires to the circuit will be dead, but the bus bar will still be hot. The bus bars are always

energized unless the main breaker has been turned off or the main fuse has been removed.

■ Keep the cover on. Unless you are working on or inspecting a service panel, keep the cover attached so that there is no possibility that you will accidentally touch wires.

■ Make a map of your circuits (page 47) and post it on the inside panel door so you can easily see which breaker or fuse needs to be disabled.

■ Store stuff away from the panel. Keep flammable objects, including hanging clothes, at least 1 meter or 3 feet away. Have a charged flashlight handy.

■ Always wear rubber-soled shoes. If the floor by the panel is at all damp, lay down some boards and lay a rubber mat on top of the boards.

■ Never let anyone clip temporary lines into the panel. Welders and floor sanders sometimes want to clip 240-volt extension lines directly onto your hot and neutral bars. This is dangerous!

Older fuse panel

An older home that has not been remodeled may have a 60-amp fuse box like the one shown. It supplies fuses for only four circuits—not enough to meet modern code for a kitchen alone. It also has two pull-out fuse blocks, which have two cartridge fuses each. The top fuse block is the main shutoff, and the bottom fuse block supplies the only 240-volt circuit allowed on the system. This box will be sufficient only for a home with very modest electrical needs. Most homeowners will want to update to a 100- or even a 200-amp breaker box. An upgrade may be required before the house is sold or in order to qualify for financing.

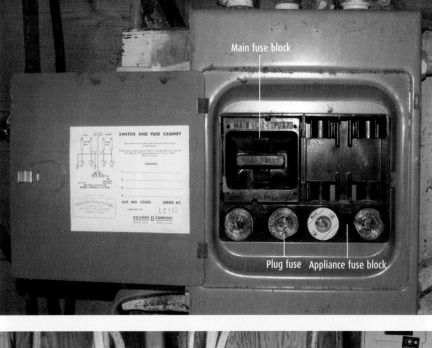

Main fuse block

Plug fuse   Appliance fuse block

Subpanels

If your main service panel does not have enough room to meet the house's needs, a subpanel may have been installed. You may find one near the main service panel, or it could be located on a different floor where it may control the outlets on that floor. A subpanel allows for the addition of new fuses or circuit breakers. This is safe as long as the wires leading from the main panel to the subpanel are thick enough and they are attached to a breaker that is correctly sized for a subpanel. For instance, if the subpanel needs 40 amps, the breaker on the main panel for the subpanel should be a 40 amp breaker. If the subpanel carries 30 amps, 10/3 cable should run from the main panel to the subpanel. There should be a main shutoff in the subpanel, which controls all the power entering it. A 40-amp subpanel should use 8/3 cable. Unfortunately, subpanels are sometimes installed incorrectly. If you are unsure of your subpanel's amp rating or whether it is wired correctly, have it inspected by a professional electrician.

Service panel

Subpanel

Double-pole feeder breaker

Feeder cable

Receptacle and switch wiring

Remove an electrical cover plate and pull out a switch or receptacle, and you'll find an arrangement involving a few wires going directly to the device. Or, you may find a multicolored tangle of wires, some related to the switch or receptacle and some not. Here are some of the most common wiring configurations you'll find behind electrical cover plates.

Switches that come with grounding terminals must be grounded to the system and the electrical box as seen in the photograph on the right. (For more information on grounding, see page 11.)

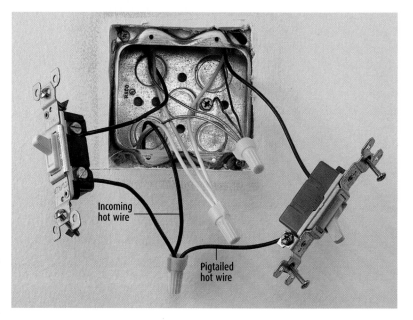

Incoming hot wire

Pigtailed hot wire

SWITCHES SHARING A HOT WIRE

Switches that share a hot wire are on the same circuit. Two pigtails (page 35) branch off from the incoming hot wire and connect to each switch. Another hot wire runs from each switch to a light. White wires are spliced. If the switch has a ground terminal it must be grounded both to the system and the grounding terminal in the box. When wiring switches make sure the box is big enough to accommodate the switches, cables, and wire nuts.

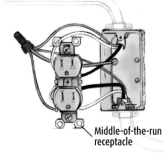

Tab broken off

A SPLIT RECEPTACLE

Also known as a "half-hot" receptacle, this is connected to two hot wires. The brass tab joining the brass terminals has been broken off. With the tab broken, each hot wire energizes one plug. Some split receptacles have each plug energized by a different circuit so that you can plug in two high-amperage appliances without the danger of tripping a breaker. Others are wired so that half the receptacle is controlled by a wall switch, while the other half is hot all the time. See page 144 for more information.

CLOSER LOOK

MIDDLE-OF-THE-RUN RECEPTACLE

A receptacle with one cable that carries power into the receptacle and one that carries it to another device is called a "middle-of-the-run receptacle." Usually two black wires are connected to the brass terminals and two white wires to the silver terminals. Or the blacks and the whites may be joined, with a pigtail at each splice. Each pigtail is attached to the receptacle. If only one cable enters the box, the receptacle is at the end of the run. The black wire is attached to the brass terminal, the white wire is attached to the silver terminal, and the ground wire is attached to the receptacle.

End-of-the-run receptacle

Middle-of-the-run receptacle

Don't strip wires midway to make connections like this

WIRES STRIPPED MIDWAY

You may find wires that have 1 inch of insulation stripped along the lengths, rather than being cut and each end stripped. Some electricians use this technique to save time. If the connections are tight, this is a safe arrangement. **However, for your own work, avoid this shortcut.** Wire often gets nicked or scraped in the process. Use pigtails instead (page 35).

Aluminum wire is silver in color

ALUMINUM WIRE

Aluminum wire, which is silver in color and thicker than copper wire, is not widely used because it expands and contracts, loosening connections. Make sure the receptacle is rated CO/ALR. **(See page 50 for how to keep an aluminum system safe.)**

⊘ SAFETY ALERT

SHOCK DEFENSE: MAKE SURE ALL CIRCUITS TO THE DEVICE ARE OFF

Before removing a fixture or a device, flip off the circuit breaker and test for power (pages 30-31), or turn off a light switch. Be aware, however, that boxes may contain wires from more than one circuit. To be safe test all wires for power with a voltage detector.

When removing the plate, grasp only the rubber handle of the screwdriver. When removing the device, pull gently, holding the plastic rather than metal parts. Don't dislodge wires. Wear rubber-soled shoes.

Colored wires

WHAT COLORED WIRES MEAN

Colored wires are sometimes used by electricians to indicate different circuits. When this is done correctly, a circuit uses its own wire color—say, brown or purple. By turning off the breaker attached to the brown wire, you turn off power to all devices attached to brown wires. **(Do not assume yours is wired this way. Always test to make sure power is off.)**

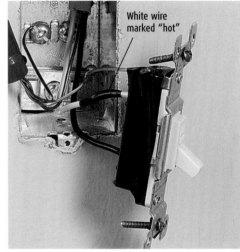

White wire marked "hot"

WHY WHITE WIRES MAY BE MARKED

When power runs into the fixture box rather than the switch box, another cable brings a black and a white wire into the switch box. When the switch is on, both wires are hot, so the white wire may be painted black with a marker or wrapped with a bit of electrician's tape. Do not remove the tape or scrape away the paint, or you will give the false—and dangerous—signal that the white wire is neutral.

Two ways to wire a switch

Power may run first to the switch box, or it may run first to the fixture box. In either case the wiring must be configured so that the switch can interrupt the hot wire (when the switch is turned off) or allow power to flow through the hot wire (when it is turned on). The hot wire coming from the power source is sometimes called the "feed wire."

With "through-switch" wiring, power runs first to the switch. Two cables enter the box, one from the power source and one from the fixture. The feed wire is connected to one of the switch terminals; the black or colored wire leading to the fixture is connected to the other terminal; and the white wires are spliced. At the fixture the two wires are attached to the fixture.

With "end-line" wiring power goes to the fixture and a cable runs from the fixture to the switch. At the fixture the power source's white wire and the switch cable's black wire are connected to the switch. The feed wire is connected to the switch cable's white wire, which is taped or painted black to indicate that it is actually a hot wire. At the switch only one cable enters the box. The white wire is painted or taped black, and both wires are connected to the switch.

Electricians and inspectors differ on marking white wires with black tape to indicate they are actually a hot wire. This is a practice that may be controlled by local codes. It is best to ask at your local home center or call up the inspector's office to inquire about what local inspectors will look for.

Ungrounded switches and fixtures

Until fairly recently it was common to wire light fixtures and their switches without connecting the grounds. (The extra protection of grounding was considered unnecessary, since a light does not pose the hazards that a receptacle does.) Today's tougher electrical standards call for all switches and fixtures to be grounded. If you have ungrounded switches or fixtures, it is safe to leave them alone, but you should certainly connect the ground wires if they are available.

"THROUGH-SWITCH" WIRING

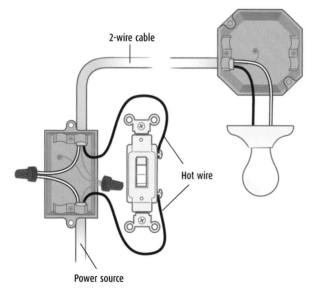

2-wire cable

Hot wire

Power source

"END-LINE" WIRING

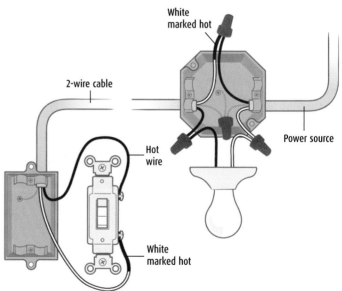

White marked hot

2-wire cable

Hot wire

Power source

White marked hot

Basic tools and skills

Chapter 2 highlights

Equipped with a basic understanding of household electricity, you may be tempted to dive right into your project. After all, how hard can it be? Grab a utility knife, some tape, and a pair of pliers, and start splicing and twisting, right?

Some homeowners who tackle wiring projects with this attitude successfully complete the repairs they set out to make. But there's no guarantee that their work will meet the standard requirements for safety and longevity.

Professional electricians perform their highly detailed work accurately and safely. They ensure the tightness of connections so there's no chance of them coming apart. They cover all bare wires to avoid the danger of shorts.

With the help of this book, the right tools, and some practice, you can maintain and upgrade your home's electrical system with confidence and reliability that rival the pros.

TOOL SAVVY

THE RIGHT STUFF
Although you'll need carpentry tools to cut and patch holes for installing cable and boxes, don't use them as substitutes for tools designed specifically for electrical work. The right tools protect you from shocks, ensure secure splices and connections, and make the job more enjoyable.

Resetting breakers

CLOSER LOOK

HOW BREAKERS TRIP

Service panels and breakers are made by a number of manufacturers, so there are various ways to reset breakers. Here are some common types of breakers.

This type flips halfway toward OFF when it trips. To reset it, turn it off, then on.

This breaker flips off all the way. Just flip it back on to reset it. On some a red button displays or pops out, showing that the breaker has tripped.

This breaker model has a button that pops out when it trips. Push the button in to reset.

The fuses or circuit breakers in the service panel form the first line of defense for your home, protecting you and your family from fire and shock. If a house is wired correctly, with no circuits overloaded, you may never have to open your service panel except to shut off power while working on an electrical project.

If a circuit in your home frequently blows a fuse or trips a breaker, check pages 48–49 for tips on how to eliminate circuit overloads.

Learn how to shut off and restore power from the service panel. Map your circuits and tape an index in your service panel (page 47). Always leave a clear pathway to the service panel.

If a circuit breaker trips often, even though you don't seem to be running too many appliances or lights, the problem may be the wiring or the circuit breaker. It's easy to test a breaker (see below).

Testing a breaker

1

TEST THE BREAKER

If you suspect that a faulty breaker is tripping for no apparent reason, touch the prongs of a voltage tester to the breaker's terminal screw and a ground. If there is no power, the breaker is faulty. Or try this test: **Shut off the main breaker.** Loosen the setscrews on the suspected breaker and a nearby breaker of the same amperage. Switch the wires, tighten the setscrews, and flip the main breaker back on. If the original breaker trips unreasonably while connected to a different circuit, replace the breaker.

2

REPLACE THE BREAKER

Shut off the main breaker to be safe. Loosen the setscrew on the damaged breaker, then pull out the wire. Pull out the breaker by hand. Make sure you touch only plastic, never anything metal. Pull out one end of the breaker to loosen it, and then pull out the whole breaker. Buy a new breaker of the same amperage and size, made by the same manufacturer. Slip the wire into the new breaker and tighten the setscrew. Push the breaker in until it snaps in place like the ones around it. Restore power.

Changing fuses

A lways replace a blown fuse with a fuse of amperage appropriate for the circuit. A living area usually requires a 15-amp fuse; an appliance area needs a 20-amp fuse. A 30-amp fuse is used only for a range or dryer circuit, or for a line to a subpanel. Installing a fuse of higher amperage may get the circuit going again, but it puts your house at risk because the fuse won't blow when wires get dangerously hot.

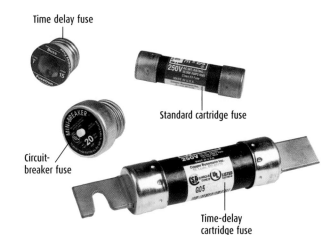

Time delay fuse

Standard cartridge fuse

Circuit-breaker fuse

Time-delay cartridge fuse

Types of fuses

A time-delay fuse holds itself together for a second or so during a momentary surge of power—for example, when a refrigerator motor turns on. The fuse will blow if the circuit remains overloaded.

An S-type fuse has a socket adapter that screws into the fuse box socket where it becomes permanently lodged. Once screwed in it is impossible to install a fuse of a different amperage.

A circuit-breaker fuse has a push button that pops out when the circuit overloads. Instead of replacing the fuse, you push the button back in to restore power. Many electricians don't think they're reliable; others consider them safe.

Why a fuse blew

If the metal strip inside the fuse is broken completely, the circuit overloaded: Too many appliances and lights were running at the same time. If the fuse window is blackened, the cause is a short circuit—meaning that somewhere wires are touching each other or a wire is making contact with metal. Inspect switches, receptacles, and fixtures—and fix the problem right away.

Short   Overload

Working with cartridge fuses

1

REMOVE THE FUSE FROM THE BLOCK

If a 240-volt circuit in a fuse box blows, the fuses are probably located inside a fuse block. Turn off the power. Grab the wire handle and pull out the block. Use a fuse puller to remove each cartridge fuse.

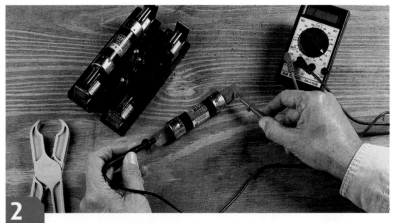

2

TEST THE CARTRIDGE FUSE

(Be careful. If you have just removed the fuse, its metal parts may be hot.) To see whether a cartridge fuse has failed, touch both ends with the probes of a continuity tester or multitester

(pages 30–31). If the fuse tests positive for continuity, it is good. If not, it has blown. Take it to a home center or hardware store and buy an exact replacement.

Basic tool kit

Compared to power tools used for carpentry work, the cost of electrical tools is a drop in the tool bucket. Buy everything you need. If you spend a little more to buy professional-quality tools, you'll find that they'll help you work faster and produce better connections.

The following section describes the tools you'll need to make all the inspections, repairs, and installations described in this book through page 104. (You may also need a few basic household tools such as a hammer, standard pliers, and a keyhole saw.) More advanced tools required for installing new electrical lines are described on pages 106–107. **Be sure all your metal tools have insulated grips.**

Tools you'll need

With **wire strippers** you can remove insulation from wires neatly and without nicking the metal. Get a pair with a spring that opens the jaws.

A **wire stripper/cutter** cuts wire like a pair of scissors and has a hole for stripping wire. Professional electricians often use this tool, or lineman's pliers, to strip wires instead of using wire strippers. It takes practice to do this without damaging the wire. **Side-cutting pliers,** or diagonal cutters, make it easy to cut wire and to snip off stripped plastic sheathing.

With **lineman's pliers** you can cut wire and easily twist them together. Buy a high-quality pair that is fairly heavy in the hand, smooth-operating, with precisely aligned cutting edges for easy snipping of wires. Use **longnose pliers** to twist a tight loop in a wire end before attaching it to a terminal. Make sure the pair you buy is sturdy enough to handle household wiring—some are intended for finer wires used in electronics.

Among the many precautions you can take to protect against electrical shock, using **rubber-gripped screwdrivers** when doing electrical work is one of the most important. Don't use screwdrivers with plastic handles only. They can crack, creating a shock hazard. The handles should be large enough so that you will not be tempted to grab the metal shaft while you work. (Four-in-one screwdrivers are especially unsuited to electrical work because they have a metal shaft that runs through the handle.)

Keep a reliable **flashlight** handy because you may have to work in the dark.

Every home center has a bin of inexpensive **electrical tape.** It'll do the job, but far better is the more expensive, professional-quality tape—it's thicker, more adhesive, and longer lasting.

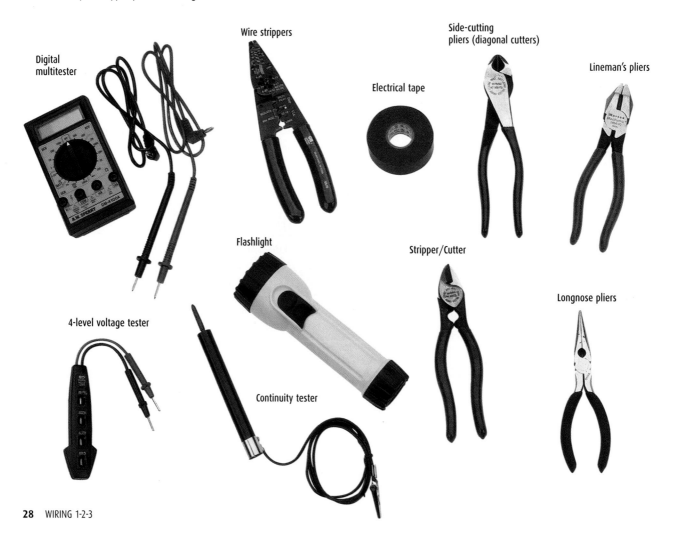

Digital multitester

Wire strippers

Side-cutting pliers (diagonal cutters)

Electrical tape

Lineman's pliers

Flashlight

Stripper/Cutter

Longnose pliers

4-level voltage tester

Continuity tester

Selecting testers

Even if you do not plan to do much electrical work, buy a **GFCI (ground fault circuit interrupter) receptacle analyzer** (it handles standard receptacles as well). It will quickly tell you whether the receptacles are safe.

There are various tools you can use to test for the existence of power. A **continuity tester** checks the reliability of fuses, switches, and sockets with the power off. A four-level voltage tester—better than the cheaper, single-level version—indicates if the power is on or off. A **digital multitester** is useful for appliance repair as well as electrical work. It performs the tasks of both a continuity tester and a voltage tester.

A **voltage detector** senses power, even through wire and cable insulation, so you can see whether wires are live before you work with them. With a **two-part circuit finder**, you can easily find out which circuit a receptacle is on. (Testers are described in detail on pages 30–31.)

Basic tool care

Protect tools from moisture; rust causes them to lose their effectiveness. Make sure that the plastic insulation on each tool is in good shape so that your hand does not touch any metal part. If a cutting tool loses its edge so it's a struggle to cut wire, replace the tool.

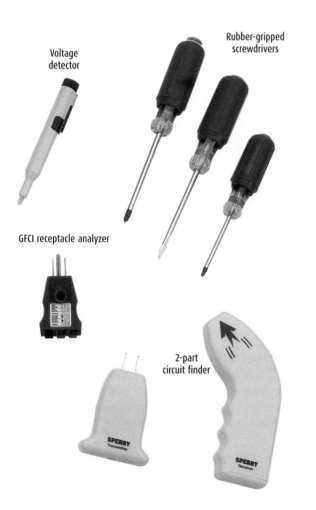

Voltage detector

Rubber-gripped screwdrivers

GFCI receptacle analyzer

2-part circuit finder

TOOL SAVVY

ELECTRICIAN'S TOOL BELT

Though a basic carpentry tool belt will keep your electrical tools close at hand, **an electrician's tool belt is specially designed for keeping often-used electrical items within easy reach.** Even if you work on only a half-dozen boxes and devices, a belt will save time.

FIBERGLASS STEPLADDER

Never stand on a metal ladder while working with or near electricity. Use a fiberglass ladder, like the one shown above, or a wood ladder that's labeled "nonconductive." These ladders protect you from shock. Although they are also heavier than aluminum ladders, they are more stable.

WORK SMARTER

SQUARE DRIVE SCREWS

Slotted screws can be difficult to set, especially in tight spaces. Square drive screws (with a square slot in the head) require a special head for the screwdriver but offer a more positive driving action with far less slippage.

Using testers

Reliable testing is essential to electrical work. Testers tell you whether the wires you are working on are hot; whether a switch, receptacle, or fixture is in working order; and whether a receptacle is wired safely.

Don't skimp on electrical testing tools. You might not need a fancy multitester, but avoid inexpensive tools such as single neon testers. They can quickly burn out or easily break, making you think there is no power when there really is.

If you buy a multitester, invest in a digital model rather than one with a dial. A digital tester is easier to use and is far less likely to give the wrong reading.

Examine your tester regularly to be sure it provides accurate information. To confirm that it's working, poke the probes of a voltage tester into a receptacle you know to be live, and make sure the tester lights up. Touch the probes of a continuity tester together. If the tester lights up, it's working. If it doesn't light up, it may need a battery or a bulb. Keep testers dry and safe from harm.

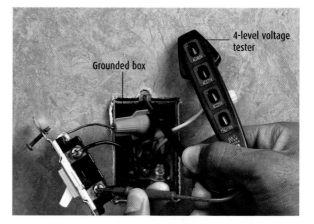

Grounded box

4-level voltage tester

A VOLTAGE TESTER INDICATES THE PRESENCE OF POWER

A four-level voltage tester is safer and more reliable than one-level versions. **Always confirm that a voltage tester is working by trying it on a circuit that you know to be live.** Touch the tester's probes to a hot wire and a grounded box, to a hot wire and a neutral wire, or insert them into the slots of a receptacle. If the tester light doesn't come on, the circuit is shut off.

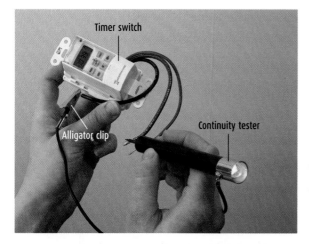

Timer switch

Alligator clip

Continuity tester

A CONTINUITY TESTER TELLS YOU WHETHER A DEVICE OR FUSE IS DEFECTIVE

Disconnect the device from all household wires. Attach the tester's alligator clip to one terminal and touch the probe to the other terminal. If the device switch is working, the tester light will glow when the switch is turned on and go out when the switch is turned off. To test the wiring in an appliance or lamp, touch both ends of each wire. The tester light will glow if the wire is unbroken. (To test a fuse, see page 27.)

A RECEPTACLE ANALYZER TELLS YOU WHETHER YOUR RECEPTACLES ARE SAFE

When you plug this analyzer into a receptacle, one or more of three lights will glow, telling you whether the receptacle is working, grounded, and polarized (page 11). Buy a tester for the type of receptacles you have in your home. While some analyzers will test ground fault circuit interrupter (GFCI) receptacles as well as standard receptacles, others analyzers test standard receptacles only.

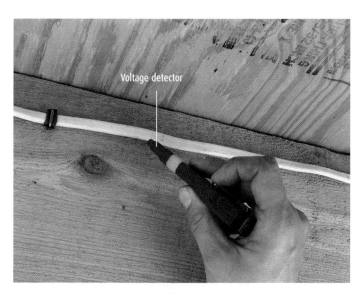

Voltage detector

A VOLTAGE DETECTOR SENSES POWER—
EVEN THROUGH WIRE AND CABLE INSULATION

This handy tester lets you check whether wires are live before you work on them. The probe doesn't need to touch a bare wire or terminal. Press the detector button and hold it on or near an insulated wire or cable to see if power is present. If there's power a light comes on.

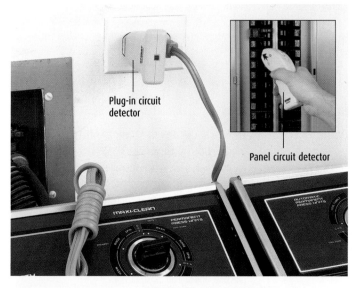

Plug-in circuit detector

Panel circuit detector

CIRCUIT DETECTORS INDICATE WHICH CIRCUIT A RECEPTACLE IS ON

Plug one part of the circuit detector into the receptacle. Open the service panel door and point the other part of the tester at the circuit breakers. The detector will glow to indicate the correct circuit. **Even after switching off the circuit, check for power at the receptacle before working.**

TOOL SAVVY

Set to volts

TO TEST FOR VOLTAGE

A multitester tests 120-volt, 240-volt, or low-voltage circuitry. Multitesters have negative and positive probes. **Test for voltage by touching each probe to a wire, terminal, or receptacle slot.** You can also touch one probe to the black wire and the other to a ground, such as a metal box. The display should show between 108 and 132 volts for a 120-volt circuit, and between 216 and 264 volts for a 240-volt circuit. Low-voltage circuitry can register as low as 4 volts.

TO TEST FOR CONTINUITY

A multitester can test a switch, receptacle, fuse, or light fixture to see whether its circuitry is damaged. **Shut off the power and remove the device.** Test for continuity by turning the dial to an "ohms" setting and touching each probe to a terminal on the device. If you test a switch, turn it ON. If the multitester needle shows zero resistance, the device is in good shape. An infinity reading means that the device is defective.

Stripping and splicing wire

⟁ PROJECT DETAILS

SKILLS: Using wire strippers, dikes, or lineman's pliers
PROJECT: Stripping and splicing two wires

🕐 TIME TO COMPLETE

EXPERIENCED: 1 min.
HANDY: 3 min.
NOVICE: 10 min.

✓ STUFF YOU'LL NEED

TOOLS: Wire strippers, lineman's pliers, or side-cutting pliers
MATERIALS: Wire, electrician's tape, wire nuts

🌐 REAL WORLD

SPLICING WIRES

It's possible to makes splices without twisting the wires together by holding the wire ends next to each other and twisting on a wire nut. Some might believe that this method is just as strong, but it only takes one loose wire to shut down a whole circuit and it could take hours to find the faulty wire. Take the extra time and twist the wires together before twisting on the wire nut.

With practice you'll soon learn to remove insulation and connect wires with ease. Keep in mind that cutting into metal wire while stripping will weaken it. If wires are not joined tightly, the electrical connection will be compromised and could cause a short.

To work with new cable, you'll first have to remove the sheathing. (See pages 118–121 to see how to remove sheathing from various types of cable.)

Use a wire nut (page 14) to join wires. Twist the wires together before adding the wire nut.

When splicing two wires together, strip about 1 inch of insulation. If the wire will be joined to a terminal, remove about ¾ inch.

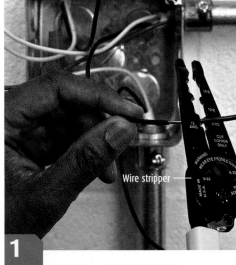

Wire stripper

1

OPTION A: STRIP WIRES WITH A WIRE STRIPPER TOOL

Don't use a utility knife; it will probably nick the wire. Choose a pair of wire strippers and practice with them until you're comfortable using them. To use a wire stripper, slip the wire into the correct hole, squeeze, twist, and pull off the insulation. The insulation should come off easily.

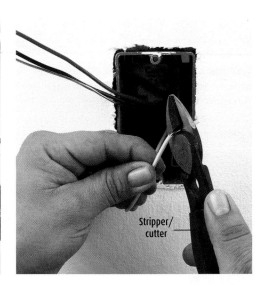

Stripper/ cutter

OPTION B: USE A WIRE STRIPPER/CUTTER

Many electricians consider wire strippers too slow. They prefer tools that are sometimes called "dikes." These include lineman's pliers, side-cutting pliers, or a stripper/cutter, with a single stripping hole. It takes time to learn to use these tools without nicking the wire. Press down with just the right amount of pressure to cut through the insulation and not the wire. Maintain the same pressure and twist until the insulation is cut all the way around. Ease up on the squeezing pressure, and pull off the insulation.

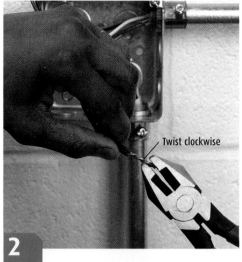

2

TWIST WIRES TOGETHER

Hold the stripped wires side by side. Grab the ends of both with lineman's pliers. Twist clockwise, making sure that both wires turn. Twist them together like a candy cane; don't twist one around the other. The wires should form a neat-looking spiral. Twist several times, but don't overtwist or you might break the wires.

Twist clockwise

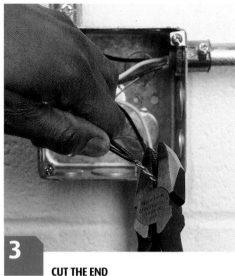

3

CUT THE END

Using the lineman's pliers or side-cutting pliers, snip off the end of the twist. Leave enough exposed metal so that the wire nut will just cover it—about ½ inch usually does it.

WORK SMARTER

JOINING SOLID TO STRANDED WIRE

To join stranded wire (often found on light fixtures and specialty switches) to solid-core wire, **give the strands several twists** between your thumb and forefinger to consolidate the strands. Then wrap the stranded wire around the solid wire, again with your fingers. **Check that the stranded wire protrudes past the solid wire ⅛ inch or so.** Twist on a wire nut, and tug both wires to make sure you have a solid connection. Finally, wrap the bottom of the wire nut with electrician's tape.

4

CAP WITH A WIRE NUT

Select a wire nut designed for the number and size of wires you have spliced (page 14). Slip the nut on as far as it will go, and twist clockwise until tight. Test the connection by tugging on the nut—it should hold securely. For extra protection, you may wish to wrap electrician's tape around the bottom of the cap. However, be aware that some inspectors do not like taped wire nuts. It's best to know your local codes and the inspector's preferences beforehand.

Wire nut

SPLICING THREE OR FOUR WIRES

When twisting three or four wires together, hold them parallel and twist them all at once with lineman's pliers. (Don't twist two together and then try to add a third.) Choose a wire nut designed to accommodate the number and size of wires you have spliced (page 14) and twist the nut on as shown in Step 4.

Twist all the wires at once

Lineman's pliers

Joining wire to a terminal

PROJECT DETAILS

SKILLS: Bending and fastening electrical wire
PROJECT: Joining two wires to terminals

TIME TO COMPLETE

EXPERIENCED: 1 min.
HANDY: 3 min.
NOVICE: 7 min.

STUFF YOU'LL NEED

TOOLS: Longnose pliers, side-cutting pliers, wire-bending screwdriver
MATERIALS: Wire, device with terminals

J oining wire to a terminal is an important skill and a key step in most electrical projects. Do this step properly to ensure the device works and doesn't develop a short.

Making the right connection

Electricians wrap the wire nearly all the way around the screw to make a connection that is completely reliable. With some practice you can make joints just as strong. Bend a wire in a circle loop, slip it under the screw head, tighten the loop, and tighten the screw.

Many devices come with terminal screws unscrewed. Screw in any unused terminal screws so they won't stick out dangerously, creating a shock hazard should the terminal touch a metal box.

Screw in any unused terminal screws so they won't stick out dangerously, creating a shock hazard.

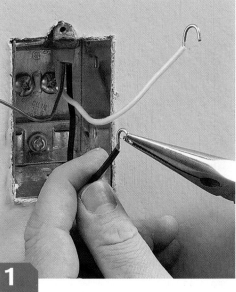

1

START A LOOP

Check that power is shut off. Strip about ¾ inch of insulation from a wire end (page 32). Using longnose pliers or the tip of a pair of wire strippers, grab the wire just above the insulation and bend it back at about a 45-degree angle. Move the pliers up about ¼ inch beyond the insulation and bend again in the opposite direction, about 90 degrees.

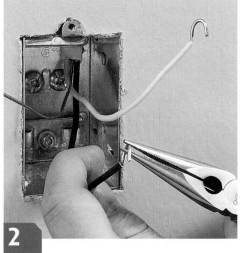

2

OPTION A: BEND A QUESTION MARK

Use a longnose pliers to form a near-loop with an opening just wide enough to slip over the threads of a terminal screw. Move the pliers another ¼ inch away from the insulation, and bend again to form a shape that looks like a question mark.

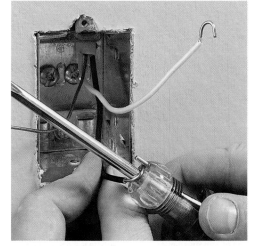

OPTION B: USE A WIRE-BENDING SCREWDRIVER

This simple tool makes perfect hooks every time. Just push the stripped wire between the screwdriver shaft and the stud at the base of the handle. Twist the handle to make a perfect loop.

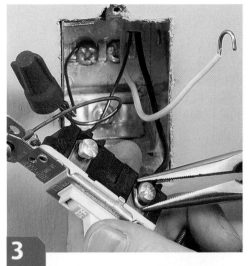

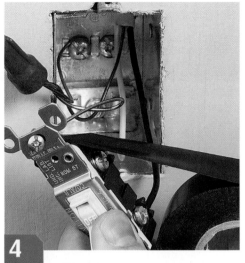

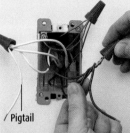

USING PIGTAILS

Codes prohibit attaching two wires to one terminal. If you need to attach two wires to one terminal, cut a "pigtail" wire 6 inches long, and strip both ends. Splice the two wires to the pigtail, and join the pigtail to the terminal.

Pigtail

3

SQUEEZE THE LOOP AROUND THE SCREW

Make sure the terminal screw is unscrewed enough to become hard to turn. Slip the loop over the screw threads, with the loop running clockwise. Use longnose pliers or wire strippers to squeeze the loop around the terminal, then tighten the screw. Install the switch.

4

WRAP WITH TAPE

Some electricians wrap electrician's tape around the body of the device to cover the screw heads and exposed wires. The thinking is to not only ensure the wires stay attached, but to also keep the terminals from touching the box. However, some inspectors do not like this practice since they cannot see your work. Before using tape check with the inspector.

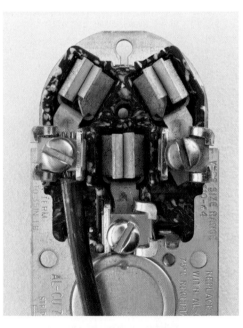

CONNECTING TO A 240-VOLT RECEPTACLE

Be certain that power is shut off—there is a dangerous level of power here. Strip about ½ inch of insulation from the wire end. The wire should be straight, not looped. Loosen the setscrew, poke the wire into the hole, and tighten the screw. (See page 145 for installing a 240-volt receptacle.)

SKIP THE PUSH-IN OPTION

Most professionals don't trust this method even though it saves time. Many receptacles and switches have holes in the back for easy connection of wires. Once you've stripped the insulation (a strip gauge shows you how much), you poke the wire in. To remove a wire, insert a small screwdriver into a nearby slot to release the clamping mechanism that holds the wire inside. The system works, but the resulting electrical connection is not as secure as a connection made using a terminal screw. Take the extra minute to do it right.

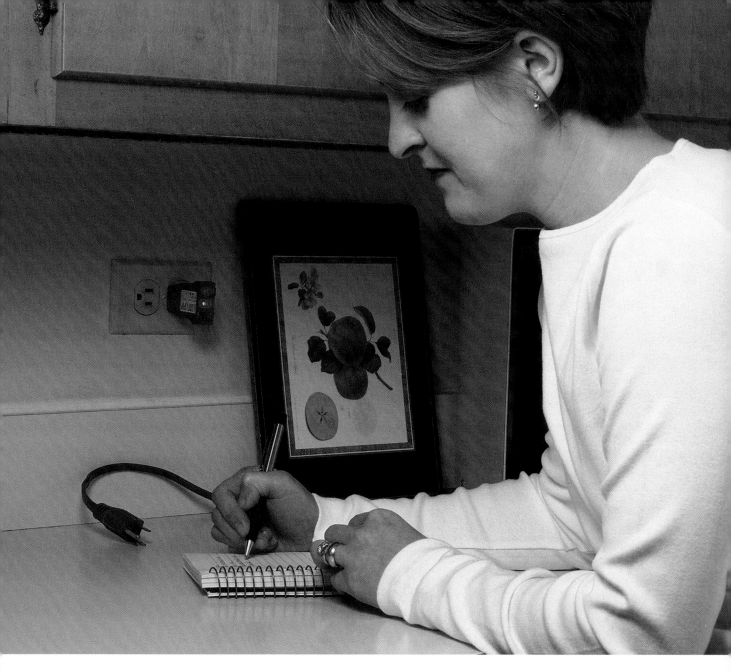

Chapter 3 highlights

Inspecting your home

ou can correctly assess the safety of your home even if you aren't a professional with a clipboard and a head full of electrical codes. Many problems inspectors find will be just as obvious to you once you learn how to find them.

If you see evidence of unprofessional electrical work in one area of your home, chances are good that a previous homeowner made some amateur installations and probably didn't consult codes or have the work inspected. Be on the lookout for other instances of substandard work.

This chapter begins with a "walk-around" inspection of your home, instructing you to examine fixtures, receptacles, and switches in plain sight. Later the chapter demonstrates how to open your service panel and electrical boxes to inspect wires and terminals.

Each section identifies common household problems and refers you to a page describing how they can be fixed.

Meeting code

Local building codes and regulations are imposed to protect you and your family from shock and fire, and to make sure your wiring works reliably for decades. See pages 108–109 for more detailed information about codes.

When you don't need code

Codes change over the years as new hazards are discovered and new products are introduced. It's possible that some of the wiring in your home fails to conform to current regulations. Usually that's not a problem, as long as it conforms to the rules that existed when the wiring was installed. But any new work, even if it connects to old work, must meet code.

If you repair a fixture or replace one fixture with another without running new cable, there's no need to consult codes. Even if local regulations require you to get a permit for every fixture replacement, most inspectors will not want to be bothered with such small changes.

When to consult codes

If, during the course of an installation or inspection, you see wiring that's improperly connected and you don't know how to fix it, or if you see wiring that you do not understand, call in a pro or check with your electrical safety authority.

When you install new service in your home (make an installation that involves running new cable), you must get a permit and be sure to work according to code. (See page 108 for tips on working with inspectors.)

The CEC and local codes

Codes vary from area to area. In fact, sometimes the regulations in neighboring cities can differ. However, all local codes are based on the Canadian Electrical Code (CEC). The CEC provides precise details about materials and installation—sometimes far more than you need to know about residential electrical installations. Copies are often available at your local library. The CEC is updated every few years to reflect changes in both products and installation techniques.

As you consult these books, remember that local codes prevail. Your local building inspection department will probably have brochures or leaflets that describe the most common electrical codes for residences.

BUYER'S GUIDE

HIRING A PRO

Most professional electricians are qualified, honest, and charge fairly. Unfortunately, a few take advantage of homeowners' lack of knowledge and general fear of electricity. Too often unscrupulous contractors target the elderly. Word-of-mouth can be a great way to find reliable contractors, but even sharp consumers may be unaware they received shoddy work or overpaid. For a large job **get quotes from at least three contractors.** Their bids should include a list of "specs"—everything to be installed and how it will be installed.

Check that the contractor is licensed for your area and is covered by insurance. This way, if there is a fire or if a worker is injured on your property, you will not be held liable. If the work involves running new cable, the contractor—not the customer—should get a permit.

Read the section in this book about the installation you will pay for. Don't be afraid to ask the electrician to explain the work being done. Question everything that looks substandard. In particular have the contractor explain how the installation is grounded.

A walk-around inspection

PROJECT DETAILS

SKILLS: Careful observation, basic electrical knowledge
PROJECT: Inspecting a medium-size home

TIME TO COMPLETE

EXPERIENCED: 3 hrs.
HANDY: 4 hrs.
NOVICE: 5 hrs.

STUFF YOU'LL NEED

TOOLS: Flashlight, receptacle analyzer
MATERIALS: Paper and pencil

O nce you know what to look for, most household wiring problems are easy to find and fix. Make a whole-house inspection by checking closets, the attic, the basement or crawl space, and the garage. Globes for light fixtures will be the only things you have to remove. Prioritize everything that needs to be done and immediately take care of all potentially hazardous problems.

Inspecting receptacles for problems

1
LOOK FOR DEVICES THAT LACK COVER PLATES
If the cover plate to a switch or receptacle is missing, replace it immediately. Lack of cover plates presents a dangerous situation: Children might reach into the electrical box, where live wires lurk. An adult fumbling for the switch at night could receive a shock as well. Replace any missing cover plates.

Crack

2
BEWARE OF CRACKED RECEPTACLES
A crack on the outside may mean that a receptacle's inner circuitry is in danger of shorting out. New receptacles are inexpensive and easy to replace (page 73).

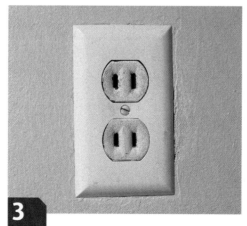

3
UPGRADE UNGROUNDED RECEPTACLES
Receptacles with only two slots and no grounding hole are ungrounded. Homeowners got by with ungrounded wiring for decades, but grounding provides a necessary level of protection. If you can't install grounded receptacles, add ground fault circuit interrupter (GFCI) receptacles (page 74).

SAFETY ALERT

NOT ON SAFE GROUND!
These grounding adapters, while once available, are illegal in most areas. If the receptacle itself isn't grounded through the system, screwing in the adapter will only give you a false sense of security. See pages 11 and 17–18 for information on proper grounding procedures.

4

WIGGLE SWITCH TOGGLES

If there seems to be too much play in the switch toggle—especially if you hear a pop when the switch is turned on or off—the device should be replaced (pages 66–68).

5

TEST A GFCI

Just because a ground fault circuit interrupter (GFCI) receptacle is supplying power doesn't mean it will protect against shock. A GFCI can lose its protective capacity. Test each GFCI by pushing the test button. The reset button should pop out. If it doesn't, replace the GFCI receptacle (page 74).

6

STANDARD RECEPTACLES IN DAMP AREAS

A wet receptacle is a shock hazard, so current codes call for ground fault circuit interrupters (GFCIs) in bathrooms, near sinks, and outdoors. See page 74 for instructions on installing a GFCI. Some areas now have codes that require GFCIs within one meter of a water source such as a sink on kitchen counters or in bathrooms. Check with your local authority to determine if and where you are required to use GFCIs.

7

CHECK FOR GROUNDING AND POLARIZATION

If a receptacle analyzer indicates that a receptacle is not grounded, **shut off the power** and remove the cover plate and the receptacle (page 73). Compare the wiring with the examples shown on pages 11 and 18. If a wire is loose, reattach it. If a receptacle is not polarized, switch wires so that the hot wire is connected to the brass terminal and the neutral wire is connected to the silver terminal. If you are not sure what is wrong, call a pro.

⊘ **SAFETY ALERT**

Plastic insert

KID-SAFE RECEPTACLES

Although kids sometimes pull them out, the simplest and cheapest protection is to push a plastic insert (above) into each unused outlet.

Most importantly, teach children to respect electricity and to stay away from all receptacles.

Inspecting fixtures and boxes for problems

1

CHECK FOR UNSECURED GLOBES

After replacing a lightbulb it's easy to tighten a setscrew before the globe is properly nested into place. With a little vibration, the globe could crash to the floor. When replacing a globe, unscrew the setscrews a bit more than necessary for removing the globe. Slip the globe up and make sure its lip is above all the screws before you tighten them. Check again after tightening.

2

DETERMINE IF THE BULB WATTAGE MATCHES THE FIXTURE

It's easy to overlook the stickers inside light fixtures that state the maximum allowable wattage. Bulbs with too-high wattage will overheat fixtures. At best you'll have to change bulbs more often; at worst overheating can cause a fire. If you need more light, install a new fixture (pages 84–85) with a higher wattage allowance.

BUYER'S GUIDE

CHECK YOUR INSURANCE
Some insurance policies have exclusions stating that the insurer does not have to pay for fire damage if the home had certain defects in its wiring. It's in your financial interest, as well as in the interest of safety, to **make sure your electrical system is free of obvious defects.**

If you find a problem, be sure to shut off the power before fixing it.

3

AVOID BARE LIGHTBULBS IN CLOSETS

Too often light fixtures in closets don't have globes. Sweaters, comforters, cardboard boxes, and other flammables placed too near bare bulbs can catch fire. The best solution is to replace your closet light with a fixture that has a globe covering the bulb. Or install a surface-mounted fluorescent light (page 102).

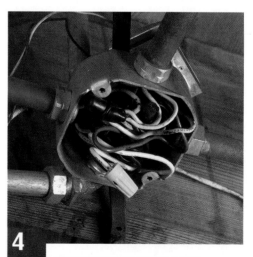

4

MAKE SPACE IN CROWDED BOXES

If a junction box is so crowded that it prevents the cover plate from being tightened all the way, install a box extender (page 213), or replace the box with a larger one.

Checking cords and wires for problems

1

CHECK FOR BROKEN OR BENT GROUNDING PRONGS

Appliance and tool grounding plugs are installed for your safety. Do not remove or bend back grounding prongs—you will negate an important safety feature. (See page 11 for an explanation of grounding.) Replace a plug that has a bad prong (pages 209–210).

2

DON'T OVERLOAD RECEPTACLES

This many-armed monster is awkward and unsafe. Using too many appliances at once can overheat the receptacle. Install another receptacle (page 141).

Don't just tape a damaged cord —be sure to replace it! And never run an extension cord under a carpet or area rug!

3

WATCH OUT FOR DAMAGED CORDS

A cord with less-than-perfect insulation can cause shock or start a fire. All lamp cords and appliance cords should be free of nicks; you should see no bare wire. Run your fingers along each unplugged cord. If you feel cracks or if the cord is brittle, replace it (pages 206–207). Pay special attention to the cord near the plug, where insulation is most often damaged. Arc Fault Circuit Interrupters can protect you from this kind of dangerous situation (page 76).

$ BUYER'S GUIDE

TAME THOSE CORDS

A tangle of cords near a desk can become unwieldy, and a stray cord poses a tripping danger. **Run the cords through a plastic sleeve or corral them with a removable strap.**

Checking cords and wires for problems *(continued)*

3

INSPECTING YOUR HOME

4

CHECK CABLE ENTERING A BOX WITHOUT A CLAMP

Cable and wire must be firmly held because vibration can cause rubbing—which can harm insulation. Metal boxes in particular have sharp edges that can nick insulation. (Plastic boxes do not usually require clamps. Staple the cable to a stud or joist within 12 inches of the box.) **Shut off power to the box,** unhook the wires, and attach the cable with a cable clamp (pages 119 and 121).

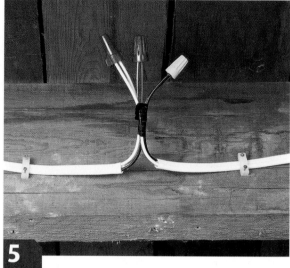

5

FIX EXPOSED SPLICES

Exposed connections can easily be bumped and loosened, running the risk of a short or fire. That's one of the reasons all wire and cable splices must be within an approved electrical box—either a junction box, a switch or receptacle box, or a fixture that is designed to be used as an electrical box. (To add a box, see pages 114–115 and 136.)

6

SECURE LOOSE CABLE. NEVER USE CABLE AS A HANGING ROD

Codes in some areas permit exposed NM (nonmetallic) cable in basements and garages, while other areas require armored cable or metal conduit. Whatever type of cable you have, it should be tightly stapled to a surface so it cannot accidentally be pulled out.

7

CHECK KNOB AND TUBE WIRING

This old style of wiring is still in use in many homes. As long as the wires are completely undisturbed and the wire insulation is in good shape, it can be used. But the insulation can get brittle and easily damaged. Have a pro evaluate it for safety. If you ever replace or extend this type of wiring, do not use more knob and tube hardware. Instead use standard cable clamped to electrical boxes (pages 118–124).

Checking the service entrance

Electricity from the power company is usually delivered to a house through two black insulated wires, each of which is hot and carries 120 volts, plus a bare wire, which serves as the neutral. The wires lead to the service entrance, which is the place where the power company's wires are attached to the house and run to the electric meter.

If the wires run overhead, they usually attach to a service head, which is shaped and insulated to keep the wires dry. From there the wires enter conduit that runs to the electric meter. This conduit may run outside the roof line (as pictured right) or run along the side of the house and through the soffit and roof. This may be determined by your local building codes. On an older home, the wires may attach to a porcelain insulator that is screwed into the house.

Prior to the service cap or insulator, you'll see a utility splice on each wire, where the company's wires stop and the house's wires begin. Overhead wires should not droop down lower than 10 feet above the yard. If the wires are rubbing against a tree, the tree should be trimmed by the power company.

An underground entrance typically has high-voltage wires from the power company running to a transformer that rests on a concrete pad. Three insulated wires run underground through watertight conduit and up the side of the house to the meter. If you have this setup, be sure to contact the power company before you do any digging in your yard, or you may accidentally nick a live wire.

Do not touch a service head or any other outdoor connections. The wires leading up to the utility splice are the responsibility of the power company, and the other connections should be handled only by a professional electrician, since the power cannot be shut off. Make a visual inspection to see that all the pipes and wires are tightly connected and all the connections are watertight. If you see anything suspicious, call the power company. They will make an inspection for free.

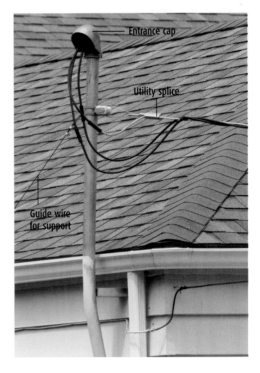

Entrance cap

Utility splice

Guide wire for support

Underground entrance

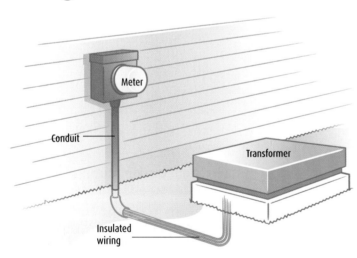

Meter

Conduit

Transformer

Insulated wiring

Make it watertight

Check here

Inspect your meter to make sure that the conduit and wires are tightly connected and will not allow moisture in. The power company will make a free inspection if there is anything of concern to you.

Inspecting boxes for problems

PROJECT DETAILS

SKILLS: Shutting off power
PROJECT: Inspecting one box

TIME TO COMPLETE

EXPERIENCED: 5 min.
HANDY: 10 min.
NOVICE: 15 min.

STUFF YOU'LL NEED

TOOLS: Voltage tester or multitester
MATERIALS: None required

Be cautious when opening and inspecting a box for potential problems. **Kill power to the box at the service panel before you begin work.** Remember, however, that there is always the potential that more than one circuit goes to a box, so work carefully. Use rubber-gripped tools, wear rubber-soled shoes, and do not touch bare wires. See pages 66 and 73 for instructions on opening a switch box and a receptacle box.

WORK SMARTER

OPENING A JUNCTION BOX
Junction boxes have flat metal cover plates and are usually found in basements, garages, or utility rooms. They generally hold six or more wires spliced with wire nuts. If possible, **trace the cables from the junction box back to the service panel.** Follow the hot wires in the service panel to figure out which circuit or circuits need to be shut off.

It may not be possible for you to shut off the power before opening a junction box, if, for example, you can't follow the cable. Also wires from two or more circuits may run through a single junction box. So even if you've shut off power, act as if power is still on. Loosen the two screws holding the cover plate, and ease off the plate. If you need to test for power, gently pull out wires so that no two splices are closer together than 1 inch. Unscrew the wire nuts and touch the probes of a multitester or voltage tester to both neutral (white) and hot (black or colored) wires (pages 30–31).

LOOK FOR OVERCROWDING
Using a rubber-gripped screwdriver, back out the screws holding the box cover plate until the cover is loose enough to remove. Too many wires crammed into too small a box can lead to shorts. See pages 114–115 to select the right size box.

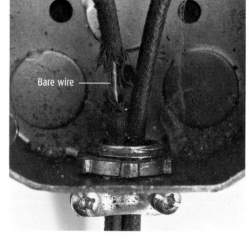

Bare wire

CHECK FOR OLD, CRACKED INSULATION
If wire insulation is hard and brittle, **shut off the circuit** and wrap the damaged insulation with a hot-shrink sleeve (page 213). If all the wiring in your house has brittle insulation, you may need to hire an electrician to rewire your house.

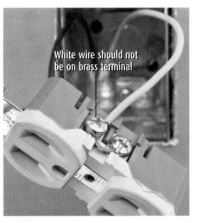

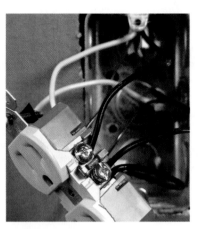

LOOK FOR EXPOSED WALL MATERIAL AROUND BOXES

An electrical box should be flush with the finished wall; if not, it poses a fire hazard. To solve this problem, replace the box or install a box extender (page 213).

CONFIRM POLARIZATION—WHITE WIRES GO TO SILVER, BLACK TO BRASS

If the white wire is connected to a brass terminal and the black one is connected to a silver terminal, the receptacle isn't polarized. An appliance or light plugged into it may be energized even when switched off. **Reverse the wires so white goes to silver and black goes to brass.** (See page 11.)

WATCH FOR TWO WIRES ON ONE TERMINAL

Two wires should not be attached to the same terminal: Not only do they make a poor connection, they can pop off and short. Remove the two wires and make a pigtail connection (page 35).

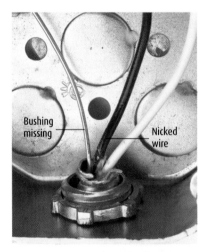

CHECK ARMORED CABLE CONNECTORS

The cut ends of armored cable are sharp and can slice through wire insulation. Even if no damage has been done, install a plastic bushing (page 121) wherever one is missing. If a wire has been nicked, cover it with a hot-shrink sleeve (page 213).

ENSURE THAT BOXES ARE SECURE

When electrical boxes are not securely anchored, wiring or connections can be damaged. If a loose switch or receptacle box is next to a stud, pull out the device, drill a hole through the side of the box, and drive a screw through the box and into the stud. If it is not near a stud, replace the box with an "old-work" box that clamps to the drywall or plaster (pages 132–133).

CHECK THAT GFCI RECEPTACLES ARE CORRECTLY WIRED

Wires coming from the power source should connect to the LINE terminals, and wires leading out to other receptacles or fixtures should connect to the LOAD terminals (page 74). Also note that the box is not grounded and should be replaced.

Inspecting a service panel

PROJECT DETAILS

SKILLS: Understanding a service panel (page 19)
PROJECT: Inspecting one service panel

TIME TO COMPLETE

EXPERIENCED: 15 min.
HANDY: 20 min.
NOVICE: 30 min.

STUFF YOU'LL NEED

TOOLS: Screwdriver, flashlight, voltage detector
MATERIALS: None required

E ven if your service panel was installed correctly, substandard wiring may have been added later. Inspect the entire panel, but pay special attention to new additions. Look for a melted breaker, burned wires, or a burned bus bar. Call an electrician if you see any sign of scorching or overheating. If you can't read the size of an old wire, carefully compare the thickness of its copper with newer wires. If you see three or more wires attached to a breaker, call in an electrician: Codes might allow you to make a pigtail connection (page 35) inside a panel.

CHECK WIRE THICKNESS
A #14 wire connected to a 20-amp breaker poses a dangerous situation. A 20-amp breaker is designed for a #12 wire or larger. A #14 wire can overheat and even melt insulation or start a fire before the 20-amp breaker trips. Replace the breaker with one that is 15 amps. Consult a professional electrician if this causes the breaker to trip often.

SAFETY ALERT

OPENING A PANEL
Study the safety precautions on page 20 before opening a panel. Switch off the main power in the box before attempting any work. The outer cover includes the door. Loosen or remove screws at the bottom, sides, and top. Lift out the cover. You'll probably see the wires and their connections to the breakers and the neutral bar. Remove the second cover if you need to remove a breaker. Don't touch any wires.

Troubleshooting your fuse box

CHECK YOUR SERVICE PANEL FOR THESE SIGNS OF TROUBLE:

■ Rust in the fuse or breaker box may indicate that the box is getting wet. This can be very dangerous. Make sure the box is dry at all times.

■ A 30-amp fuse may indicate that a fuse higher than recommended was installed because that circuit kept blowing fuses. Also check 20-amp fuses to make sure they shouldn't be 15-amps. If the wire leading to the fuse is not #10 or thicker, the fuse should be lower in amperage—15 amps for #14 wire and 20 amps for #12 wire.

■ Constantly blown fuses are an annoyance—and they indicate that a circuit is overstressed. See page 48 for tips on balancing circuit loads.

■ Without an index, or circuit map, it can be challenging to figure out which circuit to shut off or turn back on. See opposite page for how to map circuits.

■ In some areas a panel attached to a flammable surface is considered a fire hazard; nonflammable material is required between the panel and wood.

■ Open knockouts also present a fire danger. Buy push-in "goof plugs" designed to fill the open knockouts.

Mapping circuits

When making a repair or new installation, knowing which circuit controls which outlet speeds the job and helps ensure safety. That's why electrical codes require service panels to have an index telling which receptacles, lights, and appliances are on which circuit. If your panel has no index, creating one will take some time. Prepare by turning on all the lights in the house. Plug a light, fan, or radio into as many receptacles as possible, and switch them on. Turn on the dishwasher and open the door of the microwave oven. With the whole house switched on, you are ready to map.

1 MAP THE LOCATIONS OF ALL OUTLETS

Draw a rough sketch of each floor in your house, noting the location of every receptacle, switch, light, and appliance. (You may want to use the symbols shown on page 110). On the service panel place a numbered piece of tape next to each breaker or switch.

2 IDENTIFY CIRCUITS

To communicate with your helper, use a pair of walkie-talkies or two cellular phones. Start at the top of the panel. Switch off the circuit and have your helper identify the room without power. On the map jot down the number of the circuit next to each outlet that is turned off. Repeat these steps for each circuit.

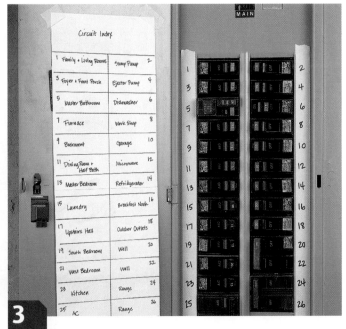

3 DRAW UP THE INDEX

Write an index that accounts for all the fixtures, receptacles, and hardwired appliances in your home. Attach the index to the inside door panel of the circuit breaker or fuse box. You may be surprised to find that some circuits travel through several rooms. This can be confusing, but it is not dangerous.

Avoiding circuit overloads

The total power used by all of a home's light fixtures, lamps, appliances, and tools is called "demand." When demand exceeds the safe capacity of a circuit, the circuit is overloaded.

Breakers and fuses

It's usually easy to tell if a circuit is overloaded: The breaker trips frequently or the fuse keeps blowing. This probably means that wires are also overheating, posing a threat to your home.

Sometimes the solution is simple: Move one high-amperage appliance (such as a microwave oven or toaster) to a receptacle on another circuit. If the overloads stop then the problem is solved. If not, you may need to install a new circuit (pages 192–193).

Overloading problems often occur on 120-volt circuits, which serve multiple receptacles and lights. Most 240-volt circuits serve only one receptacle or appliance. If a 240-volt circuit regularly overloads, change the wiring.

To better understand troublesome circuits and to prepare for adding new electrical lines, the chart below shows how close the circuits are to being overloaded.

Checking watts and amps

If the service panel does not have an accurate index, map the house and add an index (page 47). Find a circuit's amperage rating by looking at the circuit breaker or fuse. Add up the wattage of every lightbulb on the circuit. Note the amperage or watt rating for every appliance and tool plugged into receptacles as well. This information should be printed somewhere on the appliance. Examples are illustrated on the opposite page. Some appliances vary widely in ratings, so check appliances individually. Older appliances usually have a higher rating.

Safe capacity

Codes require that appliances and fixtures on a circuit do not exceed "safe capacity," usually defined as the total capacity minus 20 percent. (See the chart, below left.) If the total demand exceeds a circuit's safe capacity and you can't solve the problem by plugging an appliance into a receptacle on another circuit, install a new circuit (pages 192–193). If a circuit suddenly becomes touchy—tripping the breaker at the slightest provocation—check to see if the breaker is functioning correctly (page 26).

Calculating circuit capacity

Here are two ways to calculate circuit capacity. First, if you know the amperage and voltage of the circuit, you can determine the total capacity by doing this calculation:

Amps × Volts = Watts
For example, if you have a 15-amp, 120-volt circuit, total capacity in watts is 15×120, or 1800 watts ($15 \times 120 = 1800$). With a 20-amp, 120-volt circuit, total capacity is 2400 watts (20×120).

Or work the other way around:
Watts ÷ Volts = Amps
If all the bulbs in a pendent light fixture add up to 600 watts, the light is using 5 amps ($600 \div 120 = 5$). If such a fixture hangs in your kitchen, don't run a toaster (at 6–13 amps) on the same 15-amp circuit or you might overload the circuit.

Some electricians use this general rule: Allow 100 watts for each amp. That means allowing no more than 1500 watts on a 15-amp circuit and no more than 2000 watts on a 20-amp circuit.

WORK SMARTER

SAFE CAPACITY FOR 120-VOLT CIRCUITS

To be sure your circuit won't overload, check individual appliances to determine the watts required by each appliance and fixture on a circuit. Total the usage to make sure it is within the safe capacity shown here.

AMPS	TOTAL CAPACITY	SAFE CAPACITY
15A	1800 watts	1440 watts / 12 amps
20A	2400 watts	1920 watts / 16 amps
25A	3000 watts	2400 watts / 20 amps
30A	3600 watts	2880 watts / 24 amps

Wattage and amperage ratings

These ratings are examples only. Check appliances individually.

TELEVISION
50–300 watts/0.4–2.5 amps

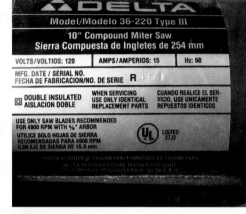

CIRCULAR SAW
1200 watts/15 amps

REFRIGERATOR
700–1200 watts/5.8–10 amps

MICROWAVE OVEN
900–1500 watts/7.5–12.5 amps

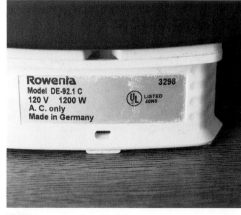

IRON
1000–1200 watts/8.3–10 amps

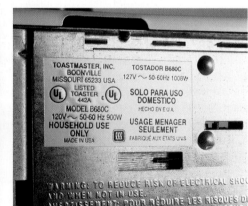

TOASTER
800–1600 watts/6.6–13.3 amps

⊘ **SAFETY ALERT**

ALLOW FOR MOTOR SURGE
During the first few seconds a motor is started, it uses significantly more power than during normal operation. A circuit supplying appliances with motors—a refrigerator, freezer, air-conditioner, or fan, for instance—needs extra capacity to handle occasional power surges. Window air-conditioners and refrigerators should probably be plugged into receptacles that have their own circuits.

🌐 **REAL WORLD**

WATT CHEER!
It's not difficult to overload a circuit and cause it to blow, especially during the holidays when decorative lights are hung and additional guests are in the house. Be mindful of the type of wattage the strings of lights require and make sure that the circuit can handle the wattage. Consider installing an outdoor circuit just for decorative lights.

Aluminum wiring

When copper prices increased in the early 1970s, builders in many areas switched to aluminum wire. Homeowners soon discovered, however, that aluminum posed a fire hazard, especially when connected to brass or copper terminals or wires. By the time aluminum wire was banned, thousands of homes had been wired. Because aluminum expands and contracts over time, it can loosen from terminals, causing faults. Also, where aluminum is attached to brass or copper, it oxidizes, degrading the connection.

Consider replacing aluminum wires with copper if the wires run through conduit or Greenfield. You (or an electrician) can install new wires by attaching them to the old wires and pulling them through the conduit (page 123). However, if the aluminum is encased in NM or armored cable, replacing it will be difficult and costly.

Preventive maintenance for aluminum wiring

To check the condition of your aluminum wiring, you'll need to systematically open every switch box, receptacle box, fixture, hardwired appliance, and junction box in your home.

Shut off power to a circuit and open its boxes. If a switch or receptacle has CO/ALR written on it (center right), it is safe to connect aluminum wires to it. If the device is a standard receptacle, replace it with a CO/ALR device. (Buy them at electrical supply stores if your home centers do not carry them.) How to replace devices is described on pages 66–73.

Or use a more time-consuming but less costly method (bottom right): Disconnect an aluminum wire from its terminal, snip off the bare wire ends, restrip the wire, and connect it to a short pigtail made of copper. Squirt antioxidant onto the wire ends. Then twist the wires together and attach an Al/Cu wire nut, which is made for this purpose. Connect the copper pigtail to the standard switch or receptacle.

Make sure that throughout the house all aluminum-to-copper or aluminum-to-brass connections are brushed clean of corrosion (look for a powdery white coating, especially on devices near damp areas); coat the connections with antioxidant. Check each device, backing off the terminal screws, adding the antioxidant, and firmly retightening the screws. Aluminum breaks easily. If a wire end is cracked, snip it off and restrip. Never use the holes on the back of the receptacle for back wiring if you have aluminum wiring.

Check all connections to terminals annually, and tighten them as needed.

Bare wire is dull silver

Look for "AL"

CHECK WIRING
Aluminum wire is marked "AL." The stripped wire is a dull silver color. Aluminum is a soft metal and strains easily. Look for cracks in the bare wire.

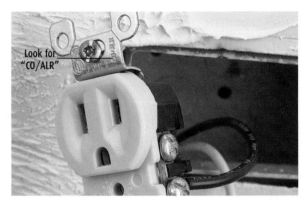

Look for "CO/ALR"

CHECK DEVICES
All switches and receptacles should have CO/ALR stamped on them. If not, replace them with a CO/ALR device. Check every switch and receptacle.

Antioxidant

APPLY ANTIOXIDANT
To keep the aluminum from developing a nonconductive layer of oxidant, especially where aluminum is joined to copper, snip off bare wire ends, restrip, and coat the wires with antioxidant. Use Al/Cu wire nuts, and attach to copper pigtails.

Planning lighting

Chapter 4 highlights

Before you choose light fixtures, draw up a lighting plan. Keep in mind that lighting does more than just illuminate. Lighting also:

■ **Enhances activities.** Reading, food preparation—even cleaning—becomes easier and more pleasurable when the lighting is ample but not glaring.

■ **Highlights decorative features.** By changing or redirecting lights, you can emphasize artwork, favorite pieces of furniture, or other decorative features. You can even position lights to make a room seem larger. Outdoor lighting can dramatize built-ins and plantings.

■ **Sets a mood.** By building versatility into a room with a variety of fixtures and dimmer switches, you can easily adjust the lighting to suit the occasion.

■ **Provides safety.** Well-placed lights help make stairs and hallways safer; outdoors, lighting can even discourage intruders.

Choosing ceiling fixtures

The broad range of overhead fixtures can be roughly divided into ones with eye-catching decorative features (like the ones shown on this page) and ones that are hardly noticeable but provide general illumination (like the flush ceiling fixtures shown on the opposite page). Track lights fall in between. All come in a wide variety of styles. Here are the basic types and features to choose from.

Pendent lights

Lights that hang down from the ceiling are called pendants. Use them for general lighting, to illuminate a dining room table, or to light up a work surface.

A chandelier or other type of pendant usually can't illuminate a large room on its own. That's because a chandelier often hangs at eye level and would produce an unpleasant glare if it were bright enough to light an entire room.

Pendent lantern

Pendant

- **Pendent shades.** Use a pendent shade to focus light on a specific space, such as a small table, a countertop, or a narrow work area. A pendent light with a glass shade will provide general lighting as well as directed light. A metal shade focuses light more directly. Older styles of pendent lights hang by decorative brass chains, with a neutral-color lamp cord running through the chain. Newer fixtures use a plain chrome-color wire for support, with the cord running alongside.
- **Pendent lanterns.** These lights resemble the old glass lanterns that protected candles from wind. Use them in narrow areas like foyers and stairways. Hang these at least 6 ½ feet from the ground so that people can walk under them. Center a pendent lantern width-wise in a narrow room. If it is near a large window, place it so it will look centered from the outside.
- **Chandeliers.** Originally designed as candleholders, chandeliers usually have five or more lightbulbs. Look for a model that is easy to clean; complex designs can be difficult to dust. Keep it in scale—a chandelier that is too small will appear to be dwarfed by the room. When choosing a unit to hang over a dining room table, select one that is about 12 inches narrower than the table. If it is any wider, people may bump their heads on it when they stand up from the table. In an entryway maintain proportion by installing a chandelier that is 2 inches

Chandelier

wide for every foot of room width—for example, use a 20-inch-wide light in a 10-foot-wide room.

Get the height right. A common mistake is to hang a chandelier too low. A chandelier should hang about 30 inches above a tabletop. The length of the chain will depend on your ceiling height.

Track ceiling fixtures

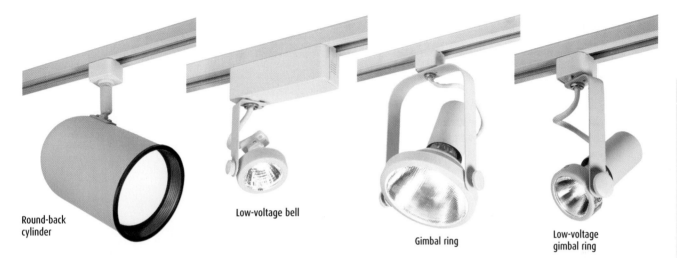

Round-back
cylinder

Low-voltage bell

Gimbal ring

Low-voltage
gimbal ring

CHOOSING TRACK LIGHTS

A single track lighting system can combine general lighting and accent lighting. When choosing a lamp make sure it can handle the lightbulb of your choice and that it will fit onto your track. Incandescent lamps such as a **round-back cylinder** or a **gimbal ring** produce a broad, intense beam. Low-voltage halogen track lights such as a **low-voltage bell** or **low-voltage gimbal ring** produce a more intense, less broad area of light. They have their own transformer, so they can attach to a standard-voltage track. (However, these low-voltage lights require a special dimmer switch; a standard dimmer will damage the lamps.) A track that partially encircles a room at a distance of 6 feet or so from the walls will disperse light more effectively than a single track running through the middle of the room.

Flush ceiling fixtures

Fluorescent
flush-mount

Halogen
flush-mount

Semiflush-mount

Two-head spot

CHOOSING FLUSH FIXTURES

A single flush fixture in the middle of the ceiling is the most common way to light a room. These fixtures usually produce enough light to adequately illuminate a 12×12-foot room with an 8-foot ceiling or a 16×16-foot room with a 10-foot ceiling (the higher the fixture, the broader the spread of its light). They hug the ceiling, consistently distributing light. Newer fluorescent ceiling fixtures with electronic ballasts look like incandescents, save energy, and have tubes that rarely burn out. A semiflush fixture hangs down a foot or so from the ceiling. It diffuses light through the globe as well as upward like a cove light, evenly illuminating a room. Halogens offer more intense light. Two- or three-head spotlights provide some of track lighting's versatility. Point the lights horizontally for general lighting, or angle them downward to highlight certain areas of the room.

Selecting bulbs and tubes

The color of a lightbulb or a light fixture globe or shade significantly affects the mood of a room. Lighting that is slightly red or yellow is considered "warm," while blue-tinged light is "cool." Incandescent bulbs produce warm light; many fluorescents are cool—if not downright cold.

Choose the color of your home's lighting according to the color of your furnishings. If you have pure white walls or cabinetry, warm lighting will make them beige. Cool light directed at brownish natural wood may give it a green tinge.

Fortunately, whether you have a fluorescent or an incandescent fixture, you can switch from cool to warm light, or vice versa, by changing the bulbs or tubes.

BUYER'S GUIDE

NEW LIGHT ON FLUORESCENTS
Fluorescent lighting is economical but often harsh and cold. For a slightly higher cost, you can buy tubes that deliver light similar to that of an afternoon sun. The lower the Kelvin temperature of a tube, the warmer its light will be. A tube marked "3000K," for example, delivers warm color, while a "5000K" tube will make a room feel cool. "Full-spectrum" or "wide-spectrum" tubes have low Kelvin ratings.

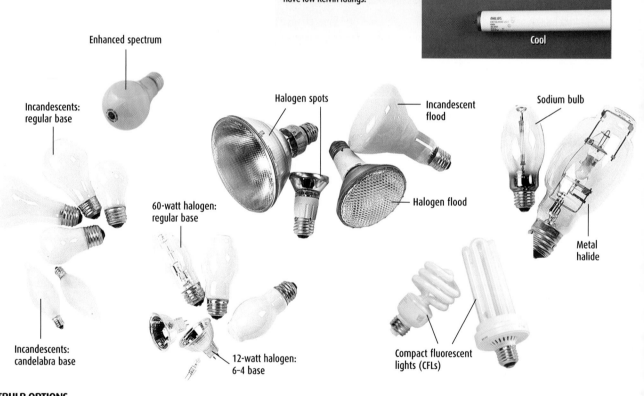

Sunshine or daylight

Aquarium/plant

Warmer than cool but cooler than aquarium

Cool

Enhanced spectrum

Incandescents: regular base

Halogen spots

Incandescent flood

Sodium bulb

60-watt halogen: regular base

Halogen flood

Metal halide

Incandescents: candelabra base

12-watt halogen: 6–4 base

Compact fluorescent lights (CFLs)

LIGHTBULB OPTIONS

■ **Incandescent bulbs** are the most common but have comparatively short lives and are not very energy-efficient.

■ **Compact fluorescent lights (CFLs)** that screw into incandescent sockets are by far the most efficient choice to save money in the long run. Choose from among several shapes and degrees of warmth.

■ **Halogen bulbs** generally last longer and are more efficient than incandescents, but they burn hot. Halogens come in many styles, so make sure the bulb base fits in your fixture.

■ **Reflector bulbs** direct either a wide or narrow beam of light, depending on the bulb. A "spot" bulb projects a flashlight-like beam. A "flood" bulb illuminates a wider area. The second

number on the stamped label indicates the degree of the beam spread.

■ **HID (High-Intensity Discharge) lamps** such as sodium, metal halide, and mercury vapor produce very bright, economical light outdoors.

■ **Enhanced spectrum bulbs** are tinted blue for a more vivid and natural-feeling light.

Planning kitchen lighting

The right lighting plan can make your kitchen more cheerful and inviting, increase the safety of food preparation, and highlight cabinetry and other design features. As you plan remember that surfaces like ceramic tiles and semigloss paint reflect light. This can be beneficial, but in the wrong place they can bounce bright light into your eyes.

■ **Ambient lighting** produces a daylight effect. Flush ceiling fixtures or track lights spread light more evenly than recessed can lights or pendants. Cove lighting creates ambient light originating from several directions. Windows and skylights are great sources of light during daylight hours, but they need help in the evening or in gloomy weather. A dimmer switch or two on your ambient lighting will make it easier to strike the right balance.

■ **Task lights** under kitchen cabinets or in other strategic areas illuminate common kitchen tasks such as food preparation and dishwashing. A range hood with a light eases stove-top cooking as it vents odors.

■ **In-between lights** illuminate kitchen work spaces while providing generous amounts of ambient light. These lights include recessed can lights over a sink, pendent fixtures above an eating area, and track lights in a semicircle near cabinetry.

Ambient lighting

Task lights

In-between lights

Track lighting

Pendent task lighting

Fluorescent light over work area

Rope lighting

LIGHTING YOUR EATING AND PREP AREAS

Ensure that ambient lighting is positioned so that it amply illuminates work areas. To supplement ambient light, install fluorescent or undercabinet halogen lights over work surfaces. If there are no cabinets above, use track lighting, sconces, recessed can lights in the ceiling, or halogen trapeze lights. Pendent lights work well for task lighting but are not practical above a sink because they hang down too low.

Strings of rope lights placed along the kickplate add an accent and highlight your flooring.

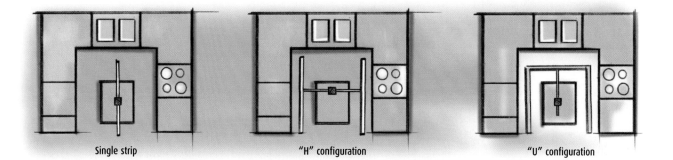

Single strip

"H" configuration

"U" configuration

SHAPING UP WITH TRACK LIGHTING

Many kitchens feature a single strip of track lighting running through the center of the ceiling. This kind of light provides adequate illumination but can sometimes bounce off wall cabinets and produce an uncomfortable glare—especially if the cabinets are shiny or light in color. The lights can cast a shadow over a person preparing food at the countertop, contributing to poor visibility.

Instead of installing a single strip of track lighting along the ceiling, wrap the tracks around the room in an "H" or a "U" pattern. Install the tracks about 3 feet out from the wall and 2 feet out from the wall cabinets. The lamps will then shine down over the shoulders of people working at counters, or toward the center of the room—providing both task lighting and ambient light.

PLANNING LIGHTING

4

LIGHTING COUNTERTOPS

Place fluorescent or halogen undercabinet lights so they will illuminate the countertop but not shine in a person's eyes. If the light fixtures are chunky, consider installing a 2-inch strip of wood along the underside of the cabinet to shield the glare.

USING COVE LIGHTING

This is an easy and inexpensive way to add an elegant lighting touch to a kitchen. Fluorescent fixtures placed on the top of a wall cabinet wash the wall and ceiling in a glow that disperses even light throughout the kitchen.

Lighting for healthy plants

SUPPLEMENTING NATURAL LIGHT

Nothing brightens a kitchen window like potted flowers or herbs. Most plants need at least 4 hours of direct sunlight a day. Unless your window provides this kind of exposure, you may need to supplement your room's natural light with artificial rays. Install incandescent or fluorescent bulbs or tubes that are labeled full- or wide-spectrum. As supplements to filtered window light, these lights need to be on only for several hours a day. Keep them a foot or more away from your plants to avoid drying out the leaves.

If your room provides little sunlight or none at all, you will have to install supplemental lighting at close range. To grow healthy plants focus these lights on your plants and leave them on for all or most of the day.

Lighting a bathroom

A n average-size bathroom needs a ceiling fan/light in the center of the main room, a moisture-proof ceiling light over the shower/bath, and lights over the sink.

■ Ambient lighting is typically provided by an overhead light combined with a vent fan. Make sure the fan's blower is powerful enough to adequately vent your bathroom (pages 161–163). For a little more money, you can also purchase a low-wattage night-light or a fan-forced heater unit. Some people prefer a heat lamp near the tub or shower for additional heat while drying off after bathing.

■ Bathroom mirror lighting deserves careful thought.

A horizontal strip of decorative lightbulbs above the mirror provides lots of light but may shine in your eyes. A fluorescent fixture with a lens provides more even light but may lack warmth. Sconce lights placed on either side of the mirror are the best source for lighting your face for shaving or applying makeup. When planning circuits don't forget to install a ground fault circuit interrupter (GFCI) receptacle near the sink.

■ Shower lighting supplements what little light comes through the shower curtain or glass door. Consider installing a recessed canister light with a watertight lens placed directly above the shower.

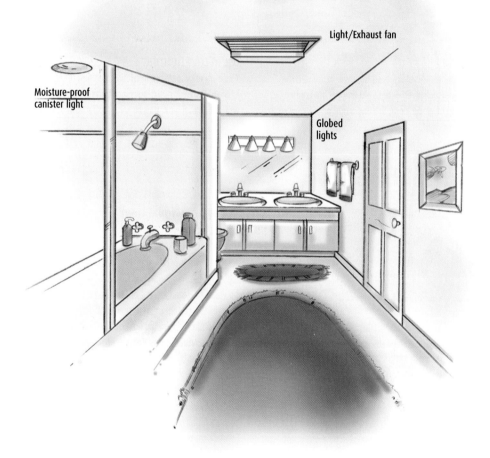

Moisture-proof canister light

Light/Exhaust fan

Globed lights

LIGHTING UP YOUR BATHROOM

The darker the color of your bathroom walls and fixtures, the more light you need. Light from a window may be sufficient for daytime use. But for nighttime and early-morning use, the shower, in particular, might need one or two moisture-proof canister lights. (Codes limit them to 60 watts each if the shower is enclosed.) Above the sink install moisture-resistant globed lights that won't shine in your eyes. Overhead install a single fixture that efficiently and stylishly combines a light, exhaust fan, and perhaps a night-light and a heater.

Lighting living areas

Living rooms, dining rooms, great-rooms, and large bedrooms all benefit from both ambient and task lighting. Rather than installing a single lighting component, think in terms of the total effect of the room. "Layering" several types of lights makes a room more comforting and inviting. The goal is flexibility, so you can set a variety of moods by brightening or dimming the entire room or part of the room.

- Highlight a piece of art or cabinetry or accentuate wall texture with lights to give the room warmth and interest.
- Put at least one of the components on a dimmer switch, and install several lights that are optional, but not necessary. Don't be afraid to install too many lights; you don't have to have all of them on at the same time.
- Install an in-between light such as a dining-area chandelier to brighten the dinner table and provide some ambient light.
- Modern codes require AFCI circuit breakers for all circuits supplying plug outlets in bedrooms(see page 76).

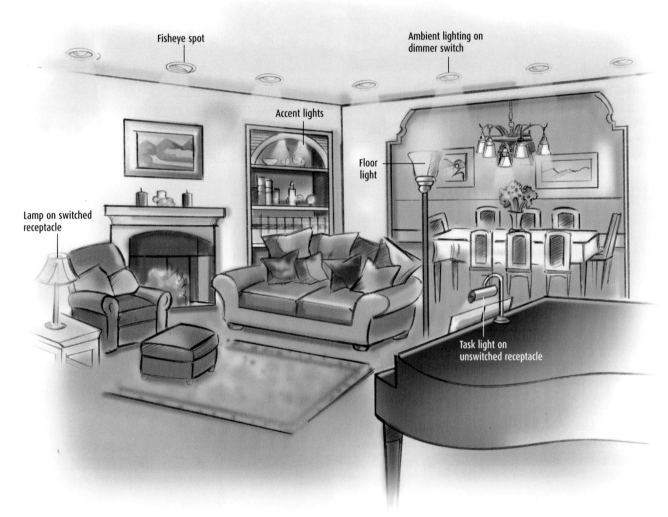

Fisheye spot

Ambient lighting on dimmer switch

Accent lights

Floor light

Lamp on switched receptacle

Task light on unswitched receptacle

SHOWING OFF A GREAT-ROOM WITH GREAT LIGHTING

The lighting plan for this large family room includes a grid of recessed canister lights for general lighting and a centrally located chandelier over the dining table. A recessed light with fisheye trim spotlights a wall painting. The table lamp and floor lamp are controlled by wall switches. Accent lights brighten shelves. The task light on the piano is on an unswitched receptacle.

LIGHTING UP CABINETS
Achieve a stunning effect with lights placed inside glass-doored cabinets. If the shelves are also glass, the light will glimmer as it filters down. Use small fluorescent fixtures—which stay cool—and control them with a special fluorescent dimmer switch.

CHOOSING A BEDSIDE LIGHT
For bedtime reading a swivel light that mounts on a wall has great advantages over a table lamp. You can point the light directly at your book, and it won't take up space on the end table.

Lighting room by room

Provide very bright light in areas used for work and study. In rooms designed for entertaining, less light is called for.

- **Eating/Dining areas.** A bright pendent light is appropriate for a breakfast nook or other informal eating area, but a table used for fine dining should have indirect, subtle light. Point recessed or track lights away from the table. Position a chandelier so it does not shine in diners' eyes.
- **Hallways and stairways.** These areas require enough light so people won't trip. You may need lights at the bottom and top of a stairway. A 75-watt ceiling fixture every 12 feet is sufficient for a hallway. Increase the wattage if elderly people live in your home. Wall sconces work well in these areas.
- **Study.** A single reading lamp can create an uncomfortable glare on book pages. Provide one or two additional sources of light, such as ample overhead lighting or a second lamp.
- **Work rooms/hobby areas.** Start with overhead lighting that distributes light evenly throughout the room. Then add nonglare lights above work surfaces and flexible lamps for specific tasks.

INSTALLING SCONCE LIGHTING
Lights that mount on the wall can make a room feel larger and a hallway wider. Use sconces for accents rather than for ambient lighting. Place low-wattage bulbs in them, unless you want to highlight the wall above.

Planning for recessed lighting

Recessed canister lights vary in intensity and angle. The higher your ceiling the more floor space a light will illuminate. In general, recessed cans should be 6 feet from each other. Of course, most rooms are not sized to accommodate this, so you'll have to adjust your calculations. In the example below most of the lights are 5 feet apart. Make a similar plan for your own installation, experimenting with several configurations. Take your plans to your home center for advice.

Once you start installing can lights, you'll find that many have to be moved several inches from their ideal locations in order to avoid hitting joists (ceiling framing). Fortunately, this will not make a big difference in the overall effect.

Special techniques

In addition to providing general lighting, recessed can lights enhance decorating strategies with:

- **Wall washing.** To light up a large wall area, install cans with wall-wash trims that are 24 to 30 inches apart, and the same distance from the wall.
- **Accent lighting.** Spotlight a painting, fireplace mantle, or other feature with a can that has an eyeball trim. Place it 18 to 24 inches from the wall, centered on the object.
- **Grazing.** To dramatize an unusual vertical surface, such as a fireplace or a textured wall, place cans 6 to 12 inches from the wall and 12 to 18 inches apart. Wire them with a separate dimmer switch.

CONCENTRIC CIRCLES OF LIGHT
On graph paper make a scale drawing of your room. To get a general idea of the distribution of light, use a compass to draw circles that are scaled to about 5 feet in radius (10 feet in diameter). In this example, the center of the room will get more light than the perimeter—which is usually desirable. Generally figure that a 65-watt floodlight in a room with an 8-foot ceiling will light up a circle that is 8 feet in diameter; if the ceiling is 10 feet high, it will illuminate a 10-foot circle.

Planning security lighting

Outdoor lighting may be your home's most important security feature. It may even deter intruders more effectively than additional door locks or an alarm system.

■ Keep areas brightly lit so there are no dark pathways. Ideally two or more lights should be pointed at a potential intruder who approaches your home.

■ Install two light fixtures at each door of entry—or at least one fixture equipped with two bulbs in case one bulb burns out. Control these lights with motion sensors or timers (page 171) rather than an inside switch.

■ Install spotlights controlled by a motion sensor over the garage door and under the eaves. These discourage intruders and make it easier to carry in the groceries at night.

■ Place light posts or path lights along walkways. Control bright lights with motion sensors and low-voltage lights with a timer or photocell so they stay on all night.

■ Make it difficult to extinguish lights. Casual trespassers will usually be deterred by bright lights, but a professional thief will look for ways to shut off your security lights. Seven feet may be an attractive height for placing porch lights, but an intruder can easily reach that high. Place outdoor lights 9 feet or more above the ground.

■ Add standard-voltage light posts to fortify your property. Low-voltage path lighting can be easily disconnected.

■ Install bright lights on motion-sensor switches indoors behind a sliding glass door or large window. These will surprise intruders and alert you as well.

Entry lights on timer

Bright indoor light on timer

Eave lights with motion sensor

Post light on timer

Garden floodlights on timer

BRIGHT AND SECURE
This grouping of lights makes intruders uncomfortable, but it appears decorative enough not to broadcast its security function. Outside entry lights, spots, eave lights, and light posts allow no place to hide. A timer-controlled indoor light behind a large window makes it appear as if the occupants are home even when they're not. For ease of use control the light with timers or motion sensors.

Lighting your yard

Lighting can emphasize your yard's best features. Begin by making a sketch of your property, including plantings, pathways, and outdoor structures. Spend an evening or two with a work light and extension cord to try out some ideas. Vary the positioning. Outdoor lights may be suspended, mounted on poles, installed on the side of a deck or house, or placed under foliage. Consider these other options:

■ Try outdoor-rated rope lights. Some rope lights (page 64) are designed for exterior use. Hang them loosely from post to post on a railing, stretch them taut along a fascia board, or spiral-wrap them—barber-shop style— around a pole or post.

■ Incorporate holiday lights. Outdoor holiday lights— whether large and colorful or tiny white pinpricks—can be used year-round. Hang them high and fire them up for a party to add a festive atmosphere.

■ Use both standard-voltage and low-voltage lights. Keep some standard-voltage lights around for times when you want to see clearly at night, but give yourself the option of using low-voltage lighting as well.

■ Experiment with color. Use outdoor lenses and lightbulbs in various colors to set just the right mood. The results can be surprising, so take the time to experiment. Blue light resembles the cast of a full moon's light. Green light cast on a tree or shrub can give foliage a special luminescence. Reds, oranges, and yellows can evoke a warm, inviting feel.

Under-eaves lights with blue lenses

In-ground lights to accent tree

Brick lighting

Foliage lighting

LIGHTS THAT EMPHASIZE FOLIAGE

Aim illumination toward attractive features of your yard, such as trees and plantings. Be sure these lights don't create an unpleasant glare for passersby. Bright under-eave lights are less harsh if blue lenses or bulbs are used. A tree can appear lit from within by an in-ground spotlight shining upward. Romanticize in-ground lights by dropping a few leaves on top of them. Lights that shine through flowering plants cast interesting shadows and highlight the colors of petals. Brick lighting defines the borders of a patio or driveway. All these elements can add to your home's security (opposite page) while they beautify your lot.

Deck and patio lighting

You'll find many light fixtures designed specifically for decks and patios at your home center. Position these lights to shine up from a patio surface, point down at a deck or stair treads, or sit atop posts and provide general illumination. The simplest way to add outdoor lighting is to plug in a string of low-voltage lights. However, keep in mind that these lights look temporary and are easily damaged.

120-volt fixtures

A flexible lighting system should combine low-voltage lights with standard 120-volt fixtures. Run standard-voltage cable or conduit in trenches (pages 174–176), hide it under decking or railing pieces, or drill long holes through posts and fish it through (page 177). Plan these installations to complement security lighting (page 62).

Rope lights

Exterior-grade rope lights can be strung in fanciful patterns or in orderly straight lines. Unless you use a lot of them, they will be more decorative than bright. Plug them directly into a receptacle, or use an extension cord approved for outdoor use. Fasten them to wood posts and railings with galvanized fence staples.

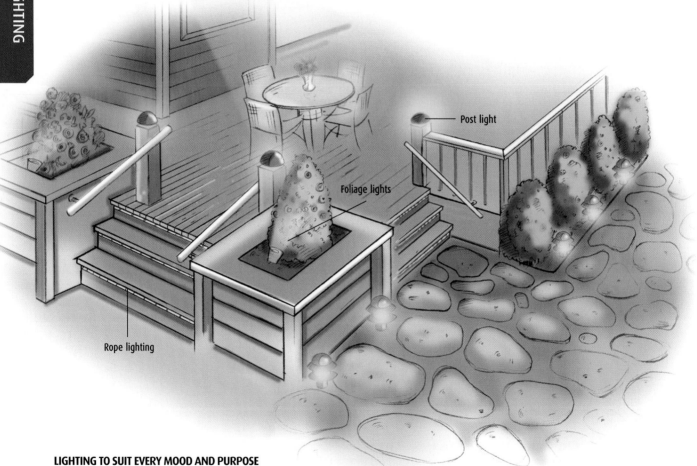

Post light

Foliage lights

Rope lighting

LIGHTING TO SUIT EVERY MOOD AND PURPOSE

Treat outdoor diners to the same even lighting you would expect them to enjoy inside. Point several eave lights at the table, positioning them as high as possible. Rope lights are great as accents and to illuminate steps to help reduce the possibility of tripping. Post lights offer gentle highlights while other lights give emphasis to specific features, such as plantings and flowers.

Switches and receptacles

Chapter 5 highlights

witches and receptacles (both of which are referred to as "devices") are the workhorses of your electrical system, often getting used thousands of times per year. Usually they are remarkably reliable, and when one does wear out, replacing it is an easy task.

This chapter will show you how to replace standard devices and how to upgrade for special purposes. The two most common upgrades are a dimmer switch, which allows you to control the level of light, and a GFCI receptacle, which provides added protection against the possibility of shock. Many other types of special-duty switches are available to enhance your control over lighting. All these devices are nearly as easy to install as a standard switch or receptacle.

This chapter also covers GFCI and AFCI circuit breakers, which protect all the outlets on a circuit in two different ways. Be sure to follow local codes and install GFCI and AFCI circuit breakers where required.

Replacing a switch

5

SWITCHES AND RECEPTACLES

PROJECT DETAILS

SKILLS: Stripping wire and attaching wire to a terminal
PROJECT: Replacing a standard wall switch

TIME TO COMPLETE

EXPERIENCED: 15 min.
HANDY: 25 min.
NOVICE: 45 min.

STUFF YOU'LL NEED

TOOLS: Tester, wire stripper, lineman's pliers, longnose pliers, side-cutting pliers, screwdriver
MATERIALS: New switch, electrician's tape, wire nuts

I f your switch pops when you turn it on, if it seems loose, or if your light fixture doesn't switch on even with a new bulb, it's time to replace the switch. Switches are easy and quick to install. To test a switch, see pages 77–78.

Choosing a replacement

If the switch has two wires connected to it (it might also have a ground wire) and a toggle marked ON and OFF, it is a single-pole switch—the most common type. If three wires connect to it (not counting the ground wire), it is a three-way switch (page 16).

You may choose to replace your switch with a dimmer. If so, it's not necessary to change the wiring entering the box, but you do have to connect wires to leads with wire nuts rather than screw wires to terminals (page 69).

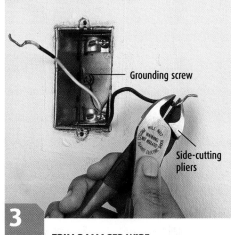

1

TEST FOR POWER

At the service panel, shut off power to the circuit supplying the switch. Remove the two screws above and below the switch toggle, and pull off the cover plate. (If it is painted over, first score around it with a utility knife.) Test with a 4-level voltage tester to make sure that power is off.

💲 BUYER'S GUIDE

STURDY DEVICES FOR HEAVY USE

If a switch is used constantly, pay a little extra for a device labeled "commercial" or "spec-rated." It has stronger contacts and is sturdier.

2

INSPECT THE WIRING

Remove the two screws holding the switch to the box. Gently pry out the switch. Pull on the wires to ensure that they're firmly connected to the terminals. If a wire is loose or broken, you've probably found the problem.

3

TRIM DAMAGED WIRE

Unscrew the terminal screws on the switch about ¼ inch (stop when they get hard to turn), and remove the wires. If a stripped wire end appears nicked or twisted, snip off the damage.

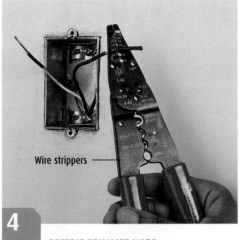

4

RESTRIP TRIMMED WIRE

Using wire strippers, strip about ¾ inch of insulation from the end of any wires that you snipped (pages 32–33). If you strip a white wire that has been painted black or marked with black tape, remark it.

Wire strippers

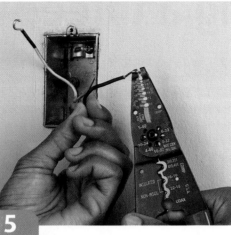

5

TWIST A LOOP

Form a question mark at the end of each wire, using the tip of wire strippers (pages 34-35) or longnose pliers. Make the loop tight enough so that it just fits around the shank of the terminal screw.

🌐 **REAL WORLD**

LOOP THOSE WIRES RIGHT THE FIRST TIME 'ROUND
Replacing a switch isn't necessarily a no-brainer. If a wire loses connection with the switch terminal, the fixture will not work. When replacing a switch the wires should be looped clockwise around the terminals.

5

SWITCHES AND RECEPTACLES

Even if your local codes don't require that a switch or box be grounded, do it anyway. A little extra protection can't hurt.

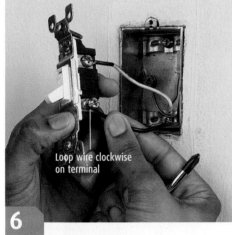

Loop wire clockwise on terminal

6

ATTACH THE WIRES

On new switches the terminals are screwed down tight. Unscrew each until it gets hard to turn. Slip a looped wire end under the screw head, with the end of the loop pointing clockwise. Squeeze the wire end tight around the terminal with longnose pliers (page 35) or the tip of wire strippers. Tighten the screw.

Mounting screw

Screw hole

7

INSTALL THE SWITCH

Gently push the wires back into the box as you push the switch back into position. Aim the mounting screws at the screw holes. Tighten the screws and check that the switch is plumb (straight up and down). The elongated holes allow for adjustments. Replace the cover plate, restore power, and try the switch.

Wrapping a switch body

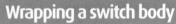

Wrap device with electrical tape

Some electricians wrap the switch with electrician's tape so that all terminals and bare wires are covered providing extra protection from accidental grounding and ensuring the wires won't come off the terminal screws. However, before doing this make sure your local codes allow it and the electrical inspector will approve it. Many inspectors will not approve a wrapped switch because they cannot see if the wires are properly attached to the switch.

Replacing a three-way switch

PROJECT DETAILS

SKILLS: Stripping wire, connecting wire to terminals
PROJECT: Replacing a single three-way switch

TIME TO COMPLETE

EXPERIENCED: 20 min.
HANDY: 40 min.
NOVICE: 1 hr.

STUFF YOU'LL NEED

TOOLS: Tester, wire strippers, lineman's pliers, longnose pliers, side-cutting pliers, screwdriver
MATERIALS: New switch, electrician's tape, wire nuts

5

SWITCHES AND RECEPTACLES

hree-way switches work in pairs to control a light from two locations—handy for controlling a light from the top and the bottom of stairways, or from either end of hallways. The toggle isn't marked OFF and ON. Either up or down can be ON depending on the position of the toggle of the other three-way. (For more on three-way switches, see pages 148–150.)

Before you begin, **shut off power to the circuit (page 6).** Disconnect wires from terminals, and restrip any damaged wires (page 32). Most of the steps for replacing a three-way switch are the same as for a single-pole switch. But with three-ways be sure to mark the wires before you remove the old device.

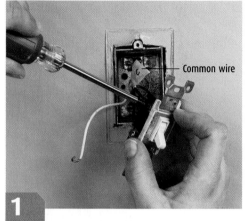

Common wire

1

TAG THE COMMON WIRE

Shut off power, remove the cover plate, and **test to make sure there is no power in the box.** Label the common wire with a piece of masking tape. The common terminal (page 149) is colored differently from the others (it's not the green ground screw) and may be marked "common" on the switch body.

BUYER'S GUIDE

THREE-WAY DIMMER

Replace only one of your paired three-way switches with a dimmer: Two dimmers won't work. The remaining switch requires a standard three-way toggle. (Fluorescent fixtures also require special dimmers.)

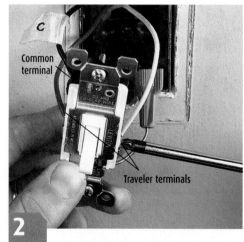

Common terminal

Traveler terminals

2

OPTION A: WIRING ONE CABLE

When only one cable enters the box, it will have three wires plus a ground. Identify the hot wire using a voltage detector (page 31), or by touching one prong of a voltage tester to a ground and the other to each wire in turn. Attach the hot wire to the common terminal, which is a different color. Attach the other two wires to the traveler terminals. Connect the grounds.

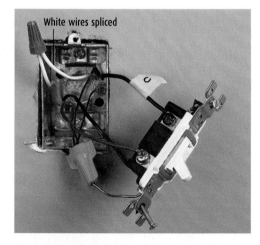

White wires spliced

OPTION B: WIRING TWO CABLES

If two cables enter the box, one cable will have two wires and the other will have three wires (plus ground wires). But despite all the extra wires, you'll find only three wire ends. Proceed just as you would for a one-cable installation (left).

Replacing a dimmer switch

PROJECT DETAILS

SKILLS: Stripping, splicing wire
PROJECT: Connecting one dimmer switch

TIME TO COMPLETE

EXPERIENCED: 15 min.
HANDY: 25 min.
NOVICE: 45 min.

STUFF YOU'LL NEED

TOOLS: Screwdriver, side-cutting pliers, strippers
MATERIALS: Dimmer switch, wire nuts, electrician's tape

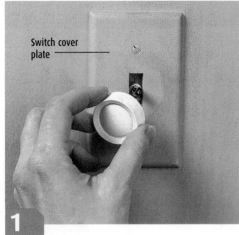

1

REMOVE THE KNOB

Shut off power at the service panel. Pull off the rotary knob with firm outward pressure. Underneath is a standard switch cover plate. Remove the cover plate. Remove the mounting screws and carefully pull out the switch body.

Switch cover plate

2

TEST FOR POWER

A dimmer has wire leads instead of terminals. Remove the wire nuts and **test for power** by touching the probes of the tester to both wires, or to either wire and the metal box, or to one wire and the ground wire. **If power is detected, shut off the correct circuit in the service panel.** (To test for continuity, see page 30.)

Wire lead

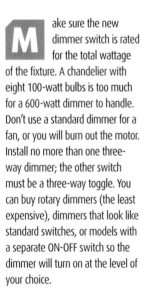

Make sure the new dimmer switch is rated for the total wattage of the fixture. A chandelier with eight 100-watt bulbs is too much for a 600-watt dimmer to handle. Don't use a standard dimmer for a fan, or you will burn out the motor. Install no more than one three-way dimmer; the other switch must be a three-way toggle. You can buy rotary dimmers (the least expensive), dimmers that look like standard switches, or models with a separate ON-OFF switch so the dimmer will turn on at the level of your choice.

3

OPTION A: INSTALLING A STANDARD DIMMER

Attach the ground wire if there is one. Strip ¾ inch of insulation from each solid house wire and 1 inch from each stranded dimmer lead. Wrap a lead around a wire with your fingers so that the lead protrudes past the wire about ⅛ inch. Slip on a wire nut and twist until tight. Test the strength of the connection by gently tugging on both wires.

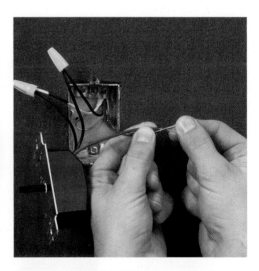

OPTION B: INSTALLING A THREE-WAY DIMMER

If you replace a three-way dimmer, tag the existing lead wires to connect the new dimmer in the same way as the old dimmer. If only one cable enters the box, attach the black wire to the common terminal and the other two wires to the traveler terminals. If you replace a three-way toggle switch with a dimmer, tag the wire that leads to the common terminal. The other two wires are interchangeable.

Installing special switches

⟲ PROJECT DETAILS

SKILLS: Stripping and splicing wires, joining wires to terminals
PROJECT: Installing one of the special switches shown here

⏱ TIME TO COMPLETE

EXPERIENCED: 15 min.
HANDY: 30 min.
NOVICE: 40 min.

✓ STUFF YOU'LL NEED

TOOLS: Wire strippers, lineman's pliers, screwdriver
MATERIALS: Specialty switch, wire nuts

5

SWITCHES AND RECEPTACLES

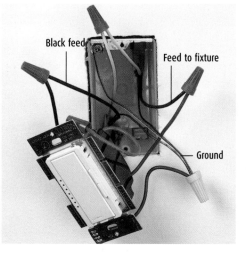

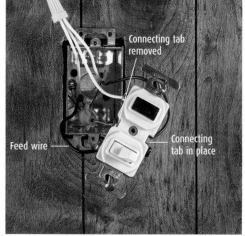

TOUCH-SENSITIVE DIMMER

With this switch you dim or brighten a light by continuing to press the switch rather than by turning a knob or operating a toggle. Connect the black lead to the black feed wire and the red lead to the black wire (or to the white wire painted black) running to the fixture. Connect the green lead to ground (page 11).

PILOT-LIGHT SWITCH

Use one of these for a garage light or an attic fan—anywhere you can't see the fixture while operating the switch. When the light glows the fixture is on. Connect the black feed wire to the brass terminal where there is no connecting tab, and the other black wire to a brass terminal on the other side. Pigtail the neutral wires, and connect one to the silver terminal.

Within an hour you can install any of several clever switches that do everything from control a circuit at a preset time to switch on a light as you walk into a room. Instead of the familiar screw-down terminals on toggle switches, most special switches have leads—short lengths of stranded wire. **Shut off power to the circuit.** To splice leads follow the directions on page 32–33.

💲 BUYER'S GUIDE

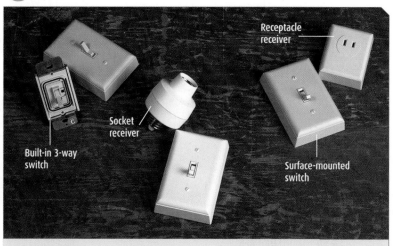

ANYWHERE SWITCH

This **switch lets you control a fixture without having to run electrical cable.** Wire the receiver inside the fixture, attach the sending switch "anywhere" on a wall, and put in a battery. You can even use these switches in a three-way setup (pages 148–150), and dimmers are also available.

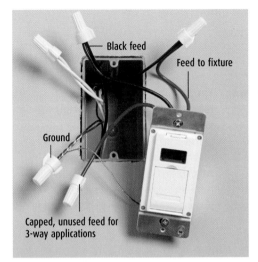

Black feed

Feed to fixture

Ground

Capped, unused feed for
3-way applications

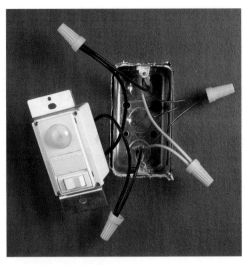

CLOSER LOOK

ONE CABLE OR TWO?

See page 24 for the two ways to
wire a switch. If only one cable
enters a switch box, then power
runs first to the fixture and then
to the switch. Two wires—a black,
and a white wire marked black—
run from the fixture to the switch.
With one cable, the black wire
leads to the fixture and the black-
marked white wire leads is the
feed wire (page 24). If two cables
enter the switch box, one brings
power and the other runs to the
fixture. Timer, combination, and
pilot-light switches are among
those that can be installed only if
you have two cables in the box.
With these types of specialty
switches there must be an
unmarked white neutral wire.

5

SWITCHES AND RECEPTACLES

TIMER SWITCH

This switch turns outdoor lights on and off one or more times
a day. It can be used to replace a standard switch or a 3-way
switch. Connect the black feed wire to the black lead and the
other black wire (which goes to the fixture) to the blue lead.
In this case the red wire is capped but would be used in the
case of replacing a 3-way switch. Connect the white neutral
wires together. Always follow manufacturer's instructions
when connecting switches.

MOTION-SENSOR SWITCH

This switch turns on when its infrared beam senses
movement. Adjust the time-delay feature to control how
long the light will stay on. Wiring is the same as for a
standard single-pole switch (pages 22–23), except that you
connect to leads rather than to terminals.

Combo switches

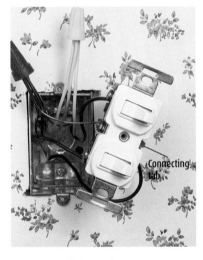

Connecting
tab

Connecting tab

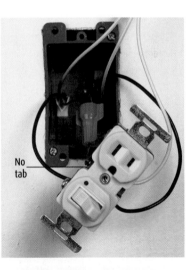

No
tab

DOUBLE SWITCH

This device allows you to control two fixtures
from a single switch box. Three cables enter the
box: One brings power and the other two run to
fixtures. Hook the feed wire to a terminal on the
side that has a connecting tab. Hook the other
two black wires to the terminals on the other
side of the switch. Splice the white wires and
the grounds.

SWITCH/RECEPTACLE

This combines a switch and a grounded
receptacle plug in a single switch box. The
device usually is wired so the receptacle is hot
all the time. Hook the feed wire to a terminal
on the side with a connecting tab. Hook the
other black wire to a brass terminal on the other
side. Pigtail the white wires and hook to the
silver terminal.

SWITCH/RECEPTACLE WITH RECEPTACLE
CONTROLLED BY SWITCH

If you want the receptacle to turn off when the
switch is off, reverse the positions of the black
wires so the feed wire is on the side that does
not have a connecting tab.

More switch possibilities

Here are some of the many special switches available at Home Depot. In addition to the switches you find on display, you can special-order most any switch made by all the major manufacturers of electrical devices. All these switches install using the techniques shown on the previous two pages.

Many high-end switches are as decorative as they are useful. Some have a wide rocker that is pushed rather than flipped. Some combine a large sliding switch with a smaller rocker switch, for a space-age look. And some switches even come in colors other than the usual ivory or white.

Dimmers

A **"smart dimmer"** flips on and off with a toggle or rocker switch, but causes the light to fade slowly when you turn it off. This has a calming effect and it allows you to leave a room with a bit of light to guide your way. An **electronic timer switch** has presets switches that keep the light on for various lengths of time. A **touch-point dimmer** responds to where the finger is placed on the switch's pad. A **toggle dimmer** combines the look of a standard switch with the capability of a dimmer. A **fan speed control** has similar controls to a dimmer but allows you to precisely control the speed of a ceiling fan. In

short, the switches pictured represent just a few of the wide variety of switches available.

Timers

Consider a **programmable timer switch**, which turns lights on and off more than twice a day. This can create the illusion that people are at home while you are on vacation. An **electronic timer switch** keeps the light on for a selected number of hours before automatically shutting it off. And a **plug-in timer** controls a lamp or any other fixture or appliance that you plug into it.

Smart dimmer

Electronic timer switch

Fan speed control

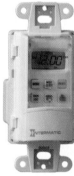

Programmable timer switch

Toggle dimmer

Touch-point dimmer

Plug-in timer

Time delay switch

SWITCHES AND RECEPTACLES

5

Replacing a receptacle

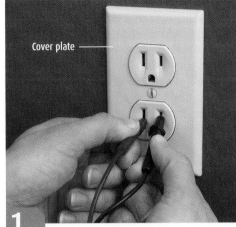

1 CHECK THAT POWER IS OFF

Turn off power to the circuit (page 6). Test to confirm. If the tester shows current, check your service panel and turn off another likely circuit. Test again and proceed only if power is off. Remove the cover plate and unscrew the mounting screws. Being careful not to touch wires or terminals, pull out the receptacle.

Cover plate

2 TEST WIRES FOR POWER

In a damaged receptacle, wires may be hot even though testing shows no power. Touch tester probes to the terminals. If more than two wires enter the box, test all wires (page 6). If you have old wiring and both wires are black, use a receptacle analyzer (page 30) to check that the neutral wire is connected to the silver terminal and the hot wire to the brass.

If a receptacle doesn't seem to work, first check that whatever is plugged into it works properly. Replace any receptacle that is cracked. Before buying a replacement receptacle, check the wiring. Usually the wires leading to a receptacle will be #14 and the circuit breaker or fuse will be 15 amp. In that case, install a 15-amp receptacle. Install a 20-amp receptacle only if the wires are #12 and the circuit breaker or fuse is 20 amps or greater.

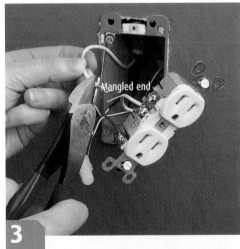

Mangled end

3 SNIP AND RESTRIP DAMAGED WIRE ENDS

Once you're sure the power is off, unscrew the terminals and pull away the wires, taking care not to twist them too much. If a wire end appears nicked or damaged or if it looks like it has been twisted several times, snip off the end and restrip it (pages 32–33).

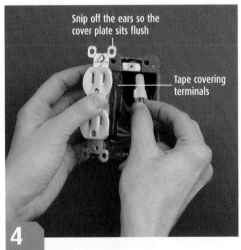

Snip off the ears so the cover plate sits flush

Tape covering terminals

4 INSTALL THE RECEPTACLE

Wire the new receptacle the same as the old, with each white wire connected to a silver terminal and each black or color wire connected to a brass terminal. Wrap electrician's tape to cover all terminals and bare wires. Gently push the outlet into the box. Tighten the mounting screws, and check that the receptacle is straight. Replace the cover plate, restore power, and test with a receptacle analyzer.

5

SWITCHES AND RECEPTACLES

Adding GFCI protection

PROJECT DETAILS

SKILLS: Stripping and splicing wires, connecting wires to terminals
PROJECT: Installing one GFCI receptacle

TIME TO COMPLETE

EXPERIENCED: 30 min.
HANDY: 45 min.
NOVICE: 1 hr.

STUFF YOU'LL NEED

TOOLS: Screwdriver, lineman's pliers, longnose pliers, side-cutting pliers, receptacle analyzer, wire strippers, level
MATERIALS: New receptacle, electrician's tape, wire nuts

A ground fault circuit interrupter (GFCI) shuts down power in milliseconds when it detects the tiniest change in current flow and codes require GFCIs in bathrooms, in kitchens near sinks, and outdoors. GFCIs are inexpensive and simple to install.

A single GFCI can protect up to eleven receptacles or light outlets on the same circuit. A GFCI circuit breaker can protect an entire circuit (page 75). If your home has ungrounded receptacles (page 11), installing GFCIs will provide protection, but won't ground your circuits.

Check your GFCIs at least once a month by pushing in the test button. (The reset button should pop out. Push it back in.) A GFCI may provide power even though it has lost its ability to protect.

Don't use a GFCI as a receptacle for a refrigerator, freezer, or any other appliance that must stay on all the time—it may trip off without your knowledge. Also do not attempt to control a GFCI with a switch.

BUYER'S GUIDE

EXTEND A GFCI BOX
A bulky GFCI can dangerously crowd a box. **Buy a box designed for raceway wiring and two 2-inch-long 6/32 screws.** Fasten the screws through the GFCI and raceway box and into the box.

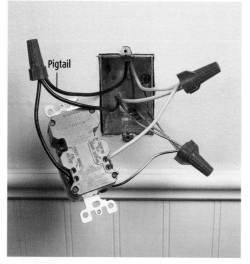
Pigtail

Incoming connected to LINE

Outgoing connected to LOAD

INSTALLING A SINGLE GFCI

Shut off the power. Make connections only to the LINE terminals. For an end-of-the-run box, connect the wires to the terminals. If the box is middle-of-the-run (shown), make a pigtail for each connection by stripping 6 inches along the ends of the wires. Splice each pigtail to the wire(s) with a wire nut, and connect it to the GFCI terminals. Put the white wire on the silver terminal and the black or color wire on the brass terminal. Be sure the box in the wall is large enough to accommodate a GFCI. Replace it if it is not.

PROTECTING OTHER OUTLETS

Shut off the power. Connect the wires carrying power into the box to the LINE terminals. Then connect the wires leading out of the box (to other receptacles or lights) to the LOAD terminals. If you're unsure which wires come from the service panel, pull the wires out of the box and position them so they will not touch each other. Restore power and use a tester to see which pair of wires is hot; connect these to the LINE terminals.

SWITCHES AND RECEPTACLES

5

Installing a GFCI breaker

The least expensive way to give a circuit GFCI protection is to install a GFCI receptacle. It can be wired to protect up to four additional receptacles (page 45).

For more reliable protection install a GFCI circuit breaker. It's more expensive, but it protects all the outlets on a circuit. Although you must feel comfortable about working on a service panel, installing a GFCI breaker can be easier than installing a GFCI receptacle. The latter is bulky and often requires a box extender.

See pages 19–21 for general safety instructions for working in a service panel. **Always shut off power to the main breaker before you begin working.**

5

SWITCHES AND RECEPTACLES

INSTALLING A GFCI BREAKER

Shut off the main breaker. (This de-energizes all the wires and circuitry after the main breaker, but the wires leading into the service panel will still be live.) Have a flashlight handy. Pull out the existing circuit breaker, loosen the terminal screw, and pull the wire out. Insert that wire into the GFCI breaker, and tighten the screw to clamp the wire tight. Detach the line's white wire from the neutral bus, and attach it to the breaker. Push the GFCI breaker into place as you would a standard breaker (page 26). Attach the curly white wire to the neutral bus bar, and restore power.

GFCI breaker

Ground bus bar

Neutral bus bar

Neutral feed

Hot feed

Installing AFCI

 n arc fault occurs when electricity is allowed to arc—to travel via a spark—usually from a hot wire to a neutral, ground wire, or anything that is grounded. Arc faults most often occur in a lamp or appliance cord with damaged insulation (see below left). It can also occur with house wiring inside an electrical box, as when a hot wire with damaged insulation touches a bare ground wire (see below middle). And a hot wire that is cracked can create an arc all by itself (see below right). The arc (or spark) creates a fire hazard as well as a danger to anyone who may touch the cord.

A GFCI receptacle will likely shut off when there is an arc fault, but an AFCI is more reliable. For that reason AFCI breakers are now required by codes for bedroom circuits that have receptacles on them, and are a good idea for living and dining rooms as well.

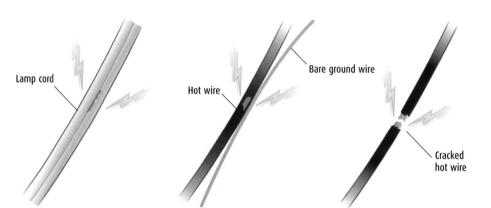

Lamp cord

Hot wire

Bare ground wire

Cracked hot wire

Installing an AFCI breaker

Install an AFCI circuit breaker just as you would a GFCI breaker (see page 75). Purchase a breaker made by the service panel's manufacturer, and make sure it is the correct amperage—15- and 20-amp breakers are usually available.

Shut off the main breaker. (This de-energizes all the wires after the main breaker, but the wires leading into the service panel will still be live.) Before you install the breaker, remove the existing circuit breaker, loosen the terminal screw, and pull the wire out. Insert that wire into the AFCI breaker's terminal hole and tighten the setscrew. Detach the circuit's white wire from the neutral bus, and attach it to the breaker. Push the AFCI breaker into place as you would a standard breaker. Attach the curly white wire to the neutral bus bar, and restore power.

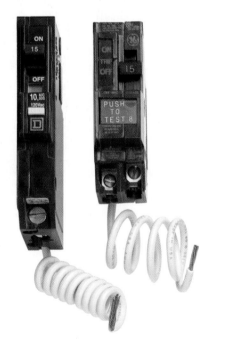

Testing switches

PROJECT DETAILS

SKILLS: Using a continuity tester or multitester, disconnecting a switch
PROJECT: Removing and testing a specialty switch

TIME TO COMPLETE

EXPERIENCED: 10 min.
HANDY: 20 min.
NOVICE: 30 min.

STUFF YOU'LL NEED

TOOLS: Voltage tester, continuity tester or multitester, screwdriver
MATERIALS: None required

TESTING A TIMER SWITCH

Timer switches vary significantly by manufacturer. Some are digital with buttons, as shown above, or analog with a rotary dial. The color of the wires on the switch also vary according to the manufacturer. To test a timer switch you will need to test the continuity of the switch when it is turned on (the continuity tester light should glow) and turned off. Check the wiring diagram of the manufacturer to know which colors of wires to touch with the tester's probes.

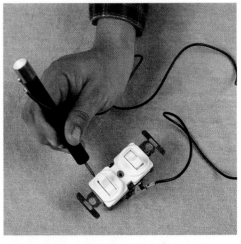

TESTING A DOUBLE SWITCH

Test each of the switches in the same way: Touch the probes to the terminals on each side of the switch. If the tester indicates continuity with the switch ON and no continuity with the switch OFF, then the switch is working. If you get any other result from either switch, replace the device.

 switch should show continuity when turned on and no continuity when turned off. With some specialty switches, however, it might be hard to know when the switch is on and when it is off. Some of the more common specialty switches are expensive enough to warrant testing before you replace them. (You may want to replace single-pole switches without testing—they're cheap to replace.) **Do not test a switch while it is wired. Shut off power to the circuit, and remove the switch.**

TESTING A SWITCH/RECEPTACLE

Begin by testing the switch. With probes touching the terminal on each side, the tester should show continuity with the switch ON and no continuity with the switch OFF. If you get different results, replace the device.

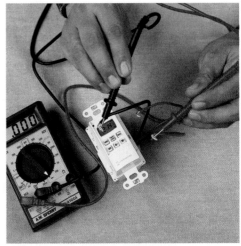

TESTING A PROGRAMMABLE SWITCH

Turn the manual override switch to ON, and touch the probes to both leads. Use a digital multitester as shown or a continuity tester (page 30) to test for continuity. Then test with the switch turned OFF. The tester should show no continuity. If your results differ replace the switch.

Testing a three-way switch

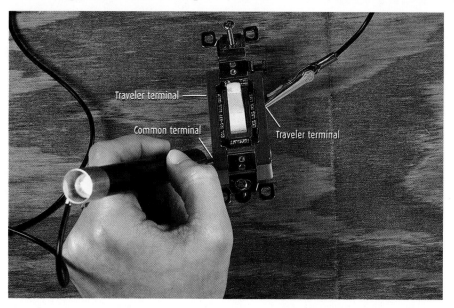

Traveler terminal

Common terminal

Traveler terminal

TESTING A THREE-WAY SWITCH
Touch one probe to the common terminal (it is a different color and may have "common" printed next to it) and one to either of the "traveler" terminals. Flip the switch. The tester should show continuity when the toggle is either up or down, but not in both positions. Keep the toggle in the ON position (the position that shows continuity) for the first traveler terminal, and move one probe from the first traveler terminal to the second. The tester should show no continuity. Flip the switch and the tester should show continuity. If any of the test results differ, replace the switch. (See pages 148–150 for more about three-way switches.)

Understanding and testing a four-way switch

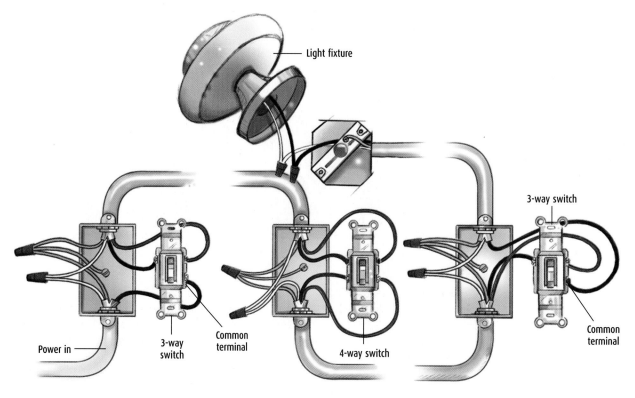

Light fixture

3-way switch

Common terminal

Power in

3-way switch

Common terminal

4-way switch

A FOUR-WAY SYSTEM CONTROLS A SINGLE LIGHT WITH THREE OR MORE SWITCHES
The first and last switches are three-ways, and the switch or switches between them are four-ways. Carefully tag all the wires before removing any of

the switches. This schematic will help if you get confused. Test the three-way switches as described above, but you'll have to take the four-way to an electrical supply store for testing. What's so complicated about a four-way? The paths of

continuity may run crosswise or diagonally from any of the four terminals to any of the others. The direction of the paths depends on the switch manufacturer so always make sure the packaging the switch comes in has a diagram you can follow.

Checking 240-volt receptacles

Stationary 240-volt appliances, such as electric water heaters, central air-conditioning units, and electric furnaces, are "hardwired." Instead of having cords with plugs, a cable runs directly from the appliance to a junction box.

Movable 240-volt appliances, such as window air-conditioners and electric ranges, are plugged into 240-volt receptacles.

Some receptacles deliver both 240-volt and 120-volt power (page 145). These are used for electric ranges and clothes dryers that need heavy voltage for heating elements and standard voltage for motors and clocks.

Specific types of receptacles are available, each with a different hole configuration so only one type of plug can fit. Ranges usually use 120/240-volt, 50-amp receptacles; dryers plug into 120/240-volt, 30-amp receptacles; air-conditioners use 240-volt, 30-amp receptacles.

TESTING A 240-VOLT RECEPTACLE

If an appliance plugged into a 240-volt receptacle gets no power or only partial power, first check the service panel to make sure that the breaker hasn't tripped or the fuse hasn't blown. To make a live test, turn on the circuit, and carefully insert the probes of a four-level voltage tester or a multitester (pages 30–31) into the two vertical slots. The meter should register around 240 volts. With one probe in a vertical slot and one in a neutral or ground slot, you should get a reading of 120 volts. If your readings differ, **shut off power to the circuit** and remove the receptacle. Make sure the wiring connections are tight. If they are not, tighten and retest. Otherwise, replace the receptacle with a duplicate (page 145). If the receptacle is working correctly, but the appliance is not, you may need to replace the appliance cord.

Switching from three-wire to four-wire

5

SWITCHES AND RECEPTACLES

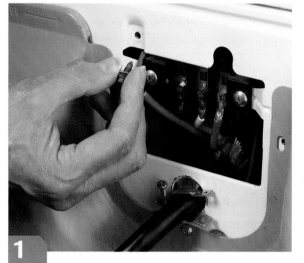

1

ATTACH THE WIRES
Kneel on a foam pad while you work. Note how the three-wire cord is attached, and wire the new cord the same way. A ground for the dryer motor often attaches to the dryer body near where the plug wires attach. Attach the cord's ground wire to it.

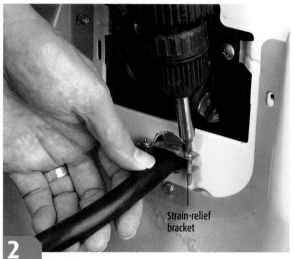

Strain-relief bracket

2

TIGHTEN THE STRAIN-RELIEF BRACKET
Don't neglect this important piece of hardware; if the dryer cord gets yanked, the bracket will protect the connections and help avoid a possible short. Fit it into the cord access hole and evenly tighten both screws firmly onto the cord.

⊙ CLOSER LOOK

Three-prong plug

Four-wire grounded receptacle

THREE PRONG PLUGS AND FOUR PRONG RECEPTACLE
Although most dryers are hard wired rather than plugged, you may run into the rare situation where the dryer was built with an incompatible plug. In that case you should determine what your local codes dictate for a dryer connection and follow them.

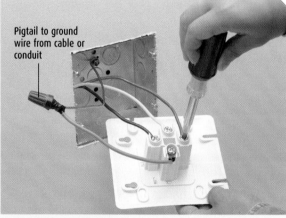

Pigtail to ground wire from cable or conduit

MOVE UP TO A GROUNDED RECEPTACLE
If your system is grounded (look for a copper wire fastened to the box and check for grounding at your service panel), **give yourself a safety edge by installing a four-wire receptacle.** Attach black to black, white to white, and red to red. With #10 wire, pigtail to the ground. If you need to run new cable for a new receptacle, see page 141.

Grounding receptacles

PROJECT DETAILS

SKILLS: Testing for power, stripping and connecting wires
PROJECT: Testing and replacing a receptacle

TIME TO COMPLETE

EXPERIENCED: 15 min.
HANDY: 30 min.
NOVICE: 45 min.

STUFF YOU'LL NEED

TOOLS: Voltage tester or multitester, wire strippers, screwdriver, longnose pliers
MATERIALS: Grounded receptacle, electrician's tape

1 TEST AN UNGROUNDED RECEPTACLE FOR GROUND

Scrape off any paint from the mounting screw. Insert one probe of a voltage tester or multitester into one receptacle slot, and touch the other to the mounting screw. Repeat the test for the other slot. If voltage is present the box is grounded and you can install a three-hole receptacle.

2 TEST AGAIN

If the first test is negative, remove the cover plate and repeat the first test, but touch the metal box, rather than the mounting screw, with one probe. If power is now indicated, you can install a grounded receptacle.

f a receptacle is ungrounded (with two slots only, and no grounding hole), its box may actually be grounded. If so, you can install a grounded receptacle. Do not install a grounded receptacle if the box is not grounded—you'll give the false impression the box is grounded when it is not. (For a description of grounding, see page 11.)

If a box is ungrounded, ground it by running a #12 green insulated or bare copper wire to a cold-water pipe and connect it using a special grounding clamp. Or install a GFCI receptacle (page 74), which will provide greater protection than grounding alone.

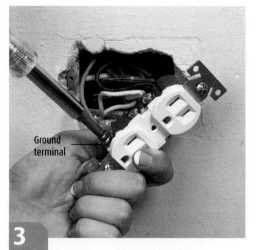

Ground terminal

3 INSTALL A GROUNDED RECEPTACLE

Snip off the stripped wire ends, which could break if they are bent again, and restrip. See page 18 for wiring directions. Be sure to test with a receptacle analyzer. If the test shows the receptacle is not polarized, switch the wires.

⊘ **SAFETY ALERT**

AVOID GROUNDING ADAPTERS

This type of adapter is illegal. It's not much work to install a grounded receptacle, **so there's no good reason to use an adapter.**

Adding surge protection

Once in a while, power supplied by your utility company may suddenly increase for a few milliseconds. This "surge" does not affect most electrical components, but it can damage sensitive electronic equipment, such as computers and televisions. A surge on your telephone line can destroy your modem and damage your computer. So buy surge protection. The higher a device's "joule" (a unit of strength of energy) rating, the better the protection. A surge arrester or protector will work only if the electrical system is grounded.

5

SWITCHES AND RECEPTACLES

POWER STRIP SURGE SUPPRESSOR

An inexpensive device like this protects against surges and makes it easy to organize all those cords in a home office. Just plug it in. To protect a modem and computer, spend a little more for a device with a phone connection or a DSL cable.

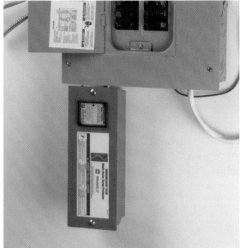

WHOLE HOUSE SURGE PROTECTION

Installed directly on your service panel, a whole house surge protector gives all the wiring in your house protection from surges in power in the local lines. Surges can come from lightning strikes that hit the wiring near your home. However, if your home is hit directly, even a whole house surge protector may not protect your more delicate circuitry such as your computer.

WORK SMARTER

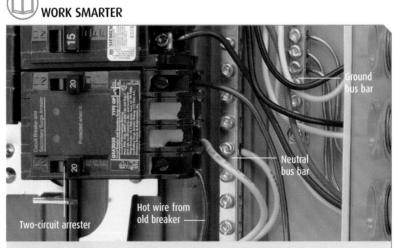

Ground bus bar

Neutral bus bar

Hot wire from old breaker

Two-circuit arrester

ARRESTER IN BREAKER BOX

To install an arrester that covers two circuits, shut off the main breaker. **Remove two circuit breakers.** Switch the breaker toggles to OFF. Push the arrester breaker into place (page 26). Transfer the black wires from the old breakers to the terminals of the arrester breaker. Attach the curly white wire to the neutral bus bar (make sure there are no kinks). **Restore power and switch the arrester breakers on.** Another type of surge arrester protects the entire panel.

Ceiling lights and fixtures

Chapter 6 highlights

O ften the quickest and easiest way to make a stunning improvement to a room is by installing a new ceiling light fixture. Most new lights are quick to install, though some will require an hour or so of assembly. If your home was built after World War II, chances are good that the hardware in your ceiling box is compatible with the new fixture. If it is not, you can purchase special mounting parts that allow you to connect old to new.

If you have an existing surface-mounted ceiling fixture that is controlled by a wall switch, you can install another surface-mounted light. Also consider track lights and Eurostyle lights of various types, both of which attach easily. If you want a ceiling fan, you may need to replace the existing box with a stronger fan-rated box that is firmly attached to framing.

Upgrading a ceiling fixture

PROJECT DETAILS

SKILLS: Stripping and splicing wires, connecting wires to terminals, attaching a fixture, connecting to terminals
PROJECT: Attaching a new fixture to an existing box. Allow more time if you need to buy the correct mounting parts, replace incoming cable damaged by heat, or patch the ceiling

TIME TO COMPLETE

EXPERIENCED: 20 min.
HANDY: 40 min.
NOVICE: 1 hr.

STUFF YOU'LL NEED

TOOLS: Voltage tester or multitester, wire strippers, lineman's pliers, longnose pliers, side-cutting pliers, screwdriver, stepladder
MATERIALS: New light fixture, electrician's tape, wire nuts

SAFETY ALERT

SAVE THAT INSULATION
Don't remove the fiberglass insulation at the top of a ceiling fixture, even if it seems to get in the way. It's there to protect the wires from overheating.

Before you replace the fixture, check that the canopy of the new fixture (the part that snugs up to the ceiling) will cover any imperfections in the drywall or plaster. If you have a thin "pancake" box, replace it with a remodeling box (pages 132–133).

Determine which mounting hardware you'll need before buying a new fixture. **Turn off the power at the service panel (page 6)** and remove the fixture. Enlist a helper to support the fixture while you remove the mounting screws that hold the canopy in place. Gently pull down the fixture.

Working as if the wires are hot, unscrew the wire nuts. **Test that the power is off,** and then undo the wires. Note the type of mounting hardware, or remove it and take it along when buying a new fixture. The new fixture will probably include mounting hardware (usually, a strap). You may be able to reuse existing hardware.

Always push the house wires up into the box. Never place them in the fixture's canopy, where they may be harmed by heat.

1 WIRE A FLUSH-MOUNTED FIXTURE
Tug on the hardware to make sure the box is firmly attached. Don't depend on the wires and wire nuts to support it while you work. Rest the fixture on a stepladder, or make a hook from a wire coat hanger and temporarily suspend the fixture from the mounting strap. **With the power off,** splice white to white wires and black to black wires, using wire nuts (page 14). Tuck the house wires up into the box.
Note: Sometimes you will find that two black wires come with the fan or fixture. If this is the case, the smooth wire is hot and the ribbed wire is the neutral.

2 MOUNT THE FIXTURE
Slide a mounting screw through the fixture and up into the threaded hole in the strap. Start one mounting screw, fastening it halfway in, then start the other screw. With a screwdriver or a drill and screwdriver bit, drive the mounting screws tight.

Special alignment

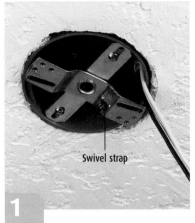

1

ADD A SWIVEL STRAP
Use a swivel strap (also called an offset crossbar) if you need to twist the canopy into exact alignment. This is most often a consideration when installing a fixture with a geometric canopy.

2

MOUNT A FIXTURE THAT NEEDS ALIGNMENT
Wire the fixture, and tuck the house wires up into the box. Screw both mounting bolts into the threaded holes of the strap. Line up the fixture-mounting holes with the bolts and attach the fixture, using the decorative mounting nuts.

Center-mounted

Center stud

1

USE A CENTER STUD FOR CENTER-MOUNTED FIXTURES
A center stud, sometimes called a nipple, may have wires running through it (for a pendent fixture) or around it (for a center-mounted fixture). A variation uses a center nipple, which screws into the strap.

2

INSTALL A CENTER-MOUNTED FIXTURE
The center stud should be long enough to go through the strap and the fixture, but not so long that it pokes into the box or hits the globe. Attach the wires and fold them into the box as you slide the canopy up and over the stud. Snugly secure the canopy with the nut.

Older installation

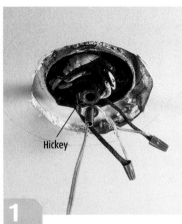

Hickey

1

ADD A HICKEY IN OLDER INSTALLATIONS
An older home may have a ⅜-inch pipe running through the middle of the ceiling box. To install a pendent fixture, add a hickey to make the transition from the pipe to a new fixture. Feed the fixture leads through the hickey, and tuck the house wires up into the box.

2

ADD A MEDALLION
Hickeys are found in old houses with plaster and lath ceilings. The fixture canopy usually won't cover damaged plaster around the ceiling box. Adding a medallion saves you the trouble of patching and painting while adding a decorative feature.

Installing track lighting

PROJECT DETAILS

SKILLS: Laying out a track and anchoring with screws, stripping and splicing wires

PROJECT: Installing a track lighting system

TIME TO COMPLETE

EXPERIENCED: 2 hrs.
HANDY: 4 hrs.
NOVICE: 6 hrs.

STUFF YOU'LL NEED

TOOLS: Voltage tester, wire strippers, lineman's pliers, drill with screwdriver bit, tape measure, hacksaw

MATERIALS: Track system with lights, wire nuts, screws, plastic anchors

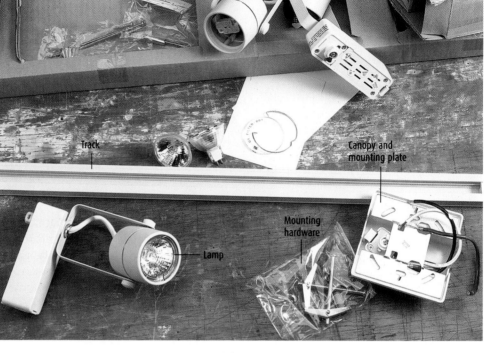

PURCHASING A TRACK SYSTEM

Work with a salesperson; explain the size and configuration you want. Buy a kit that includes track, mounting plate, end cap, and canopy. You also may have to buy additional track and end caps as well as L- or T-fittings for the corners. Choose the lights and bulbs when you buy the tracks. You can put different types of lamps on the same track, but be sure to purchase lamps made by the same manufacturer as the track—otherwise, the two may be incompatible.

A track system is the most versatile of all ceiling fixtures. You can configure it in many ways, choose from several lamp styles, and position the lamps to suit your needs. To begin installation remove the existing ceiling fixture to locate the track.

If you don't have an existing ceiling fixture that is switched, see pages 146–147 for how to install a new one.

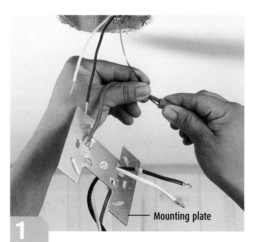

1

INSTALL THE MOUNTING PLATE

Shut off power at the service panel. Use wire nuts to splice the house wires to the plate leads. Connect the ground wire to the plate and to the box if it is metal (for grounding see pages 11, 17-18). Push the wires into the box, and screw the plate to the box so it is snug against the ceiling.

2

MEASURE AND MARK FOR THE TRACK

At the mounting plate measure to see how far the side of the track will be from the nearest wall. Mark the ceiling so the track will be consistently parallel to the wall. Use a framing square to draw lines if the track turns a corner.

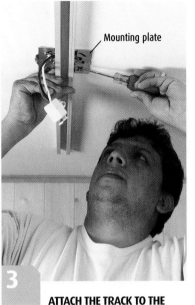

3

ATTACH THE TRACK TO THE MOUNTING PLATE

Have a helper hold the track in place against the ceiling and centered on the mounting plate. Drive the setscrews to anchor the track to the plate.

4

SECURE THE TRACK

Use a stud finder to locate joists. If the track is more than 4 feet long, have a helper hold one end while you work. Snap the track onto the plate, and drive a screw into every available joist. If there are no joists, drill holes every foot or so, insert plastic anchors, and drive screws into the anchors.

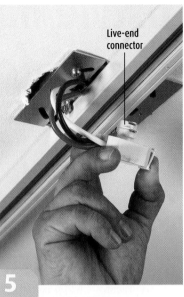

Live-end connector

5

TWIST ON THE LIVE-END CONNECTOR

Insert the live-end connector and turn it 90 degrees until it snaps into place. Align the connector's two copper tabs with the two copper bars inside the track. Snap the plastic canopy over the track and mounting plate.

6

ATTACH A CORNER

You can buy connectors to make 90-degree turns, T- shapes, or odd-angle turns. Slide the connector into the track that is already installed, slide the next track onto the connector, and attach that track to the ceiling. Cover all open track ends with end caps.

7

TWIST ON A LIGHT

This type of light twists into place in the same way as the live-end connector (Step 5). Another type has a metal arm that is twisted to tighten. Restore power, turn on the switch, and swivel the lights to position them for the best effect.

CLOSER LOOK

CUTTING TRACK

Tracks are available in standard lengths of 2, 4, 6, and 8 feet. If these sizes do not fit your needs, cut a track with a hacksaw or a saber saw equipped with a fine-toothed metal-cutting blade. Clamp the track in a vise or hold it firmly with your hand as you cut. Cut slowly and take care not to bend the track while cutting. **Reattach the plastic end piece.**

Eurostyle lights

6

CEILING LIGHTS & FIXTURES

PROJECT DETAILS

SKILLS: Anchoring screw hooks, splicing wires
PROJECT: Installing a set of halogen trapeze lights

TIME TO COMPLETE

EXPERIENCED: 1 hr.
HANDY: 2 hrs.
NOVICE: 3 hrs.

STUFF YOU'LL NEED

TOOLS: Voltage tester, wire strippers, drill, screwdriver, longnose pliers, side-cutting pliers
MATERIALS: Trapeze light kit, wire nuts

Lights to choose

At The Home Depot you will find many choices of sleek and stylish lights with a modern European flair. These fixtures tend to show off their hardware rather than hiding behind a canopy or globe. Some balance on two wires like trapeze artists, while others attach to tracks that run in curves. Most of these lights allow you to design the pattern or shape of your choice.

Trapeze lights

These halogen fixtures are energy-efficient, stylish, and—because you can easily point them to do the most good—versatile. Exposed wires or tracks are not dangerous because they carry very low voltage. Remove an existing ceiling light and attach a canopy transformer to the ceiling box (as shown in Step 2), or insert a plug-in transformer into a switched receptacle (page 146).

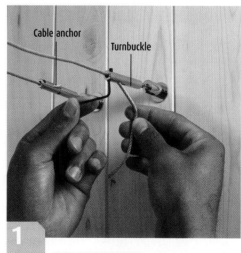

1

STRETCH THE CABLES

Shut off power. Remove the light fixture or install and run cable to a ceiling box (Chapter 9, **Installing new services**) where you plan to install the lights. Attach two cable anchors on the walls between which the unit will hang. Cut two lengths of cable to span the length of the installation. Fasten cables to the anchors and tighten the turnbuckle until the cables are taut.

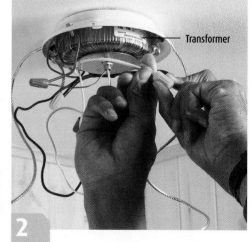

2

INSTALL THE TRANSFORMER

Install a strap on the ceiling box (pages 84-85). Mount the transformer onto the strap. Splice the canopy transformer's red lead to the house's black wire, and splice white to white wires. Ground the light by connecting the green lead to the ground wire.

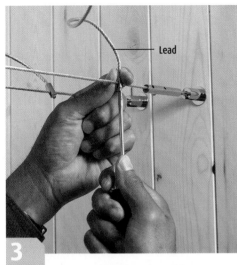

Lead

3 **CONNECT THE LOW-VOLTAGE WIRES**

You may have to cut the low-voltage leads to the right length, restrip the clear insulation, and reattach the leads to the transformer. Clamp the leads onto the stretched cables using the fasteners provided with the kit. Attach the cover to the transformer.

4 **HANG THE LIGHTS**

Hold a halogen with a cloth (oil from your skin will damage it), and push the pins into a light arm. Slip the spring clamp over a wire, position the light arm on the cable, and clip the spring clamp onto the cable. Restore power and test.

Go ahead and adjust the lights while the power is on. The voltage is so low you'll barely feel it.

Flexible track lights

1 **MARK FOR CEILING SUPPORTS**

Shut off power. Remove the existing ceiling fixture, or run wiring for a new ceiling box (Chapter 9, **Installing new services**). Working with a helper or two, bend the track into the shape of your choice. Mark the ceiling for the locations of the supports, which will hold the track in place.

2 **ATTACH THE CANOPY AND THE SUPPORTS**

Connect the wires in the electrical box to the canopy, following manufacturer's instructions; the wiring is much the same as for a ceiling fixture (see pages 84–85). Disassemble the supports, and drive screws to attach them at each of the marked locations. If there is no ceiling joist to drive the screw into, use a plastic anchor. Assemble the lower portions of the supports.

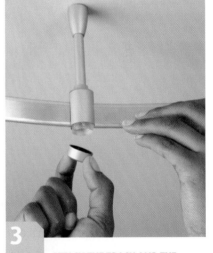

3 **ATTACH THE TRACK AND THE LIGHTS**

Again working with a helper or two, bend the track to the desired shape and slip it up into the slots in the supports. Screw on the caps loosely, make adjustments to the shape of the track if needed, then screw the caps tight. You can now attach the lights at any points along the track.

Hanging a ceiling fan

eiling fans circulate air downward to cool rooms in the summer and upward to evenly disperse heat in the winter. Observe the following guidelines to install a fan, and it will effectively circulate the air in your home without hissing, wobbling, or pulling away from the ceiling.

Planning for a fan

Before installing a fan consider these issues:

- Decide whether to wire the switch to control the fan and the light separately (page 71).
- Buy a separate light kit if your unit doesn't include one; some fans include lights, so check to be sure.
- Choose a fan-rated box that fits your situation (page 91).

- Plan how you'll cover the hole once you remove the old ceiling box. Buy a light with a canopy that's wide enough to cover the hole, or get a medallion to hide ceiling imperfections (page 85).
- Decide how many blades you want. Depending on the design of the blades, four-blade fans can move more air than five-blade models.
- Avoid "ceiling hugger" fans—they do not circulate air well. Fans should have downrods long enough (you can buy downrod extenders) to position fan blades at least 10 inches from the ceiling, but check that the blades are no lower than 7 feet from the floor.
- Use only a speed control switch. If you install standard dimmer switch it can burn out the fan motor.

Removing the old box

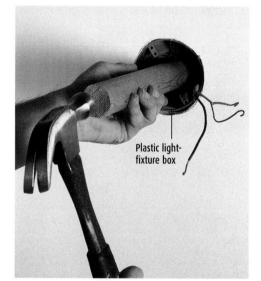

Plastic light-fixture box

REMOVING A CEILING BOX
Shut off the power. Sometimes you can remove screws or nails and pry out the box. Or you may have to carefully cut away drywall or plaster to get to fasteners. If the box is nailed to a joist, cut around the box to enlarge the hole, and tap the box loose using a piece of wood and a hammer. You may be able to cut through fasteners with a reciprocating saw or a metal-cutting keyhole saw. Take great care not to slice through any cable.

REMOVING AN OLD PANCAKE BOX
In an old home with plaster ceilings, you may encounter a pancake box like this. **Shut off the power.** Unscrew any nuts or screws that are holding the box in place, and pry out the box. You may need to cut away some wood lath to make room for the new box.

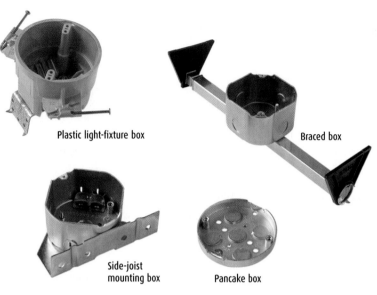

Plastic light-fixture box

Braced box

Side-joist mounting box

Pancake box

CUT THROUGH FASTENERS

If a box is attached to the side of a joist, first use a drywall saw or utility knife to cut around the box and expose the wiring and the fasteners. **Shut off the power.** Cut through the nails or screws with a reciprocating saw, taking care not to nick any wiring.

FAN BOXES TO CHOOSE

Be sure to purchase a fan-rated box, which has thick threads for attaching the fan's mounting plate. Some boxes mount directly below a ceiling joist, some mount to the side of a joist, and some use a brace that attaches to a joist on either side.

Installing a braced box

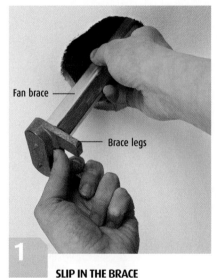

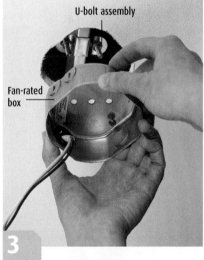

1 SLIP IN THE BRACE

Check the joists for any wiring or plumbing runs that might be in the way before you install the brace. Test-fit the box on the brace; then take it apart again. Push the brace through the hole and spread it until it touches the joists on both sides with the legs of the brace resting on top of the drywall or plaster.

2 TIGHTEN THE BRACE

Measure to make sure that the brace is centered in the hole. Position it on the joists at the correct height so the box will be flush with the surface of the ceiling. Use an adjustable wrench or channel-type pliers to tighten the brace until it is firm.

3 ATTACH THE BOX

Attach the U-bolt assembly to the brace so that the assembly is centered in the hole and the bolts face down. Thread cable through the cable connector and into the fan-rated box. Slip the box up so the bolts slide through it. Tighten the nuts to secure the box.

WHEN FRAMING IS ACCESSIBLE, ATTACH A CEILING BOX TO A JOIST...

Install this type of box in unfinished ceilings or ceilings with a large hole. Drill pilot holes and drive in 1¼-inch wood screws to attach it to a joist.

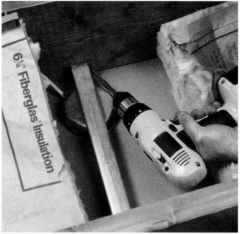

OR INSTALL A BRACED BOX FROM ABOVE

Buy a new-work ceiling fan box with a brace. Slide the box along the brace to position it. Tighten the clamp. Attach the brace by driving in 1¼-inch wood screws.

Screwing from below

If you have a joist in the middle of the hole (as may be the case if you removed a thin "pancake" ceiling box), attaching a fan box from below will be easy. Buy a thin fan-rated box, and clamp the cable to it. Hold it in place and drill pilot holes; then drive in 2-inch wood screws. (Don't use drywall screws or "all-purpose" screws—they break too easily.)

Attaching the plate

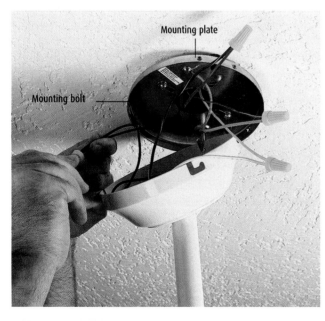

Mounting plate

Mounting bolt

INSTALL THE MOUNTING PLATE

Thread the wires through the center of the mounting plate. If the box has mounting bolts that poke through the plate, fit the mounting plate over the bolts and fasten it with the nuts provided. If separate bolts are provided, push each one through the mounting plate as shown. When both bolts are in place, tighten the plate onto the ceiling.

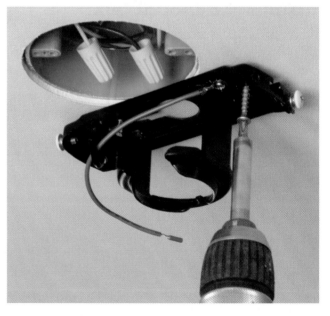

OPTION: ATTACH THE PLATE TO A JOIST

If it is difficult to install a new fan-rated box, consider this technique: Attach the fan's mounting plate with screws driven into a nearby joist rather than attaching it to the box. If the fan's canopy will not cover the box, add a ceiling medallion.

Installing the fan

Canopy — Downrod

Bulb-shape fitting

1

ASSEMBLE THE DOWNROD AND CANOPY

On a worktable ready the fan for installation, following manufacturer's instructions. Run the fan leads through the downrod (or downrod extender), and tightly screw on the downrod. Remember to tighten the setscrews. Slip on the canopy, then install the bulb-shape fitting at the top of the downrod. It will rest in the canopy when the canopy is attached to the ceiling. Be careful not to mangle the wires. Do not attach the fan blades yet.

2

WIRE THE FAN

Temporarily hang the fan from the hook on the mounting ring. Connect the copper ground wire to the green wire attached to the fan base. If you have only two wires, connect both the black lead (for the fan motor) and the blue or striped lead (for the light) to the black house wire, and the white lead to the white house wire. If you have three-wire cable, connect black to black, white to white, and red to the blue or striped light lead. Check the manufacturer's directions. You may choose to install a remote-control unit (page 95).

CLOSER LOOK

SWITCHING THE FAN AND LIGHT

You probably have two-wire cable (not counting the ground wire) running into the ceiling fixture. If so, you have four options to control the fan and the light:

■ Hook the fan to the two wires so the wall switch turns the fan and the light on or off at the same time. Use the pull chains on the fixture to control the fan and light individually. This is convenient enough if you don't need to change fan speeds often.

■ Purchase a fan that has a special fan/light switch that requires only two wires. These fans are expensive, however, and the switches

have been known to turn the fan on by themselves —a potentially dangerous situation if you're away for a few days.

■ Install a remote-control switch, as shown on page 95. This is rather costly, but far less work than running new cable.

■ Control the fan and light separately by using a double wall switch. Run three-wire cable from the fixture to the switch using the red wire to power the fan and the black wire to power the light. Connect the wires as shown in **Combo Switches** under **Double Switch** on page 71.

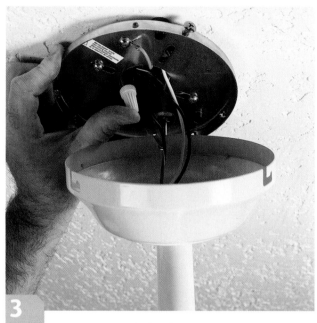

3 ATTACH THE CANOPY TO THE MOUNTING PLATE

Use a helper to support the fan motor while you drive the screws. Push the wires and wire nuts up into the box to keep them from vibrating against the canopy when the fan is running. Clip the canopy onto the mounting plate and tighten the screws.

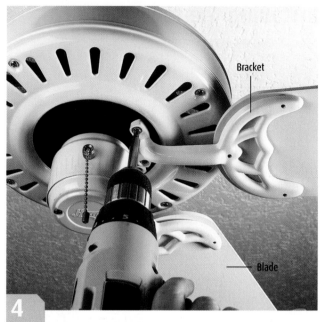

4 ATTACH THE BLADES

If the brackets are not all of uniform shape, return them and get replacements. Screw a bracket to each fan blade. Make sure the side of the blade that you want to show faces down. Attach each bracket to the motor with two screws. Drive the screws slowly to avoid stripping. Don't bend the brackets as you work.

5 WIRE THE LIGHT KIT

When you remove the plate on the bottom of the fan, you may see a tangle of wires. Don't worry; just find the blue or striped lead and the white lead, and connect them to the light kit leads. Screw the light kit up to the fan. Some light kits require a spacer ring between the fan and the light. The spacer ring should come with the kit or the fan.

Fan light options

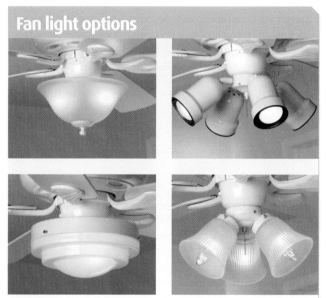

Some ceiling fans come with a light kit, but you can also purchase light kits separately. With many styles available you can find lighting to match your décor. Be sure that the lights you choose allow for bulbs of a high enough wattage to adequately light your room. In most cases a kit with three or four separate lights will provide more wattage than a single light.

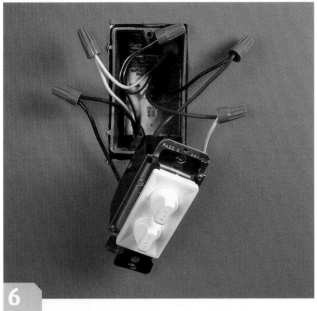

6

OPTION A: IF POWER RUNS TO THE SWITCH

Shut off power to the switch. A three-wire cable usually runs from the fan to the switch, and a two-wire cable brings power to the switch. Follow the manufacturer's instructions; wire colors vary. Most likely you'll splice the black wire bringing power to the black switch lead, and splice the two white wires together. Then splice the black wire from the fan and the red wire from the light to the switch's fan and light leads.

OPTION B: IF POWER RUNS TO THE CEILING BOX

If the switch box has only one cable—the one from the fan—then power runs to the ceiling box. Usually you'll find a black-marked white wire that brings power from the fan to the switch; however, the previous installer may not have marked it. If unmarked, wrap tape around its end and splice it with the switch's black lead. Splice the red wire (from the light) and the black wire (from the fan) to the switch's light and fan leads.

If the fan wobbles

If a fan does not turn smoothly, first make sure that all the screws are tightened firmly, and check that the downrod is seated correctly in the mounting bracket; you should not be able to twist it while pulling down. Also measure down from the ceiling to make sure that none of the blades are warped, and replace any that are. If none of these measures solves the problem, use a fan balancing kit, which is usually included in the box with a new fan or which can be purchased separately.

BUYER'S GUIDE

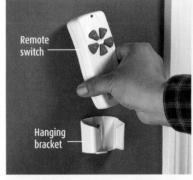

WIRELESS REMOTE SWITCH

If you have only two wires running from the switch to the fan box, a remote control will let you control the fan and light separately. Before you install the canopy, hook up the receiving unit with both fan and light leads (black and blue or striped) spliced with the remote's black lead, and the white wire spliced to the white lead. Make sure the little dip switches are set the same on

the switch unit and the receiving unit. Install the canopy. Put a battery in the sending unit, and attach a hanging bracket on a wall. If the ceiling fixture was originally switched, the two wires sending power to the fan are still controlled by that switch. The sending unit controls the fan or light, or both, only when the wall switch is on.

Installing recessed lighting

PROJECT DETAILS

SKILLS: Installing cable, connecting to power, wiring a switch, and stripping and splicing wire
PROJECT: Running cable and installing 4 lights with a switch, in a finished ceiling

TIME TO COMPLETE

EXPERIENCED: 1 day
HANDY: 1.5 days
NOVICE: 2 days

STUFF YOU'LL NEED

TOOLS: Stud finder, drill with long bit, drywall saw or hole-cutting drill attachment, voltage tester or multitester, wire strippers, lineman's pliers, screwdriver, safety glasses
MATERIALS: Can lights and trims, switch box and switch, cable and clamps, electrician's tape, wire nuts

R ecessed canister lights, also called "pot lights," use 60- to 150-watt floodlight bulbs. They're ideal for task lighting, highlighting artwork, or grouped to illuminate whole rooms. (See page 61 for tips on planning.) **Cans get hot. Some codes require them at least ½ inch away from wood and other flammables but local codes may dictate a greater distance. Always follow manufacturer's instructions.**

If the joists are exposed, use a new-work can light (page 99). For ceilings already covered by drywall or plaster and lath, buy a remodel can (below) that clips into a hole cut in the ceiling. It's also called an old-work, or retrofit, can. To install a remodel can, follow the steps beginning on page 98.

Choosing canister lights

Can lights are designed to suit specific situations. Here's how to choose the right one:

- If there's insulation in the ceiling, buy IC (insulation compatible) lights. **Standard recessed lights will dangerously overheat when surrounded with insulation.**
- Use bulbs of the recommended wattage or lower. **Bulbs with too-high wattage will dangerously overheat.** When putting a number of cans on a dimmer, add up all the wattage and make sure your dimmer is rated to handle the load.
- If you have less than 8 inches of vertical space above the ceiling, purchase a low-clearance canister.

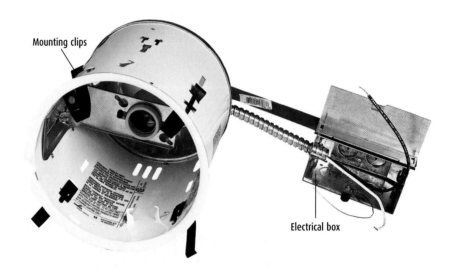

Mounting clips

Electrical box

ANATOMY OF A CAN LIGHT
A standard remodel canister fixture has an approved electrical box, suspended far enough from the light so it will not overheat. A thermal protector shuts the light off if it becomes too hot (for example, if you use a bulb of too-high wattage). If you have less than 8 inches of vertical space above your ceiling, purchase special cans designed to fit into this smaller space. Be sure they are IC (insulation compatible) rated so there will be no danger of overheating.

CEILING LIGHTS & FIXTURES

Cans for tight spaces

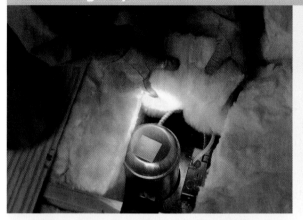

A can light that is rated insulation compatible (IC) will not overheat even if wrapped in insulation, and it is cool enough so you don't have to worry if it comes in contact with wood. Some codes require a "blue boot," or cover, that is placed over in addition to a vapor barrier over that to keep insulation away from the heat. Ask about your local codes for can light installation. If the joists are only 2×6 there are special low-clearance fixtures for the small space, as shown above. You can also buy special canister lights for a sloped ceiling, which allow you to point the light straight down.

💲 BUYER'S GUIDE

Eyeball trim

Open trim

Reflector trim

Watertight lens

Black baffle trim

White baffle trim

TRIM OPTIONS

Some canister lights come with an integral trim, but most can accept various types of trim. Be sure to purchase a trim made by the manufacturer of your canister light. An **open trim** exposes the lightbulb. Use a **watertight lens** in a shower or bathroom. A **reflector trim** makes the light a bit brighter. An **eyeball trim** can be swiveled to point where you want it. A **black baffle** makes the bulb less noticeable, while a **white baffle** makes it brighter. Place a wall-washer near a wall, to dramatize a textured wall.

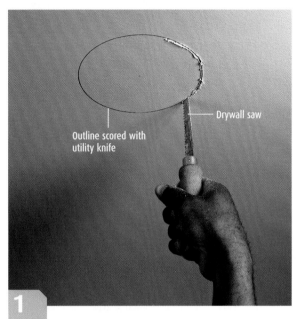

Outline scored with utility knife

Drywall saw

Saw is made to cut a standard box diameter

Arbor attaches to saw, fits in drill chuck

1 OPTION A: CUT THE HOLE

Lightly mark all light locations. Use a stud finder to make sure they do not overlap a joist. Or drill a hole and poke a bent wire up into it to make sure the hole is entirely between joists. Use the template provided with the light to draw a circle on the ceiling. Draw and cut each hole precisely. If the hole is even a little too big, the can may not clamp tightly. Wearing safety glasses, cut the line lightly with a utility knife; then cut along the inside of the knife line with a drywall saw. Take care not to snag any wires that may be in the ceiling cavity.

OPTION B: USE A HOLE-CUTTING SAW

This tool saves time and cuts holes precisely. You don't have to draw the outline of the hole on the ceiling; just mark the center point. Check to see that you will not run into a joist. Check that the lights fit snugly without having to be forced into place. Note: This tool is costly (the saw and the arbor are sold separately), but it's worth the price if you have more than six holes to cut through plaster. A less expensive tool (inset) is available for cutting through drywall only.

16 inches of extra cable

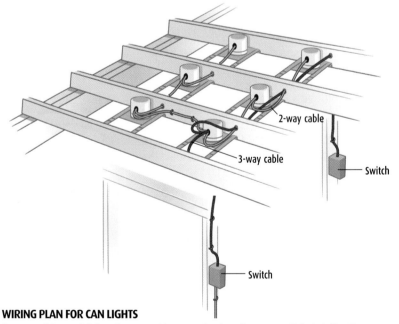

2-way cable

3-way cable

Switch

Switch

2 ROUGH-IN THE WIRING

Run cable from a power source to a switch box and then to the first hole, allowing at least 16 inches of extra cable to make wiring easy. (See pages 117–131 for how to run cable.) Work carefully and use a drill with a long bit to avoid cutting additional access holes (pages 128-131) that will need patching later.

WIRING PLAN FOR CAN LIGHTS

Run power into a switch box, then run cable to the cans in a serial manner. If you want to control the lights from two different switches (as shown), see page 68 for installing three-way switches. Where possible run cable alongside joists rather than across them.

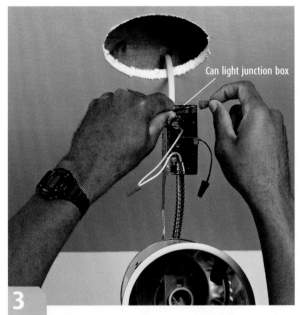

Can light junction box

3 WIRE THE LIGHT

Open the light's junction box. Usually there's a plate that pops off. Run cable into the box and clamp it. Strip insulation and make wire splices—black to black, white to white, and ground to ground (pages 32–33). Fold the wires into the box and replace the cover.

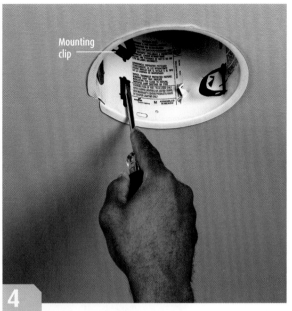

Mounting clip

4 MOUNT THE LIGHT

Most remodel cans have four clips that clamp the can to the ceiling by pushing down on the top of the drywall or plaster. Pull the clips in so they do not protrude outside the can. Slip the can's box into the hole; then push the can body up into the hole until its flange is tight to the ceiling. With your thumb or a screwdriver, push each clip up and outward until it clicks and clamps the fixture.

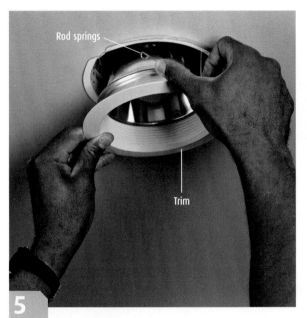

Rod springs

Trim

5 ADD THE TRIM

Most trims are mounted with coil springs or squeezable rod springs (as shown). If you have coil springs: Hook each spring to its assigned hole inside the can (if it is not already there). Pull out each spring and hook it to the trim; then carefully guide the trim into position. If you have rod springs, squeeze and insert both ends of each spring into their assigned holes; then push the trim up.

CLOSER LOOK

Tab

Plaster ring

Sliding mounting bars

MOUNTING A NEW-WORK CAN LIGHT

If ceiling joists are exposed, this is an easy installation. On a workbench attach the plaster ring to the fixture. Adjust it to compensate for the thickness of the ceiling drywall that will be installed later. At the ceiling slide the mounting bars outward so they reach joists on each side. Hammer the four tabs into the joists. Add 1¼-inch screws for extra strength.

Undercabinet halogen lighting

I f your cabinets are already installed and you need to light the countertop surface below, consider a halogen light kit that plugs into a receptacle. Not all codes allow this type of installation so you may not find the kind of kit pictured below in your local store. Most kits do come with installation instructions and if those vary from what is shown below, follow the manufacturers instructions.

A typical kit includes a transformer, cord, cord switch, several lights that attach to the underside of shelves or cabinets, and detailed instructions. There is little in the way of real wiring; most of the connections can be made by poking one component into another. Most of the work will be running the cord through holes and stapling it out of sight.

If you don't like using a cord switch, plug the kit into a receptacle controlled by a switch. If you don't already have a switch-controlled receptacle, see page 71 for how to wire one.

You can also purchase halogen lights that install with new cable, like the fluorescent undercabinet lights shown on pages 103–104. This may be a better option if the cabinets have not yet been installed.

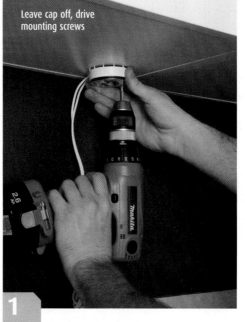

Leave cap off, drive mounting screws

1

ATTACH THE LIGHTS

Position each light near the back of the cabinet, but follow manufacturer's instructions for placement so you do not overheat the wall. Measure to be sure the screws will not poke through to the inside of the cabinet above. Drive screws to fasten each light.

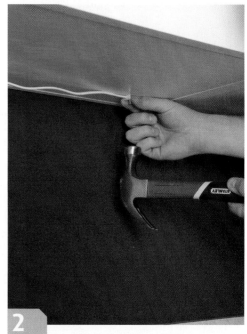

2

ROUTE AND STAPLE THE CORD

Run cord from each light toward a central location near the receptacle you will plug into. Work carefully, so the cord is fairly taut, and staple it where it will be least visible. You may choose to drill holes in the cabinets, run cords through the holes, and make connections inside a cabinet.

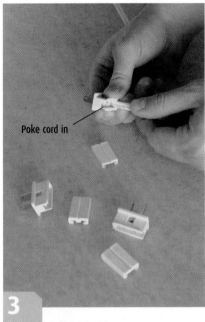

Poke cord in

3

WIRE A PLUG

To connect the cord to a plug, remove the plug's cover, poke the cord in, and replace the cover to anchor the cord and make the electrical connection. Be sure to place the ribbed wire (which is the neutral wire) as instructed.

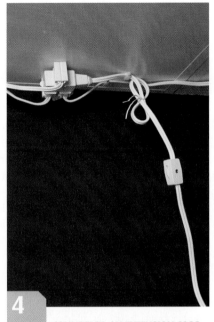

4

CONNECT TO AN EXTENSION CORD

Bundle the cords neatly, and plug them into an extension cord. You may choose to build a small wooden casing around the cords to keep them from getting bumped by plates and glasses.

5

PLUG IN

Route the extension cord to a receptacle and plug it in. In the example shown a combination switch/receptacle is wired so that the receptacle is controlled by the switch; see page 71 for how to make these connections.

Setup with a transformer

In another type of installation, a transformer is plugged into a receptacle, and wires lead from the transformer to the lights. In the example shown the transformer is plugged into a receiver module that is controlled by a remote-control switch, which can be placed anywhere in the room (see page 95). If the transformer steps the power down, smaller gauge wires can be used to run from the transformer to the lights. check the manufacturer's recommendations.

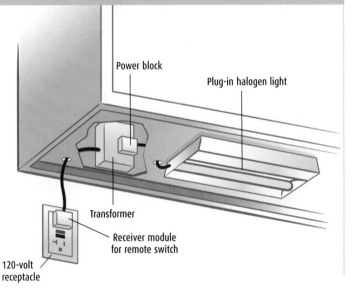

Power block

Plug-in halogen light

Transformer

Receiver module for remote switch

120-volt receptacle

Installing fluorescent lighting

PROJECT DETAILS

SKILLS: Attaching with screws, stripping and splicing wires
PROJECT: Installing a fluorescent light fixture

TIME TO COMPLETE

EXPERIENCED: 30 min.
HANDY: 1 hr.
NOVICE: 2 hrs.

STUFF YOU'LL NEED

TOOLS: Wire strippers, lineman's pliers, drill with screwdriver bit
MATERIALS: Fluorescent fixture, wire nuts, screws

INSTALLING A FLUORESCENT

Shut off power at the service panel. Remove the old fixture. Clamp the cable to a knockout in the new fixture and attach the fixture directly to the ceiling by driving screws into joists. Splice the fixture's wires to the incoming wires. Attach the cover.

CLOSER LOOK

CONSIDER FLUORESCENT LIGHTING OPTIONS

- If an old fluorescent light needs a new ballast (pages 211-212), consider replacing the fixture. Newer fluorescents with electronic ballasts are trouble-free for decades.
- Save energy costs by replacing an incandescent ceiling light with a fluorescent.
- Today's fluorescent tubes offer a greater variety of light than in years past (page 54). A diffusing lens further softens the light.

Fluorescent lights often are installed without a ceiling box: Cable is clamped to the fixture, which substitutes for a box. However, some codes require that fluorescent lights be attached to ceiling boxes. Suspend the fixture or set it in a suspended ceiling grid and make the connections. Square or rectangular fixtures with long tubes are the most common. Other fluorescent fixtures are shaped like incandescents and use circular or U-shape tubes.

Because the lights can be heavy, codes often require that a safety chain connects the light to the joists above so that should the hanging ceiling fall, the heavy light will stay in place.

INSTALLING FLUORESCENTS IN A SUSPENDED CEILING

Fluorescent fixtures fit into the ceiling grid, taking up the space of a 2×2-foot (shown) or 2×4-foot ceiling tile. For smaller fixtures install additional metal grid pieces and cut ceiling tiles to fit in either side. When you've established your power source for the lights (see pages 125–126 for how to extend the incoming line), install the grid, then attach the cable to the fixture, leaving more than enough cable to reach the power source. Connect to the power source before adding the tiles.

Adding undercabinet fluorescent lights

PROJECT DETAILS

SKILLS: Running new cable and connecting to power, attaching light fixtures, stripping and splicing wires, wiring a switch

PROJECT: Removing the backsplash, cutting holes, running cable, wiring four lights, and reinstalling the backsplash

TIME TO COMPLETE

EXPERIENCED: 1 day
HANDY: 1.5 days
NOVICE: 2 days

STUFF YOU'LL NEED

TOOLS: Multitester or voltage tester, lineman's pliers, side-cutting pliers, longnose pliers, wire strippers, drywall saw, screwdriver, drill with spade bit, utility knife, flat pry bar
MATERIALS: Undercabinet fluorescent lights, armored or NM cable, electrician's tape, wire nuts, cable clamps, cable staples, switch box, nailing plates

Undercabinet lighting brightens work surfaces and adds pleasing visual depth to kitchens.

Fluorescent lighting is a cool, low-energy light source. If you need only one or two lights, consider buying small fluorescent fixtures with cords and switches. However, you won't want to turn on three or more lights every time you walk into the kitchen. If you want a series of lights controlled by a wall switch, buy fixtures without cords or switches. Lights that are only 1 inch thick are sleeker than standard 1½-inch lights, but they are more difficult to wire and require special reducing cable clamps. Get the longest lights possible for the available under-cabinet spaces; you'll probably need several sizes.

Some codes require that you run armored cable or conduit through walls; others allow exposed armored or nonmetallic (NM) cable. Codes may require you to pull power from a source other than a countertop receptacle. Check with your building department.

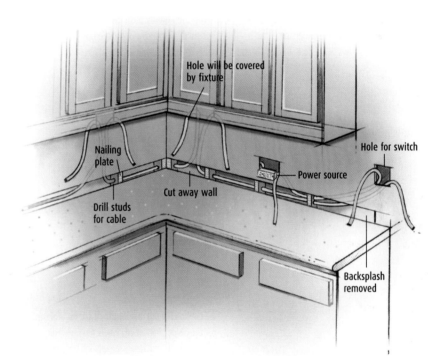

Hole will be covered by fixture

Nailing plate

Drill studs for cable

Cut away wall

Power source

Hole for switch

Backsplash removed

1 RUN CABLE

Plan the wiring so as many holes as possible will be covered when you're done. If the countertop backsplash is removable, remove it and cut a channel in the drywall or plaster that will be completely covered by the backsplash. Drill holes in the studs to accommodate cable (pages 125–127). (If you can't remove a backsplash, allow time for patching and painting the wall afterward. Or install tile between the countertop and the wall cabinets.) Examine each light to determine exactly where the cable will enter and exit. Cut narrow holes in the wall where the cable will enter the lights. Cut carefully so the hole will be covered when the light is installed. Cut a hole for the switch box, and run cable into it from a power source—perhaps a nearby receptacle (pages 129, 141–142). **Do not connect the cable to power.** Run cable from the switch box to the hole for the first light, then from the first to the second light, and so on. Let about 16 inches of cable hang from the holes so you'll have plenty of slack to make connections. Most local codes allow fluorescent lights to be used as junction boxes, so you can string the wire from light to light. Check to be sure.

2 ATTACH THE LIGHTS

Disassemble the lights, and remove the lens and fluorescent tubes. Clamp each cable to the light as you would clamp cable to a box (pages 119 and 121). Have a helper hold the light as close to the rear wall as possible while you drive screws through the light and into the underside of the cabinet. Be sure that the screws won't poke through to the inside of the cabinet.

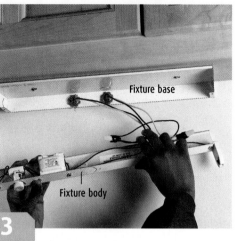

Fixture base

Fixture body

3 WIRE THE LIGHTS

Plan so that wires will not come within an inch of the ballast. Splice wires with the leads inside the light, black to black and white to white. Bend the wires so they will not get in the way, then gently push the bottom portion of the light into position. If it does not go in easily, take it down and realign the wires for an easier fit. Attach the base.

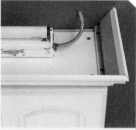

GOOD IDEA

ADD COVE LIGHTING

If your **cabinets have space above,** you can install lights there without hiding the cable.

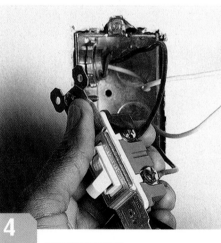

4 WIRE THE SWITCH

Install a switch box (pages 132–133). Splice the white wires together. Attach each of the black wires to a single-pole switch. (If you wish to dim the light, use a dimmer made especially for fluorescent fixtures.) Connect the ground wire to the switch and to the box if it is metal. Cover the terminals with tape. **Shut off power to the receptacle or junction box that will supply the power.** Splice white to white and black to a black or color wire in the receptacle (page 22). Restore power.

TIME SAVER

BX elbow

CABLE INSIDE THE CABINET

Cut holes in the cabinets. Lay BX or MC cable on the inside. Plan exactly where the cable will enter each light below the cabinet. Because you can't slip excess cable into the wall cabinet, you'll have to cut the cable precisely. (See pages 120–121 about working with armored cable.)

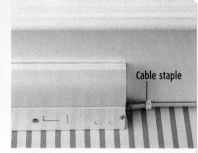

Cable staple

CABLE UNDER THE CABINET

Attach the lights under the cabinets, string cable under the cabinet, and staple the cable in place using cable staples. Measure and cut carefully so the cable is flat along the length. **Check your local code before doing this; it is not allowed in some areas.**

Planning for new services

Chapter 7 highlights

O nce you are comfortable with projects like replacing devices and fixtures, you're ready to go—not boldly, but carefully—where few homeowners dare to tread. You're ready to add new electrical service. "New service" refers to running new cable. It can be as simple as tapping into a receptacle to add a new line (page 141) or as complex as installing several new circuits in a subpanel (pages 194–195).

This chapter helps you ask the right questions and come up with the best solutions so your new installation will do what you want it to do, and do it safely. You'll learn which tools and materials to buy, how to balance loads on a circuit and draw plans, and how to anticipate code requirements.

Buying tools to run new lines

The money you pay for quality electrical tools will be minor compared to how much you'll save by doing the work yourself. To run new lines you will need most of the tools shown here as well as those on pages 28–29. Buy everything you need; the job will go more smoothly.

For cutting into walls

These tools pave the way for installing electrical cable and boxes. The right tools, along with sharp bits and blades, will do the least damage to walls, saving you patching time afterward. Consider buying a corded **power drill** with a ½-inch chuck for large bits. (A cordless drill may not have the power or capacity to drill numerous holes in walls and framing.) Have several ⅜-inch and ¾-inch **spade bits** on hand; they dull quickly. A **fishing bit** drills holes in hard-to-reach joists and studs. The **bender** helps you aim the bit where you want it to go. Once the hole is drilled, the bender has a **pulling attachment** that allows you to pull the cable with the bit.

Use a **drywall saw** to cut small holes in drywall. To cut through plaster and lath, use a **saber saw** with a fine-cutting blade, or use a **rotary-cutting tool**. A **flat pry bar** is ideal for trim removal and modest demolition. A **utility knife** is an essential all-purpose tool.

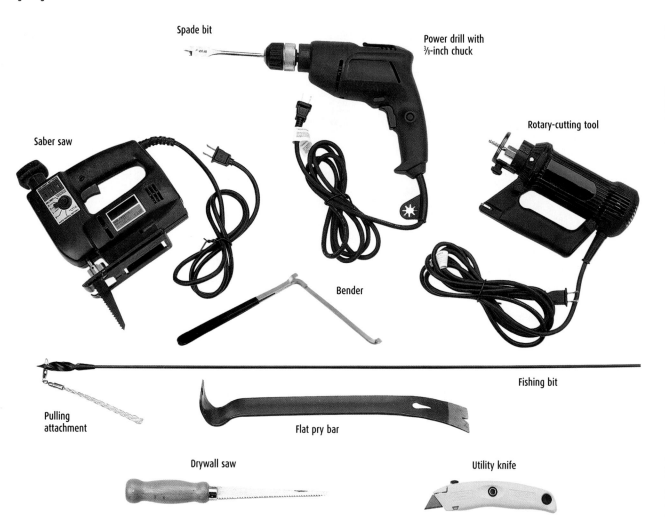

Spade bit

Power drill with ⅜-inch chuck

Rotary-cutting tool

Saber saw

Bender

Pulling attachment

Fishing bit

Flat pry bar

Drywall saw

Utility knife

Fish tapes

Hammer

Calculator

Armored cable cutter

Tool belt

Rotary screwdriver

Nut driver

Level

Conduit reamer

Magnetic sleeve and bit

Water pump pliers

Coaxial stripper

Hacksaw

Coaxial crimper

Spade for installing underground lines

For running new lines

Complete your kit with these relatively inexpensive tools. When working with armored cable, you may want to use an **armored cable cutter** (see page 120 for cutting armored cable). For figuring circuit loads use a handheld **calculator**. A **fish tape** helps you run cable through finished walls and pull wires through conduit. Sometimes you need two tapes so that you can hook them together (page 127). New fiberglass tapes are safer and easier to use than metal tapes.

Buy an electrician's **tool belt** so you won't fumble around for tools. You'll use a **hammer** to tap locknuts tight onto cable clamps. If a box or fixture has bolts instead of screws, you'll need a **nut driver**. Use a **level** to mark cutouts on walls and square up boxes.

To drive screws quickly and firmly, nothing beats a drill with a **magnetic sleeve**. Insert small screwdriver bits into its tip, and they will be magnetized so you can drive screws with one hand. With a **rotary screwdriver**, you can drive or remove small screws on cover plates, switches, and receptacles in a flash.

You may need a pair of **water pump pliers** for handling connectors. Cut conduit with a **hacksaw** equipped with a professional-quality blade that will last longer. After cutting the conduit, remove burrs with a **conduit reamer**. For coaxial cable use a **crimper** and a **stripper**. Use a **narrow spade** to excavate for outdoor cable.

Common code requirements

t's your house and you're doing the work yourself. Why should a city inspector come around and tell you what to do? Codes and inspections are a sort of collective wisdom based on the experience of nearly a century of living with electricity. Those lessons have been incorporated into electrical codes. These codes exist to prevent house fires and injury from shocks and to keep your electrical system running well.

Meeting national, provincial, and local codes

Whenever you run new electrical cable, your local building department will require you to get a permit and have the work approved by one of its inspectors. Inspectors and building departments use the Canadian Electrical Code (CEC) as the basis for most of their regulations. However, local standards often supplement or modify these basic rules.

You'll find some of the most common code requirements in the chart on the opposite page. The list is not complete, however, and you may need other sources of information.

You can buy a copy of the CEC, but it costs about $125 and is difficult to wade through. Most of its many pages deal with commercial installations that homeowners will never encounter. Many useful handbooks on the CEC are available. Buy one, or borrow one from a library, that emphasizes residential installations.

Coordinating the tasks

If you are building an addition to your house or gutting walls to remodel a kitchen or bathroom, you'll need to juggle carpentry, plumbing, and wall and floor finishing. Whether you do all or some of the work yourself, it's important that the various jobs are coordinated so that workers do not get in the way of each other and so that inspectors can see what they need to inspect. Aim for this sequence: (1) Install framing or gut the walls. (2) Run the rough plumbing, install electrical cable and boxes, and then call in the inspector. (3) Cover the walls with drywall, and paint. (4) Install the finish plumbing and electrical, and have it inspected.

Working with inspectors

Inspectors usually work with professional electricians who know codes and what is expected at inspections. Inspectors usually have a tight schedule and can't take time to educate you about what is needed. Their job is to inspect, not to help you plan your project. Take these steps to ensure that the inspections go smoothly.

■ Before scheduling an inspection, ask the building department for printed information about your type of electrical project. Make neat, readable, and complete drawings (pages 110–111), and provide a list of the materials.

■ When you present your plans, accept criticisms and directives graciously. It usually does no good to argue—and the inspector does know more than you do. Make it clear that you want to do things the right way. Take notes

while the inspector talks to you so you can remember every detail of what needs to be done.

■ Be clear on when the inspections will take place and exactly what needs to be done before each inspection. Before calling for an inspection, double-check that everything required is complete—don't make the inspector come back again. Don't cover up wiring that the inspector needs to see. If you install drywall before the inspection, you may have to rip it out and reinstall it after the inspection.

■ Some building departments limit the kinds of work that a homeowner can do; you may have to hire a professional for at least part of a job. Others will let you take on advanced work only if you can pass an oral or written test.

Codes you may encounter

Here's a quick summary of some codes that are typical for household wiring projects. Follow them as you work up your plans and write your materials list.

These guidelines should satisfy most requirements, but keep in mind that your local codes might have different requirements. You probably will want to exceed requirements in order to provide you with sufficient and safe electrical service.

The more you communicate your specific plans and techniques to your inspector, the less chance that you will have to tear out and do the job over again. It's better to be set straight by your inspector when the job is still on paper.

CABLE TYPE	Most locales allow NMD (nonmetallic) cable for all installations where the cable runs inside walls or ceilings. Some areas require armored cable or conduit. If the cable will be exposed, many local codes require armored cable or conduit.
WIRE GAUGE	Use #14 wire for 15-amp circuits, #12 wire for 20-amp circuits, #10 wire for 30-amp circuits and #8 wire for 40-am circuits.
PLASTIC AND METAL BOXES	Many locales allow plastic boxes for receptacles, switches, and fixtures; but some require metal boxes. Boxes must be flush with the finished wall. Make sure boxes are large enough for their conductors and connections(page 112).
RUNNING CABLE	NMD and armored cable must be run through holes in the center of studs or joists so that a drywall or trim nail cannot reach it. Most codes require metal nail guards as well. Some inspectors want cable for receptacles to be run about 10 inches above the receptacles. NMD cable should be stapled to a stud or joist within 12 inches of the box it enters. Once the cable is clamped to a box, at least ¼ inch of sheathing, but no more than ½ inch, should be visible in the box, and at least 8 inches of wire should be available for connecting to the device or fixture.
CIRCUIT CAPACITY	Make sure usage does not exceed "safe capacity" (pages 48–49). Local codes may be stricter.
LIVING ROOM, DINING ROOM, FAMILY ROOM, AND BEDROOM SPECS	Space receptacles every 12 feet along each wall, and 6 feet from the first opening. If a small section of wall (between two doors, for example) is more than 3 feet wide, it should have a receptacle. For most purposes, use 15-amp receptacles. For convenience, rooms should have at least one light controlled by a wall switch near the entry door. The switch may control an overhead light for living rooms or bedrooms, or one outlet of a receptacle into which you can plug a lamp. If you are adding a ceiling fan make sure the box you attach it to is designed for fans and can support the additional weight.
HALLWAY AND STAIRWAY SPECS	A stairway must have an overhead light controlled by three-way switches at the bottom and top of the stairs. If a hallway is more than 15 feet long, it must have at least one receptacle.
KITCHEN SPECS	Above countertops, space receptacles no more than 4 feet apart. Outlets near a water source such as a sink must be protected with GFCI circuit breakers. Many codes require split receptacles on 15 amp circuits in kitchens or outlets that alternate which circuit they are connected to. The codes may also require a separate 15-amp circuit for both the dishwasher and refrigerator. A microwave should have a single 20-amp circuit and use a T-slot receptacle.
BATHROOM SPECS	Any GFCI receptacle should be on its own circuit. Install the lights and fan on a separate 15- or 20-amp circuit.
GARAGE AND WORKSHOP SPECS	Install a 15-amp circuit for lights and a 20-amp circuit for tools. Install two 20-amp circuits if you have many power tools. Many areas require GFCIs in garages. Check your local code.

Mapping a job

Building departments require detailed drawings and comprehensive lists of materials before issuing permits. To save yourself and the inspector aggravation, do your best to make your drawing clear and complete.

Draw a plan

If you'll be wiring existing space, measure the rooms and make a scale drawing on graph paper. If you have blueprints for a new addition, use those. Make several copies of the floor plan so you can start over if you make mistakes. Include windows, doors, cabinets, and other obstructions.

Begin by drawing in all the switches, receptacles, and fixtures, using the symbols below. Then use color pencils to draw the cable runs. Use a different color for each circuit. Mark each cable—for example, "14/2 WG" for a cable with two #14 wires and a ground wire.

As you draw make a list of materials, tallying the number of boxes, devices, and fixtures, and roughly figuring how much cable you will need.

Don't forget

Check and double-check your drawing and your list.
- Make sure none of the circuits is overloaded (pages 112–113).
- See that switches are conveniently placed to easily turn on lights.
- Consider how each room will be used, and add devices where necessary. For instance, a home office with a computer should have a dedicated circuit.
- Make sure all your boxes will be large enough (page 114).
- Remember that if you add circuits, you may need to expand service with a subpanel (pages 21 and 194–195), a new service panel (pages 19–20), or even a new line from the utility to your house. Determine how to run cable to the service panel or subpanel.

Basic electrical symbol chart

Use these symbols as you plan your project. They'll be easily understood by your inspector.

Recessed ceiling light	Duplex receptacle	240-volt polarized receptacle	S_1 Single-pole switch	Thermostat
Ceiling light	Split-wired duplex receptacle	Isolated ground receptacle	S_2 Double-pole switch	Indoor telephone
Wall light	GFCI receptacle	Weatherproof receptacle	S_3 3-way switch	Television jack
Fluorescent ceiling light	Switched receptacle	Service panel	S_4 4-way switch	Doorbell
Fan	Fourplex receptacle	Split receptacle	Wall junction box	S_T Switch with timer	Chime

KITCHEN WIRING

14/2
14/3
14/2
14/2
12/2
14/2
14/2
14/3
14/2
14/3
14/3
5/3
14/3
14/2
14/3
14/3
14/2
14/3
14/2
14/3
14/2

15 AMP MICROWAVE
40 AMP 120/240 RANGE
15 AMP
DISPOSAL
DISH WASHER
S S₃
REFRIGERATOR
CEILING FAN/LIGHT
S₁ S₁
S₃
S₃
40 AMP CIRCUIT
PENDANT LIGHTS
S₃

MAKE A PLAN

Draw a floor plan of your project and make an extra copy or two. Use color pencils to distinguish your circuits. Add symbols for the various devices (they'll be useful when making your materials list). When you're satisfied with your plan, make a clean version to copy for the city and for your own use.

Loading circuits correctly

When planning to add new service to your home, ask three important questions: First, will any individual circuit become overloaded as a result of adding service? Second, is your service panel large enough to accommodate any new circuits you will be adding? And finally, is the power entering your home from the utility company sufficient for your needs?

Loading individual circuits

If you will be extending an existing circuit to add a receptacle or a light fixture, make sure you won't overload that circuit. List all the receptacles, fixtures, and appliances on that circuit, and then add the wattage of the new service to determine whether you will be within "safe usage." (See pages 48–49 to make this calculation.)

Sizing up a service panel

If existing circuits are not large enough to accommodate the new service you want to install, or if you will be wiring an addition, install new circuits.

Open your service panel (see page 46). If you see available blank slots, adding a circuit will be easy. If all the spaces are taken up, you may be able to add service by installing a tandem breaker (page 117).

Older homes with fuse boxes often receive 60-amp service from the utility company. If your wiring is less than 40 years old, your home probably has 100-amp service. Larger homes built in the last 15 years may have 200-amp service. The total amperage for your home is usually written on the main breaker or fuse.

Got enough power?

Circuits can add up to more than their total rating. If you add up the amperage of all the breakers in the box, you will probably find that the total is more than the overall rating of the service panel. For example, a 100-amp service panel may have breakers totaling 220 amps. This does not mean that it is over capacity.

The amperage rating tells you how much amperage each hot bus bar (page 19–21) delivers. So each vertical row of breakers on a 100-amp box delivers 100 amps. And the breakers on a single bar can exceed the total capacity, because all the lights, fixtures, receptacles, and appliances will never run at the same time.

Sizing electrical boxes

Electrical codes specify the size box needed so that the connections, wires, and switch or receptacle are not too crowded in the box. Factors that influence the size of the box include the thickness or gauge of the wire, the number of wires entering the box, the number of connections in the box, and even the type of receptacle (GFCI receptacles are larger and therefore may require a larger box).

Typically boxes are rated to hold a certain number of wires. To calculate the number of wires a box will need to hold, add the wires entering the box, excluding ground wires, and then add ½ wire for each wire nut or connector in the box. After you have this number you will then be able to ask for the correct size box when purchasing it. Two examples are pictured at right.

As a general rule, you should buy large boxes unless you don't have room in your wall or ceiling. The bigger boxes don't cost much more, and they will give you room for upgrades in the future.

A THREE WAY SWITCH
A three way switch uses two black wires, two whites, one red, and two wire connector thereby determining the size box to use.

A RECEPTACLE
A receptacle at the end of the line has only a white, a black and a wire nut connecting the grounding wires thereby determining the size of the box to use.

A home with more than 2,000 square feet will probably need more than 60-amp service. A house with less than 4,000 square feet that doesn't have electric heat or central air-conditioning probably needs no more than 100-amp service.

Computing your exact power needs

To more accurately determine whether you have enough service, compute your home's electrical usage in watts. (Remember, watts=volts × amps; page 48).

■ Add the total wattage used by all permanent appliances, such as the dishwasher, clothes dryer, and electric range.

■ Next add it all up.

■ Add the wattage of either the central air-conditioning or the heating unit, whichever is greater.

■ Divide by 230 to figure how many amps you need.

If your situation involves complex circuits, consult with the utility company. They often have services to help you to ensure safe operation of your electrical system or they can point you in the right direction.

Shopping for appliances

See the example of dishwasher below which shows both electrical energy used and estimates of yearly costs when used with electric or gas water heaters. If you are replacing an existing appliance try to buy one that requires less energy because you can be assured the new one won't overload the existing circuit. Purchase price is not the only factor to consider when buying a new appliance. Use these labels for comparing operating costs so you are a smart shopper.

 BUYER'S GUIDE

NEED MORE CIRCUITS?
Here are some options if you need more circuits than your service panel can provide.

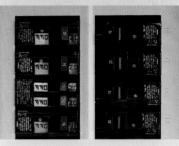

ADD A TANDEM BREAKER
You may be able to install a tandem breaker, which supplies two circuits but uses only one slot. Check local codes to see whether tandem breakers are allowed for your service panel. You may need to install a subpanel (pages 194–195) or a new service panel instead. If you need a new service panel contact a professional electrician

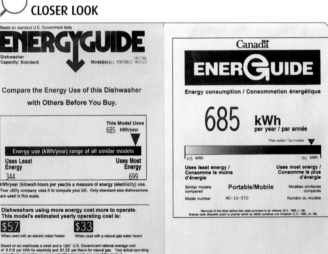

CLOSER LOOK

INFORMATIVE LABELING

All major appliances such as air conditioners, water heaters, and refrigerators are required to carry labels that will tell you how energy efficient the unit is and how much it will cost to operate for a year under normal conditions and average use. Read the label carefully before you buy.

USE A BREAKER BOX EQUIPPED FOR NEW CIRCUITS

This box has plenty of room for new circuits. A standard 120-volt breaker will take up one slot, and a 240-volt breaker will use two spaces.

7

PLANNING FOR NEW SERVICES

Choosing boxes

All electrical connections must be contained inside a box. And all boxes—including junction boxes—must be accessible. Never cover a box with drywall or paneling. Some fixtures, such as recessed cans and fluorescent lights, contain their own boxes so connections can be made inside them.

Be sure to buy boxes large enough to avoid crowding the wires (page 44).

Plastic boxes

In many areas plastic boxes are the norm for all indoor residential wiring. They are inexpensive and quick to install. To install most **new-work boxes**, position and drive in the two nails. To install **remodel boxes** (boxes installed in walls already covered by drywall or plaster), see pages 132–133.

Of course, you cannot ground a plastic box. For that reason some local codes do not allow them, or they allow them only for certain purposes.

Some plastic boxes have holes with knockout tabs, so the cable is not held tightly in place by the box. In that case you must staple the cable within 8 inches of the box. Other boxes have built-in metal or plastic cable clamps or staples. Check local codes to see whether clamps are required.

Plastic boxes are easier to damage than metal boxes. When installing a new-work box, all it takes is one wrong swing with your hammer to crack the box. Never install a box that is cracked. Buy several extra boxes just in case.

Most plastic boxes are brittle, so don't use them where they are not built into the wall. The exception is an **outdoor box** made of especially strong PVC plastic.

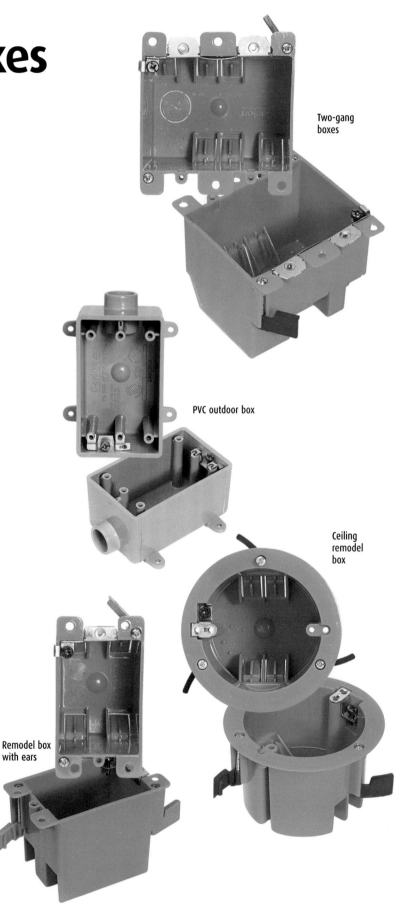

Two-gang boxes

PVC outdoor box

Ceiling remodel box

One-gang box

Remodel box with ears

Metal boxes

Even if the local building department does not require metal boxes, you may prefer them because they are stronger and provide a better ground connection. Many codes require that all junction boxes—and all exposed boxes—be metal (with the exception of an outdoor PVC box, shown on the opposite page). If a system uses conduit or armored cable and does not have a ground wire, the boxes must be metal in order to provide a grounding path to the cable or conduit.

New-work metal boxes often have nailing brackets. Position the box and drive screws or nails through the holes and into a stud or joist.

To open a knockout hole in a metal box, punch it with a hammer and screwdriver; then grab the slug from the inside with lineman's pliers and twist it off. Install a cable clamp if the box does not have built-in clamps.

Gangable boxes can be dismantled and ganged together to make space for two or more devices.

Install most **switch boxes** and ceiling boxes flush with the finished wall or ceiling surface. Install a junction box ½ inch behind the wall surface and add a **mud ring**—also called an adapter plate—which has screw holes for the cover plate. Choose a 4×4 junction box or a larger 4¹¹⁄₁₆-inch box. Make sure the cover plate or mud ring will fit the box. If a junction box holds only spliced wires and no device, cover it with a metal blank plate if it is exposed and a plastic blank plate if it will be enclosed in a wall.

Use round-cornered junction boxes called **handy boxes** if the box will be exposed on a basement or garage wall. Use metal cover plates. For a ceiling fan use a fan-rated box (pages 90–92).

1⅞-inch-deep handy box

New-work octagonal box with bracket

New-work switch box

New-work junction box

Tile mud ring

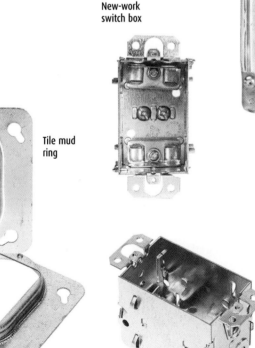

3½-inch gangable switch box

Installing straps and staples

Cable, whether hidden in a wall or exposed, must be installed carefully to keep it from being damaged. Codes specify how and where each type of cable must be anchored. A staple holds the cable firmly without damaging its sheathing. Staples with plastic parts are better because they are less likely to damage the sheathing than the once-popular metal staples. Choose the right size staples to fit the cable.

When running cable along joists or studs, secure NM or armored cable at least 1¼ inches back from the front edge of the framing member (to protect it from drywall screws), using a cable staple every 1.5 meters or 59 inches. Staple cable within 12 inches of a box that has a clamp and within 8 inches of a box that does not have a clamp. Never secure two cables with a single staple.

Use drive straps (below) for conduit; you can use one- or two-hole straps for either armored cable or conduit. When attaching a one-hole or a two-hole strap to wood, use a drill to drive in 1¼-inch screws. To anchor a strap to concrete, block, or brick, drill holes with a masonry bit and drive masonry screws into the holes.

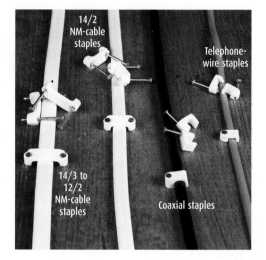

CHOOSING THE RIGHT STAPLE
A staple should hug the cable tightly without denting it. To attach it position the staple over the cable, taking care that the nails do not touch the cable, and hammer in the nails. If you have a lot of telephone cable to install, purchase a staple gun that drives in round-topped staples (page 182).

ANCHORING CONDUIT TO WOOD
Use hook-like drive straps to attach conduit to wood. Hold the drive strap next to the conduit, and pound the strap in until it firmly grips the conduit. Place straps every 4 feet and within 12 inches of a box.

ANCHORING ARMORED CABLE TO WOOD
Fasten a strap in place with a 1¼-inch general-purpose screw. Use two-hole straps to install two parallel lines. Place the cable straps every 3 to 4 feet.

Running new cable

Chapter 8 highlights

Before you start to run new lines, complete your wiring plan (Chapter 7) and get city approval for your project. Next be sure to have a basic understanding of your home's electrical system (Chapter 1) and be comfortable with basic wiring techniques (Chapter 2). You'll find that installing boxes and cable in new framing is straightforward—even fun—once you've mastered the techniques. Running new lines in old walls is more challenging, especially if there isn't an attic or crawl space in which to run the lines. With planning, a few new skills, and the right tools, you'll get the job done right.

Working with NM cable

8

RUNNING NEW CABLE

You'll find nonmetallic (NM) cable easy to cut and quick to install. Just be careful when you remove the sheathing so you don't accidentally slit the wire insulation. If you do, cut off the damage and start again; otherwise, you may get a short or a shock. Whenever possible, strip sheathing before cutting the cable to length. That way if you make a mistake, you can try again.

There are several separate conductors inside a cable. Most commonly used in residential construction are two- and three-wire cables. Two-wire cable with a ground has a black wire for power, a white wire for the neutral line, and an uninsulated copper wire for the ground. So it may confuse some homeowners when they see three "wires" in the cable. Only the two that are insulated, the black and the white wires, count for naming the cable. Thus the name 2-wire cable. If the wires in the cable are 12 gauge wires the cable is designated as 12-2 W/G with the 12 indicating gauge or size, the 2 indicating the number of wires, and the W/G indicating "with ground." It is a similar story with three wire cable. Typically in three wire cable you'll find black and red wires for power and a white wire for neutral that are insulated. If the cable has a grounding wire there will also be a uninsulated copper wire in the nonmetallic (NM) sheath.

Ground wire

1

PULL THE GROUND WIRE

Cut or pull back the sheathing so you can grab the end of the ground wire with lineman's pliers. Hold the cable end in the other hand, and pull back the ground wire until you have made a slit in the sheathing about 12 inches long. This technique is common practice among electricians, but pay extra attention because you can damage the ground wire while pulling it out.

TOOL SAVVY

USING A CABLE RIPPER

Use this tool to strip cable that is already installed in a box. Practice on scrap cable first to make sure the ripper doesn't cut too deeply and damage wire insulation.

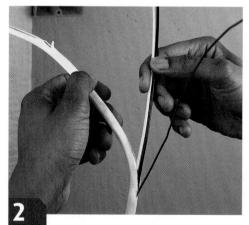

2

REMOVE THE SHEATHING

Pull the plastic sheathing back. Peel off any protective paper wrapping or thin strips of plastic, and cut them off.

Utility knife

SAFETY ALERT

SLITTING THE CABLE WITH A KNIFE CAN BE DANGEROUS
Although commonly used in a pinch, slitting the cable with a knife can nick the insulation of the wires inside the cable leading to a potentially dangerous situation. If at all possible use the cable ripper as shown in the Tool Savvy at left.

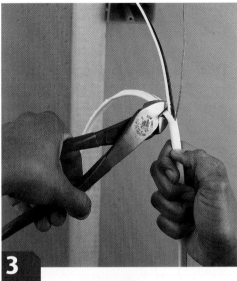

3 SNIP THE SHEATHING

Use side-cutting pliers, wire strippers, or the cutting portion of lineman's pliers to cut the sheathing.

4 PULL THE CABLE INTO THE BOX

Push the wires through the clip or clamp on the box (see right for the types you'll find). Pull the cable into the box so at least ¼ inch of sheathing shows inside.

FOUR WAYS TO ANCHOR NM CABLE TO A BOX

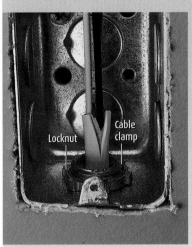

Locknut Cable clamp

CABLE CLAMP

Buy clamps made for NM cable. Remove the knockout. Screw the clamp to the cable, then slip it through the hole and screw on the locknut. Tighten the locknut by tapping with a hammer and screwdriver. Or attach to the box first, slide the cable through the clamp, then tighten the screws.

Built-in clamp

BUILT-IN CLAMP

Plastic boxes large enough to hold more than one device have internal clamps, as do most remodel boxes. Tighten the screw to firmly clamp the cable.

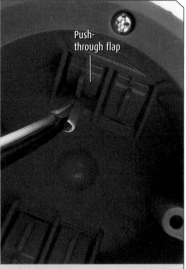

Push-through flap

POKE AND STAPLE

To run cable into many plastic boxes, you may need to push the cable past a plastic flap or knock out a plastic tab. Once you've inserted the cable into the box, staple the cable on a framing member within 8 inches of the box.

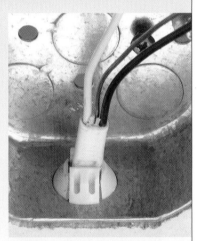

POP-IN PLASTIC CONNECTOR

Remove the knockout and push this connector in place. Then push the cable through and, if accessible, staple the cable within 8 inches of the box.

Working with armored cable

PROJECT DETAILS

SKILLS: Bending and cutting sheathing, protecting wires
PROJECT: Stripping cable sheathing and clamping it

TIME TO COMPLETE

EXPERIENCED: 5 min.
HANDY: 10 min.
NOVICE: 15 min.

STUFF YOU'LL NEED

TOOLS: Side-cutting pliers, hammer, screwdriver, channel-joint pliers, perhaps an armored cable cutter
MATERIALS: BX or MC cable, protective bushings

The features of flexible armored cable fall midway between NM and conduit. Armored cable is easier to install than conduit and less flexible than NM. It protects wires better than NM but won't turn away nails as well as conduit.

Types of armored cable

There are two types of armored cable. BX cable (also called AC90) is a type of armored cable with a ground wire. Older BX used heavy steel sheathing. Today's cable uses aluminum, which is lighter, is a better conductor, and is much easier to cut.

MC cable is like BX but with a green-insulated grounding wire. Some new building codes require using MC instead of BX for a sure ground.

Where to use it

Some codes call for armored cable instead of NM. Others require NM or conduit where the cable is exposed. Run armored cable inside walls, and protect it from nails as you would NM cable. Armored cable will bend only so far, so use NM around wall corners (page 125–127) and around door jambs (page 131).

1 BEND AND SQUEEZE THE CABLE
About 1 foot from the end, bend the cable and then squeeze the bend until the armor breaks apart slightly. If you have trouble doing this by hand, use a pair of channel-joint pliers.

Caution:
Sharp edges! Handle armored cable carefully to avoid cuts.

SAFETY ALERT

HACKSAWS CAN BE DANGEROUS
Cutting armored cable with a hacksaw is generally not recommended. It is very difficult to cut through the armor without nicking the insulation of the wires inside which could lead to a dangerous short.

USING AN ARMORED CABLE CUTTER
For large jobs you may want to invest in this tool. **Adjust the cutter for cable size, slip in the cable, and turn the handle** to make a lengthwise cut.

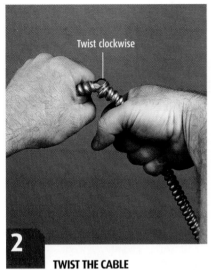

2 TWIST THE CABLE

Grasp the cable firmly on each side of the spot you want to cut. Twist the waste end clockwise until the armor comes apart far enough for you to slip in cutters. If you have trouble doing this with your bare hands, use two pliers.

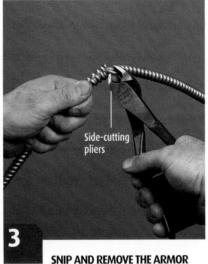

3 SNIP AND REMOVE THE ARMOR

Cut through one rib of the armor with a pair of side-cutting pliers. Slide the waste armor off the wires. Keep your hands clear of sharp edges.

4 TRIM SHARP ENDS

Remove paper wrapping and plastic strips. Leave the thin metal bonding strip alone. Use side-cutting pliers to snip away pointed ends of sheathing that could nick wire insulation.

If bushings did not come with your cable, buy them separately.

5 SLIP ON THE BUSHING

Proper placement of the bushing is important to prevent the sharp edge of the armor from cutting into the insulation around the wires. Slip a bushing over the wires. Slide it down into the armor so the bushing protects the wires from the sharp edges of the armor.

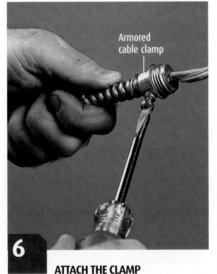

6 ATTACH THE CLAMP

Remove the locknut from an armored cable clamp. Slide the clamp down over the bushing as far as it will go, and tighten the screw. Double-check to make sure that none of the wires are in danger of being nicked by the armor.

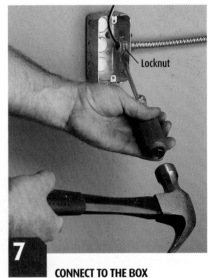

7 CONNECT TO THE BOX

Remove a knockout slug from a metal box, and poke the connector into the hole. Slide the locknut over the wires, and tighten it onto the cable clamp. On BX cable this connection is the ground—use a hammer and a screwdriver to tap the locknut tight.

Running conduit

Although not very common in residential construction, conduit is the most durable product for running wire. It's more expensive and time-consuming to install than cable, but it is no longer necessary to learn how to bend conduit. Ready-made parts make installation easier than ever. Use conduit on unfinished walls and ceilings where wiring will be exposed. Use electrical metallic tubing (EMT), or "thinwall" conduit, for most indoor installations and thicker intermediate metal conduit (IMC) for outdoor jobs. Plastic rigid nonmetallic conduit (PVC) is also used outdoors. To install it see pages 174–176.

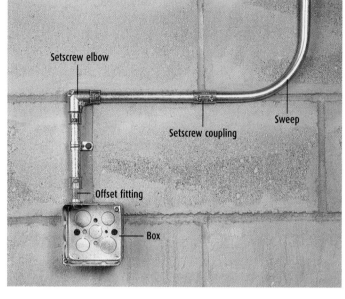

Setscrew elbow
Setscrew coupling
Sweep
Offset fitting
Box

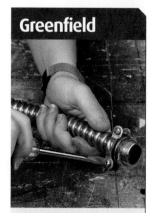

Greenfield

Also called flexible metal conduit, Greenfield is essentially armored cable without the wires. It is expensive, so use it sparingly in places where rigid conduit would be difficult to install.

ASSEMBLING THE PARTS

Take a rough drawing of your installation to a home center or electrical supply store. Ask a salesperson to help gather all the pieces you need. Generally use ½-inch conduit for up to five #12 wires or six #14 wires, and ¾-inch conduit for more wires. (Larger conduit will make pulling easier, so consider buying ¾-inch in any case.) Use setscrew couplings and elbows for indoor installations (you'll have to use compression fittings outdoors). If the conduit and the box are installed flush against a wall, you'll need an offset fitting. Use a sweep to turn most corners. At every four bends provide access to the wires by installing a box or a pulling elbow as shown on the opposite page.

Running metal conduit

1

ANCHOR THE BOXES

Place the boxes where desired. As much as possible keep the boxes level with each other so the conduit can make straight runs between them. Drive screws to anchor each box. If you are anchoring to concrete or block, use masonry screws.

2

ADD OFFSET FITTINGS AND MARK THE CONDUIT FOR CUTTING

To enable the conduit to hug the wall, install special offset conduit fittings. The conduit will insert about an inch into the fitting. Wherever possible hold conduit in place and mark it for cutting; elsewhere, use a tape measure.

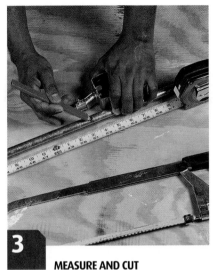

3 MEASURE AND CUT

Install the boxes first, then cut conduit to fit between them. At a corner have a helper hold a sweep in place while you mark the conduit for cutting. Use a hacksaw with a fine-tooth blade to cut.

4 REMOVE BURRS AND RUN THE CONDUIT

Ream out all burrs with a conduit reamer so the wires can slide smoothly past joints without damaging the sheathing. Attach the conduit to the fittings and boxes.

TOOL SAVVY

SQUIRT LUBRICANT

To make pulling easier on long runs, pour a bit of pulling lubricant on the wires. (Don't risk using substitute lubricants such as dishwashing liquid or hand soap. Some can dangerously degrade wire insulation over time.)

CLOSER LOOK

INSTALL PULLING ELBOWS

If the conduit will make more than three turns between boxes, install a **pulling elbow** to make fishing easier. Don't splice wires here; just use the opening to pull the wires through.

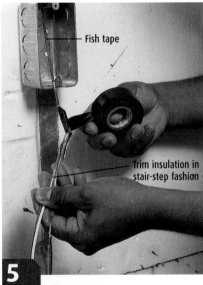

5 RUN FISH TAPE AND ATTACH THE WIRES

Feed the fish tape through the conduit in the opposite direction from which you will pull the wires. Poke the wire ends through the fish tape's loop and bend them over in stair-step fashion. Wrap firmly and neatly with electrician's tape so the joint will not bind when it goes through a sweep.

6 PULL THE WIRES

Have someone feed the wires through one end while you pull the fish tape on the other end. Pull with steady pressure. Try to keep the wires moving, rather than starting and stopping. If you get stuck back up a few inches to gain a running start.

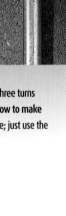

8

RUNNING NEW CABLE

PVC conduit

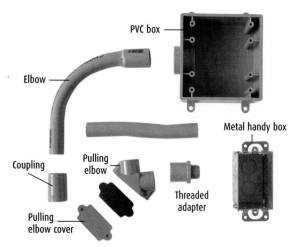

PVC box

Elbow

Metal handy box

Coupling

Pulling elbow

Pulling elbow cover

Threaded adapter

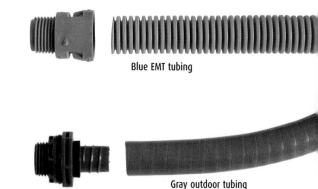

Blue EMT tubing

Gray outdoor tubing

PVC CONDUIT AND FITTINGS

When running PVC conduit you can use either PVC or metal boxes. You will need threaded adapters to connect PVC pipe to a metal box. Purchase elbows for turns. Use a pulling elbow if the pipe makes more than three turns between boxes or if you will need to get at the wires.

FLEXIBLE PLASTIC CONDUIT

Flexible conduit is a bit expensive but may be the best choice in places where it will be difficult to run solid conduit. Check to make sure it is permitted in your locale. Blue EMT tubing is lightweight and suitable only for indoor use when behind walls or in concrete where it is not exposed. Outdoor tubing is strong and impermeable to keep wires safe and dry.

Assembling the pieces

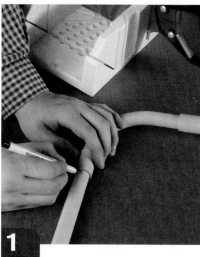

1

MAKE A DRY RUN

Install boxes as you would for metal conduit (page 122), and measure for cutting the conduit to fit between the boxes. Cut PVC conduit using a miter box and a backsaw or a power saw with a fine-cutting blade. Assemble four or five pieces in a dry run. Where needed draw layout lines that extend from a fitting onto a piece of conduit to ensure that you will install the pieces in the correct orientation.

2

APPLY CEMENT

Buy cement (and perhaps primer) approved for use with the conduit you are using. Disassemble the pieces, and glue them together in order. You may or may not need to first apply primer before applying the glue. Apply cement to the inside of the fitting and to the outside of the conduit.

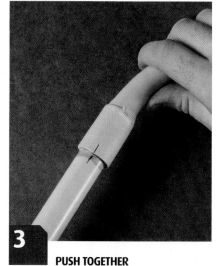

3

PUSH TOGETHER

Within a few seconds of applying the cement, push the conduit into the fitting and give it a slight twist. Hold the two pieces together for 10 seconds or so, then wipe away any excess cement. Move on to the next joint.

Wiring in unfinished framing

Running cable through bare framing members is far easier than fishing it through a wall finished with drywall or plaster and lath (pages 128–131). If the existing wall surface is flawed or if you also are installing plumbing in a remodeling job, it usually saves work to tear off all the drywall. Start anew rather than living with a roomful of small wall patches.

Installing cable that is safe and secure

Installing NM cable with plastic boxes is quick and easy—drill holes, run the cable through, and poke it into boxes. But don't run cable any old way. Safety concerns and codes dictate that it must be positioned out of harm's way, which means precise measuring and installing.

Choosing boxes and cable. Check local codes before buying materials. Codes may call for metal boxes, although plastic is fine in most areas. Assuming you will be installing ½-inch drywall after wiring, buy boxes that are easy to install ½ inch out from a stud or joist. Plan wiring carefully (Chapter 7) so you'll install the correct cables. For instance, use 14/2 for most general lighting and receptacles, 12-gauge for 20-amp circuits, and three-wire cable for three-way switches and split receptacles.

Placing holes. Local codes may specify the height at which cable for receptacles should be run, as well as where to put staples.

If an unfinished attic is above or a basement is below, run some of the cables there (pages 128-131).

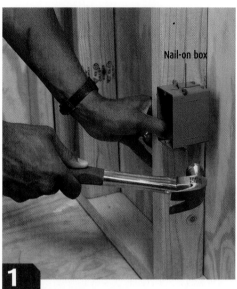

Nail-on box

1 INSTALL THE BOXES

Attach all the boxes before running cable. Receptacle boxes are usually positioned 12 inches above the floor and switch boxes 45 inches above the floor. (Many electricians set their hammer head down on the floor, using a hammer length to position floor-level receptacles.) Hold a nail-on box with its front edge positioned out from the stud the thickness of the drywall, and drive the two nails. Double-check to see that you've installed all the boxes. Walk around the room pretending to use all the switches.

SAFETY ALERT

NEVER NOTCH

In a tight spot like this, you may be tempted to whip out the hammer and chisel and chop notches in the face of the studs so the cable runs more easily. But the cable would then be dangerously exposed. Instead, drill slightly larger holes, bend the cable before poking it in, and grab it with longnose pliers. If you simply can't make the corner one trick to try is drilling a hole between the two other holes to make the corner inside the studs less acute

Corner framing

Longnose pliers

REAL WORLD

PLACE BOXES AWAY FROM FRAMING

Switch boxes should be installed far enough away from the door to allow for framing. If installed too close, the door trim may cover up the switch, which would require cutting into the drywall to move the switch box—a messy job.

2

DRILL THE HOLES

Wherever possible use a tape measure and level to mark studs and joists. Mark so holes will be in a straight horizontal line. Drill ⅝-inch holes for two-wire NM cable and ¾-inch holes for three-wire cable or armored cable. A ⅜-inch drill works fine for small jobs, but give it a rest if it overheats.

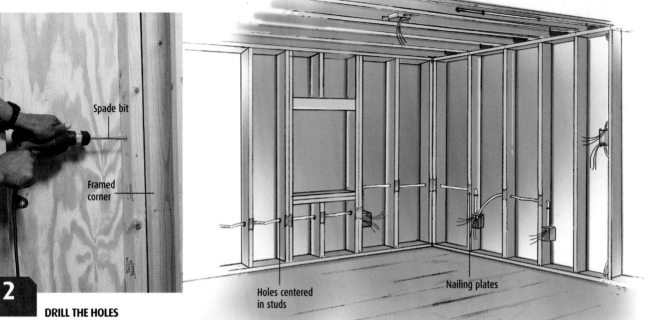

Spade bit

Framed corner

Holes centered in studs

Nailing plates

A TYPICAL CABLE ROUGH-IN

Run cable in a straight horizontal line, 1 foot above the receptacles (areas under windows are an exception) or according to local code. To keep cable out of the reach of nails, drill all holes in the center of studs and at least 1¼ inches up from the bottom of joists. Nail on protective nailing plates for extra safety (they may be required for every hole). Even if you will only hang a light, install a ceiling fan box in case you choose to add a ceiling fan later.

1 inch of play

3

PULL THE CABLE

To avoid kinks keep the cable straight and untwisted as you work. When possible pull the cable first and then cut it to length. If you must cut it first, allow plenty of extra length. Pull the cable fairly tight, but leave it loose enough so there is an inch or so of play.

Nailing plate

4

PROTECT THE CABLE WITH NAILING PLATES

These are inexpensive and quick to install. Be sure to nail one of these wherever the cable is within 1¼ inches of the front edge of the framing member. For added safety (and to satisfy some local codes), install nailing plates over every hole.

Cable staple

5

STAPLE THE CABLE AND RUN IT INTO THE BOXES

Staple cable tightly wherever it runs along a joist so it is out of the reach of nails. Staple within 8 inches of a plastic box and within 12 inches of a metal box. See page 116 for clamping methods.

8

RUNNING NEW CABLE

Special situations

Running cable through trusses

Roof and floor trusses (or engineered joists) are made to exacting specifications, and any holes you drill or notches you cut could weaken them significantly and render them out-of-code. Where possible run cable through the openings in a truss. In some cases it is best to staple cable to the exposed end of a truss, and then protect the cable by attaching a board on either side. If you need to cut into a truss, first consult with your building inspector.

Fishing through a solid corner

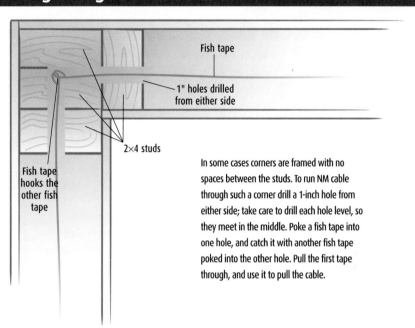

Fish tape

1" holes drilled from either side

2×4 studs

Fish tape hooks the other fish tape

In some cases corners are framed with no spaces between the studs. To run NM cable through such a corner drill a 1-inch hole from either side; take care to drill each hole level, so they meet in the middle. Poke a fish tape into one hole, and catch it with another fish tape poked into the other hole. Pull the first tape through, and use it to pull the cable.

Wiring through metal studs

Metal studs have convenient holes for running pipes and cables. Be sure to install the studs all in the same orientation and cut at the same end so the holes will line up. Insert protective plastic bushings into each hole before running the cable.

Wiring finished rooms

PROJECT DETAILS

SKILLS: Basic carpentry and wiring skills

PROJECT: To rough in for a receptacle, light, and switch

TIME TO COMPLETE

EXPERIENCED: 6 hrs.
HANDY: 10 hrs.
NOVICE: 14 hrs.

STUFF YOU'LL NEED

TOOLS: Electronic stud finder, drywall saw, saber saw, drill, hammer, screwdriver, fishing bit, fish tape, flat pry bar

MATERIALS: Cable, remodel boxes, safety goggles

You need the patience of a surgeon to run wiring through walls that are finished with drywall or plaster. At times you'll feel like grabbing a hammer and knocking big holes in the wall to get at that darned cable. But remember that patching and painting walls are tedious and time-consuming tasks, so any steps you can take to minimize wall or ceiling damage will save you work in the long run.

Follow the easiest path

If you have an unfinished attic or a basement, run as much of the cable there as possible. If a basement or attic is finished, run armored cable instead of NM.

Use an electronic stud finder to locate joists and studs that may be in the way. You may be able to move a box a few inches to avoid an obstruction. Wherever possible run cable parallel to studs or joists.

First cut holes for the boxes (pages 132–133); then run the cable. Reach into the box holes with your hand, a fish tape, or a long drill bit in order to reach the cable.

If you plan to take power from an existing receptacle for your new service, make sure you will not overload the circuit.

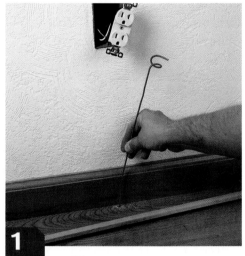

1 **TO RUN THROUGH A BASEMENT BELOW, DRILL A LOCATOR HOLE**
Directly below a box from which you want to grab power, remove the base shoe and drill a ¼-inch hole through the floor. Poke a wire down through the hole.

2 **DRILL UP THROUGH THE BOTTOM PLATE**
Using the wire as a reference point, drill a 1-inch hole through the middle of the wall's bottom plate (a 2×4 lying flat on top of the flooring above).

3 **HOOK THE CABLE**
Open a knockout hole in the bottom of the box. Strip sheathing from the cable and attach a cable clamp (remove the locknut). Form the wires into a hook. Poke a fish tape or unbent coat hanger down through the knockout hole while a helper pushes the cable up. Hook and pull up.

RUNNING CABLE BEHIND A BASEBOARD

Use a flat pry bar to remove baseboard molding. With a drywall saw cut a channel in the drywall at least 1 inch shorter than the baseboard. Drill holes through the centers of the studs and run cable through the holes. Protect all holes with nail plates.

8

GOOD IDEA

WIRING THAT'S EXPOSED BUT OUT OF SIGHT

In some situations it's OK to leave the wiring exposed. One example is cove lighting, which is placed on top of wall cabinets. Install simple fluorescent fixtures with exposed cable (codes may call for armored cable).

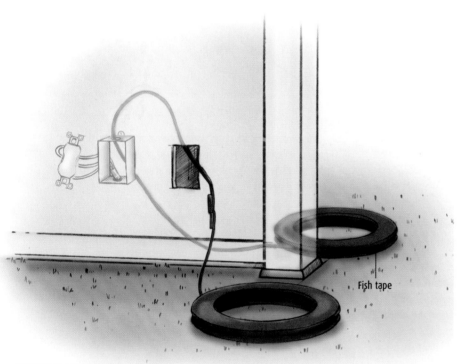

Fish tape

RUNNING CABLE THROUGH A WALL

If the new box will be more or less directly behind the existing box from which you will grab power, you can avoid wall patching. Cut the hole for the remodel box. Remove the existing receptacle and punch out a knockout in the back or bottom of its box. Run one fish tape through the existing box and one through the new hole. Hook them together. Pull the tape back through the hole, and you're ready to pull cable from the hole to the box.

RUNNING CABLE AROUND A DOOR

If you have no access above or below, this may be your only option. Codes vary on whether this type of installation is legal so be sure to check with your local electrical authority before installing cable in this manner. Remove casing from around a door and snake cable around. You may be able to slip the cable between the jamb and the stud. Or drill a hole and run the cable in the cavity on the other side of the stud.

If the attic isn't used for storage, you may be allowed to lay cable on top of the joists if you install 1×4 strips on either side of the cable.

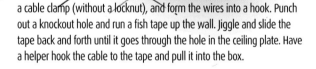

Cable clamp
without locknut

Fish tape
attached to cable

RUNNING CABLE UP, OVER, AND DOWN

If the attic is accessible, drill a hole through the top plate. Run cable down through it to the hole for the new box directly below. Drill holes and run cable through the joists, over to the spot directly above the existing box from which you want to run power. Strip sheathing from the cable, install a cable clamp (without a locknut), and form the wires into a hook. Punch out a knockout hole and run a fish tape up the wall. Jiggle and slide the tape back and forth until it goes through the hole in the ceiling plate. Have a helper hook the cable to the tape and pull it into the box.

![REAL WORLD icon] **REAL WORLD**

THE CLAMP IS WORTH THE EFFORT

Sometimes a little extra effort saves time and energy in the future. When installing cable it takes some effort to get it through the wall and into the receptacle box and it may be tempting not to attach a cable clamp, too, but inspectors will disagree. Take the time to attach the cable clamps. Attach the clamp (minus the nut) 8 inches from the cable end. Pull the wires through, and the threaded part of the clamp will seat itself nicely in the hole.

WHERE THE CEILING AND WALL MEET

When there is no access from above or below, cut notches in the drywall or plaster, like this. Drill a 1-inch hole up through the center of the top plate. Bend the cable, poke it up through the hole, and grab it from the other side.

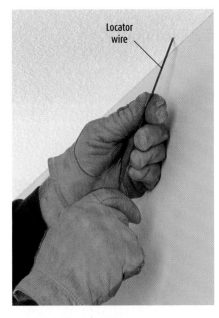

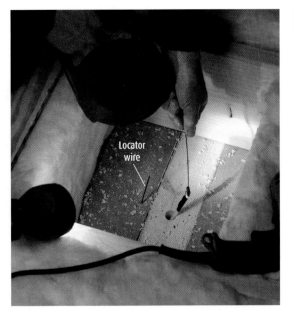

Locator wire

Locator wire

SAFETY ALERT

CUT AND DRILL CAREFULLY
Any time you cut into a wall with a saw or a drill bit, there is a possibility that you will encounter an electrical cable or a plumbing pipe. When possible drill a small hole, poke in a wire, and wiggle it around to make sure there are no obstructions. Cut with a handsaw rather than a power saw; that way you can usually feel when you encounter something. Make your cuts as shallow as possible—just deep enough to cut through the drywall or the lath and plaster. Be prepared to shut off both the water and the gas to the house in case you do puncture a pipe.

FISHING FROM THE ATTIC

To run cable up into the attic, first drill a locator hole up through the ceiling. Poke a wire up into the hole. The wire may need to extend a foot or so upward to rise above attic insulation. Go into the attic and find the wire. Near the wire drill a hole through the center of the wall's top plate. You can now run cable up or down through the wall.

Using a fishing bit

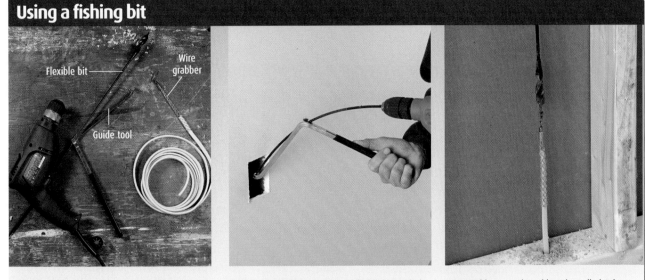

Flexible bit — Wire grabber

Guide tool

This tool is usually worth its cost because it reduces the number of holes you will need to cut and patch. It has three parts: a long, flexible bit, a guide tool, and a wire grabber that hooks to the end of the bit. First, drill the hole with the flexible

bit. Use the grabber to position the bit; it may help to have a flashlight to make sure you are, for instance, drilling through the center of a baseplate. Once the hole is drilled, leave the bit in place; don't pull it back out. At the other end slip the

wire grabber onto the cable to be pulled; it has a mesh attachment that quickly and securely grips the cable. Hook the grabber's hook onto the hole in the end of the bit, and pull the bit back to fish the wire.

Installing remodeling boxes

PROJECT DETAILS

SKILLS: Careful cutting of walls, driving screws
PROJECT: Cutting a hole in drywall or plaster and installing a box

TIME TO COMPLETE

EXPERIENCED: 20 min.
HANDY: 45 min.
NOVICE: 1 hr.

STUFF YOU'LL NEED

TOOLS: Electronic stud finder, utility knife, drywall saw, saber saw or rotary cutter, screwdriver, drill
MATERIALS: Remodeling (old-work) box, screws

When you run cable to install new devices in an old wall, you have several handy self-attaching boxes at your service. To use these remodeling boxes (also called old-work or cut-in boxes), you need only cut a hole, run the cable, clamp the cable to the box, and install the remodeling box.

To make sure you won't hit a stud or joist, before cutting a hole drill a small bore in the wall, and probe with a piece of wire.

Cut the hole carefully using one of the methods shown on this page. The hole will probably not be rectangular (page 141). The box should fit into the hole snugly, but not so tightly that you have to force it. If the hole is too wide, the box may not effectively attach to the drywall or plaster.

CUTTING A HOLE IN PLASTER WITH A SABER SAW
Cutting through a lath and plaster wall is difficult and often results in cracked plaster. Drill holes at each corner, and score the face of the plaster with a utility knife. Cut with a saber saw equipped with a fine-tooth blade. Press hard against the wall to reduce lath vibration.

CUTTING A HOLE IN DRYWALL
Use a pencil to mark the location of the hole, and score the paper surface with a utility knife. Cut along the inside of the knife-cut with a drywall saw. The resulting hole will be free of ragged edges.

CUTTING A HOLE IN PLASTER WITH A SPIRAL CUTTING TOOL
Because of its rapidly rotating blade, this tool won't rattle your lath and loosen the plaster. To use this tool, set the base on the wall and tip the blade away from the surface while you let it come to full speed. Then tilt the blade gently into the wall. Have extra blades on hand; they dull quickly on plaster.

Attaching the boxes

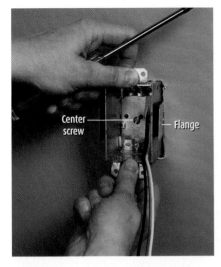

INSTALLING A BOX WITH SPRING FLANGES
If you buy this kind of box, make sure both flanges spring out firmly from the box. Push the box into the hole until the flanges are free to spring outward. As you tighten the center screw, the flanges should move toward you until they fit snugly against the back of the drywall or plaster.

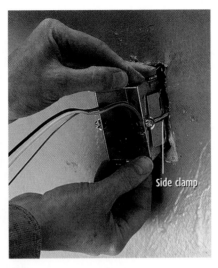

INSTALLING A BOX WITH SIDE CLAMPS
After pushing the box into the hole, tighten the screw on each side. Each clamp extends behind the wall to hold the box in place.

USING MOUNTING BRACKETS
Push a metal box with plaster ears into the hole, then slip a bracket in on each side. Center each bracket behind the wall. Pull the bracket toward you until it's tight, push the box tightly against the wall, then fold the tabs into the box with your thumb. Tighten the tabs with pliers.

CLOSER LOOK

INSTALLING A BOX WITH FOLD-OUT EARS
These plastic remodeling boxes have ears that swing out behind the drywall or plaster. Push the box into the hole, then turn the screws clockwise until the ears clamp onto the back of the drywall or plaster. Switch boxes are also available with this same wall-grabbing mechanism.

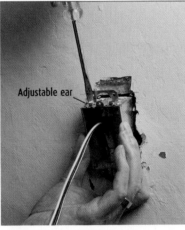

ADJUST THE PLASTER EARS
Many metal boxes have adjustable ears. Cut the hole and chip out the plaster above and below so the ears will fit. Loosen the two screws and adjust each ear so the face of the box is flush with the wall surface. Tighten the screws.

ANCHOR THE BOX TO THE LATH
Lath cracks easily, so work carefully. Drill pilot holes and drive short screws to anchor the ears to the lath. Expect to do some patching after using this method.

Patching walls

⬇ PROJECT DETAILS

SKILLS: Patching and smoothing walls and ceilings

PROJECT: Patching a medium-size hole, not including touchup

🕐 TIME TO COMPLETE

EXPERIENCED: 1 hr.
HANDY: 2 hrs.
NOVICE: 3 hrs.

✓ STUFF YOU'LL NEED

TOOLS: Putty knife, 4-inch and 8-inch taping blades, utility knife, sanding block

MATERIALS: Drywall, mesh patching tape, joint compound, spackling compound

The techniques shown on pages 128–131 help you minimize damage to walls, but patching drywall or plaster will probably be the finishing step in running cable.

Most homes built after the 1950s have walls covered with drywall—also called Sheetrock or wallboard. It's usually ½ inch thick and is fairly easy to patch. The time-consuming part is applying joint compound and smoothing the joint between the old and the new surfaces.

An older home may have lath-and-plaster walls. The lath often splits or loosens and the plaster crumbles, making patching a challenge. Older homes may have a combination of the two: Old plaster walls are often covered with ¼- or ⅜-inch drywall.

Handling textured walls

Some drywall surfaces have a textured surface that is difficult to duplicate. You can cut out the pieces carefully and replace them with the original pieces when you are done wiring. You might get away with just caulking the joints.

If a ceiling has a texture like cottage cheese, a foam product has been blown onto it. You can buy a special patching compound to repair or recoat the ceiling, or hire a pro to recoat it.

1

PATCH A SMALL HOLE IN DRYWALL

Cut a new piece of drywall to fit the hole, or reuse the piece you cut out. If you do not have a stud or joist to screw to, cut a 1×4 about 8 inches longer than the hole. Place the piece behind the hole as shown. Drive 1¼-inch drywall screws to secure the patch.

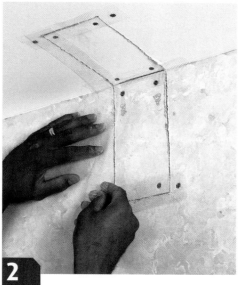

2

TAPE THE JOINTS

Cut pieces of fiberglass mesh patching tape and lay them over the joints. Apply joint compound and smooth it with a drywall taping knife. (Ready-mix joint compound is easy to use, but dry-mix compound is stronger and sets faster.)

3

SAND THE PATCH

Allow the compound to dry. Reapply the compound, feathering the edges. It will take several coats to smooth the joint. Sand the patch smooth with a drywall sanding block. Prime and paint.

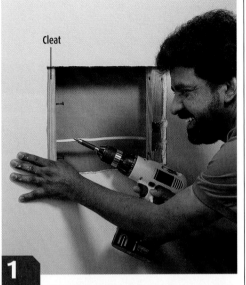

1 USE CLEATS FOR A LARGE DRYWALL PATCH

Use a level or framing square to mark out a rectangle around the damage. Your marks should span from stud to stud or joist to joist. Cut with a drywall saw. Cut 2×2 or 2×4 cleats a few inches longer than the hole. Hold them against the back of the drywall as you drive 3-inch drywall screws into the framing.

2 INSTALL THE PATCH

Cut a patch to fit, about ¼ inch smaller than the hole in each direction. Attach the patch with 1¼-inch drywall screws. Cover the joints with tape, apply joint compound (right), and sand.

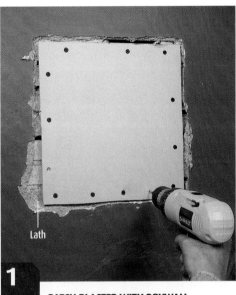

1 PATCH PLASTER WITH DRYWALL

Remove loose plaster. Tap with a hammer to excavate a rough rectangular shape. If the lath is solid, you don't need to expose studs or joists. For the patch use drywall that is the same thickness as the plaster. Cut the patch roughly to size, and attach it to the lath with 1¼-inch drywall screws.

2 FILL THE GAP WITH JOINT COMPOUND

You can mix the joint compound with perlited gypsum (see "Filling a Channel in a Plaster Wall," above). Apply mesh tape to the joints, then apply the compound. For best results apply several feathering coats of compound, scraping and sanding between coats.

WORK SMARTER

FILLING A CHANNEL IN A PLASTER WALL

You might cut a narrow channel through a plaster wall to slip a cable through. To fill the gap combine dry-mix joint compound ("90" or "45") with an equal amount of perlited gypsum. Mix the two with water, and you'll have a paste that won't sag when you apply it. Force the paste into the cavity with a putty knife. Allow it to dry then apply subsequent coats of joint compound.

REAL WORLD

BLENDING A PATCH

Pay attention to the texture of existing walls, before applying a patch to a smaller area. If the texture of the wall is rough and the patch too smooth, this will only emphasize the flaws and vice versa.

8

RUNNING NEW CABLE

Installing a junction box

1

ATTACH THE BOX

Shut off power to the wires that you will be splicing. Anchor the box with screws. To attach the box to a masonry surface, drill holes with a masonry bit. Drive masonry screws.

Grounding pigtail

2

WIRE THE BOX

Strip cable sheathing and clamp the cable, or connect conduit. Strip wires and connect them with wire nuts. If the box is metal, make a grounding pigtail and connect it to the green grounding screw.

Install a junction box wherever wires must be spliced. Keep the box accessible—never bury it in a wall or ceiling. Junction boxes are usually flush-mounted to walls or attached to attic, basement, or crawlspace framing. But you can set one inside a wall as you would a switch box; cover it with a blank plastic cover plate.

Cover plate

3

COVER THE BOX

Fold the wires into the box and attach the cover plate. To do so loosen the screws at two corners of the box, hook the cover plate on first one screw and then the other, and tighten the screws.

WORK SMARTER

USE A METAL COVER PLATE IN UTILITY AREAS

If a receptacle or switch is in an exposed box, use a metal rather than a plastic cover plate. You may need to break off the metal "ears" of the receptacle or switch. Attach the them to the cover plate first, and then attach the cover plate to the box.

8

RUNNING NEW CABLE

Installing raceway wiring

PROJECT DETAILS

SKILLS: Connecting with screws, stripping and joining wires
PROJECT: Installing a switch and fixture, or several receptacles

TIME TO COMPLETE

EXPERIENCED: 3 hrs.
HANDY: 5 hrs.
NOVICE: 8 hrs.

STUFF YOU'LL NEED

TOOLS: Drill, screwdriver, hacksaw, wire strippers, longnose pliers
MATERIALS: Box extender with cover plate, channel, fittings, fixture bases, fixture box, wire, clips, new devices, plastic anchors

Raceway wiring is an easy way to install a switch, fixture, or receptacle when cutting into a wall is difficult or appearances aren't important. It will spare you the hassle of cutting into walls, drilling holes, fishing cable, and patching the walls.

Gathering the parts

Take a drawing of your proposed installation to a home center or electrical supply source, and ask a salesperson to help you assemble all the parts. Choose metal, which is paintable, or plastic, which is not.

You'll need a starter box for each device, channel, L and T connectors, receptacle or switch boxes, and perhaps a fixture box. Buy plenty of wire. Use green insulated wire for the ground, never bare copper.

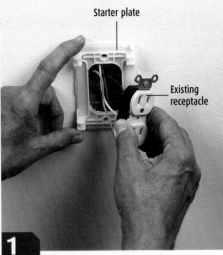

Starter plate
Existing receptacle

1 INSTALL THE STARTER BOX

Shut off power to the circuit. Pull out a receptacle and mount a starter plate on the wall behind it. Install new raceway boxes for receptacles, switches, and fixtures in the same way.

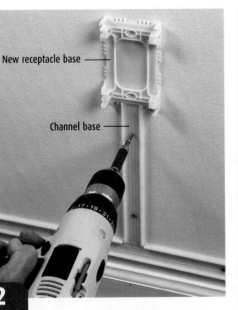

New receptacle base
Channel base

2 CUT AND ATTACH THE CHANNEL BASE

Use a hacksaw to cut pieces of channel to fit between the boxes. Attach the channel base to the wall with screws driven into studs or plastic anchors. Use fittings at all corners.

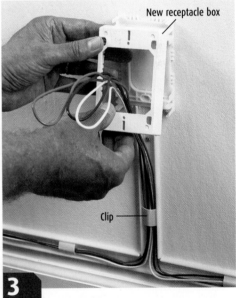

New receptacle box
Clip

3 RUN THE WIRES

Place wires in the channel base and secure them with clips about every foot. Leave 8 inches of wire at each box to make connections. Snap any device boxes onto the bases and fasten them with screws driven into studs or plastic anchors.

8

RUNNING NEW CABLE

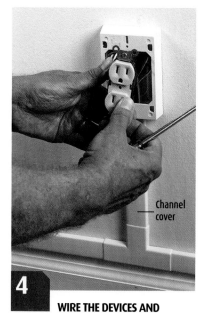

Channel
cover

4

WIRE THE DEVICES AND FIXTURES

Snap the covers onto the channel base and the corner pieces. Strip the wire ends and connect them to the terminals just as you would for standard wiring. Install cover plates, restore power, and test.

ADDING A LIGHT AND WALL SWITCH USING RACEWAY WIRING

To add a switched ceiling light to a room, you need a nearby receptacle. Install a ceiling fixture base, making sure that it is firmly attached to joists in the ceiling. Install the raceway switch base, and run a channel from the receptacle to the switch base and on to the fixture base. Run wiring and add the boxes. Make wiring connections as shown on page 142, and install the devices.

Use a similar arrangement to add a wall switch to a pull-chain light fixture. Install a raceway switch box at a convenient height. Remove the ceiling fixture and install a raceway fixture box onto the ceiling box. Run the channel and two black wires from the switch to the fixture, making connections as shown on page 146.

FISHING WIRES IN METAL RACEWAY

Metal channels do not come apart in two pieces. Install clips on the wall, and snap the channel into the clips. Fish wires through the channel. If you can't shove the wires through, you might have to use a fish tape.

$ BUYER'S GUIDE

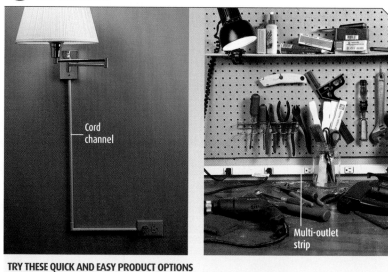

Cord
channel

Multi-outlet
strip

TRY THESE QUICK AND EASY PRODUCT OPTIONS

Cord channel (above left) encases and protects lamp cord that must be run along a wall. A **multi-outlet strip** (above right) is a sort of super extension cord, with a grounded receptacle every foot or so. No wiring is required to install these products. The channels mount to clips, or they stick to the wall with tape backing.

Installing new services

Chapter 9 highlights

Few construction projects are more satisfying than adding electrical devices or fixtures to your home. Most of these jobs take less than a day, yet make big improvements in your family's quality of life. The installations in this chapter rely on the skills and knowledge taught in the first two-thirds of the book. Refer to earlier chapters for specific instructions on the projects that follow.

Whenever adding new services, follow these important guidelines:

■ Turn off power to the circuit you are working on, and test all open boxes to make sure no power is present.

■ Be sure the new service will not overload your circuit.

■ Follow local codes for running cable and installing boxes. Obtain a permit from your building department every time you install new cable.

Tapping into a receptacle or junction box

PROJECT DETAILS

SKILLS: Testing and shutting off power, splicing wires

PROJECT: Tapping into a junction box with a new electrical cable

TIME TO COMPLETE

EXPERIENCED: 20 min.
HANDY: 1 hr.
NOVICE: 2 hrs.

STUFF YOU'LL NEED

TOOLS: Voltage tester, screwdriver, wire strippers, lineman's pliers

MATERIALS: Cable, clamp, wire nuts, electrician's tape

A junction box is often found in a basement, crawlspace, attic, or other utility area. It is often the most convenient place to grab power for new electrical service. Before you do, however, check to make sure that the circuit will not be overloaded by the new service you will install (pages 112-113).

Check the circuit before you install the new junction box to make sure the new service won't overload it.

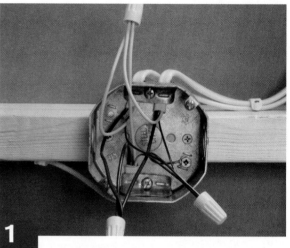

1

SHUT OFF POWER AND REMOVE THE COVER

Shut off power to the circuit. You may need to use a voltage detector to make sure that all the cables have been de-energized. Carefully remove the cover plate, and test again for power. The box shown has three cables entering it, but yours may have fewer or more.

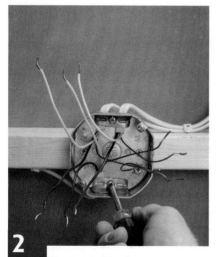

2

UNDO THE CONNECTIONS AND INSTALL THE NEW CABLE

Remove all the wire nuts and untwist the wires from each other. If any wires look in danger of cracking, cut their ends and restrip. If the box is at risk for being too crowded (page 112), pull out the cables and replace with a larger box. Run the new cable into the box, and fasten it with a cable clamp.

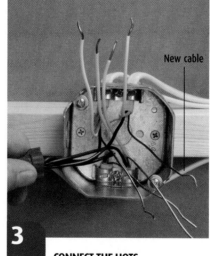

New cable

3

CONNECT THE HOTS

Twist together all the black or colored wires, and screw on a wire nut (page 14). Make sure the nut is large enough for all the wires.

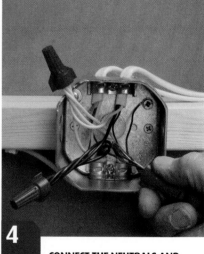

4

CONNECT THE NEUTRALS AND GROUNDS

Connect the white wires in the same way. Connect the ground wires to each other, and use a pigtail to connect to the box. Gently fold the wires into the box and replace the cover plate.

Installing a new receptacle

PROJECT DETAILS

SKILLS: Running cable through walls, stripping and splicing
PROJECT: Installing a new receptacle in a finished wall

TIME TO COMPLETE

EXPERIENCED: 20 min.
HANDY: 1 hr.
NOVICE: 2 hrs.

STUFF YOU'LL NEED

TOOLS: Drill, drywall saw or saber saw, screwdriver, lineman's pliers, wire strippers
MATERIALS: Cable and clamps, remodel box, staples, receptacle, wire nuts, electrician's tape

The easiest way to install a new receptacle is to tap an existing receptacle for power, as shown here. Before you do this make sure you will not overload the existing receptacle's circuit (pages 48–49).

If you can't pull power from a nearby receptacle, you may be able to tap into a junction box above or below the room (page 140). You also can pull power from a light fixture or switch—whichever has power entering its box.

As a last resort you may have to run cable all the way back to the service panel and install a new circuit breaker (pages 192–193).

As with many electrical projects, patching and painting walls afterward can be more trouble than the wiring. See pages 128–131 for tips on reducing damage to your walls.

Plan a cabling path that will minimize the damage to the walls.

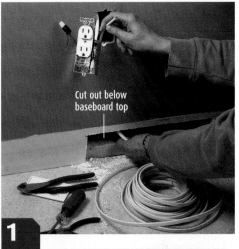

1

RUN CABLE TO THE EXISTING RECEPTACLE

Cut out below baseboard top

Choose a path that will cause minimal damage to the walls, such as running cable behind a baseboard (shown). Remove the baseboard and cut away the drywall. **Shut off power to the circuit.** Remove a knockout in the receptacle's box from where you'll take power, add a connector, then fish the cable.

Remodel box

2

RUN THE CABLE THROUGH THE HOLES

Cut a hole for the new receptacle box. Drill holes in the centers of studs for the cable to pass through. Strip 6 to 8 inches of sheathing from either end of the cable. Punch out a knockout hole and clamp the cable to the existing box. Run the cable into a remodel box and attach the box to the wall (pages 132–133). Either clamp the cable to the box or staple the cable near the box.

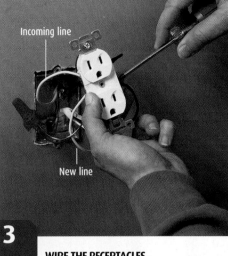

Incoming line

New line

3

WIRE THE RECEPTACLES

If the existing receptacle is at the end of the run (shown), attach the black wire to the brass terminal and the white wire to the silver terminal. If the receptacle is in the middle of the run, no terminals will be available; use pigtails to connect to power (page 35). Wire the new receptacle—white to silver, black to brass. Connect the grounds (page 11). Restore power, then test.

9

INSTALLING NEW SERVICES

Adding a wall switch

9

INSTALLING NEW SERVICES

Pull cable here...

...Then here

1 **RUN CABLE**
Shut off power to the circuit supplying the fixture. Plan a cable pathway that crosses as few studs or joists as possible. You may have to cut access holes to run cable through framing (pages 128-131).

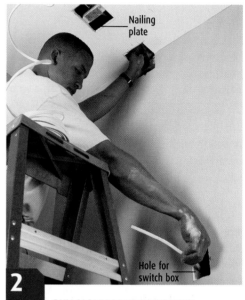

Nailing plate

Hole for switch box

2 **RUN CABLE TO THE SWITCH BOX**
Add nailing plates where you bore holes in framing. Cut a hole for a remodel switch box and pull the cable through. Strip the wires.

W iring a wall switch to a pull-chain ceiling fixture is easy; the challenge is running cable from the fixture to the switch. You may need to cut a hole near the fixture so that you can reach behind its box and clamp cable to it. Consider covering the hole with a medallion (page 85).

White wire to switch painted black

3 **WIRE THE FIXTURE**
First connect the ground (page 11). Remove the old black wire from the fixture lead, and splice it to the new white wire and mark it black. Splice the new black wire to the fixture's black lead.

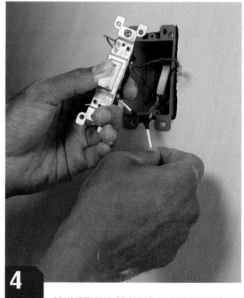

4 **CONNECT THE GROUND AT THE SWITCH**
Attach both wires to the terminals and mark the white wire black. Restore power to the circuit, and test.

Switching a receptacle

PROJECT DETAILS

SKILLS: Running cable through walls, stripping and connecting cable and wires

PROJECT: Wiring one outlet of a receptacle on a wall switch (not including wall patching)

TIME TO COMPLETE

EXPERIENCED: 2 hrs.
HANDY: 3 hrs.
NOVICE: 5 hrs.

STUFF YOU'LL NEED

TOOLS: Screwdriver, longnose pliers, wire strippers

MATERIALS: Cable and clamps, remodel box, staples, wire nuts, electrician's tape

If the receptacle you want to switch has wires attached to all four terminals, you may need to install a larger box to handle the additional wires.

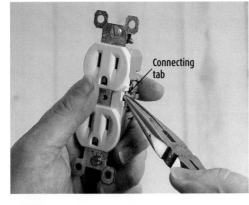

Connecting tab

You can assign either outlet of a duplex receptacle to control a floor or table lamp from a wall-mounted switch and still leave the other outlet hot all the time. This is possible because the two outlets on the receptacle are connected by tabs on either side that can be removed, as shown below. Removing the tab on the hot side (brass terminals) allows you to wire the receptacle so that only one of the outlets is switched. Grasp the tab between the brass terminals with a pair of longnose pliers and bend it back and forth to break it off. Remove the receptacle from the box to make the job easier. To run cable through finished walls and install a box for the new switch, see pages 128-133.

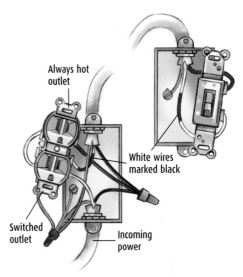

Always hot outlet

White wires marked black

Switched outlet

Incoming power

WORKING WITH AN END-OF-THE-RUN RECEPTACLE

Shut off power. Remove the receptacle and break the tab. Run two-wire cable from the switch to the receptacle. Mark both ends of the white wires black. Connect the grounds as shown. At the receptacle splice the old black wire, the new black wire, and a black jumper that is connected to the always hot terminal. Cap with a wire nut. Attach the white wire marked black to the switched terminal. Attach both the white and black wires to the switch.

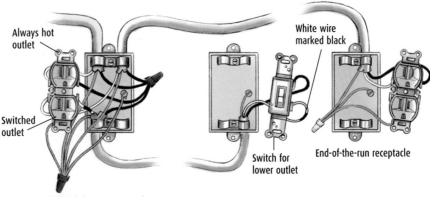

Always hot outlet

Switched outlet

Middle-of-the-run receptacle

White wire marked black

Switch for lower outlet

End-of-the-run receptacle

WORKING WITH A RECEPTACLE IN THE MIDDLE OF A RUN

Shut off power. Remove the receptacle and break off the tab between the brass terminals. Run two-wire cable from the switch to the receptacle you want to switch. Mark the white wire black at both ends. At the receptacle to be switched, remove the black wire and connect the white wire marked black to the terminal. Splice the black wires and a black jumper connected to the always hot outlet and cap the pigtail with a wire nut. Wire the switch and connect the grounds as shown above.

Splitting a receptacle

PROJECT DETAILS

SKILLS: Running cable, stripping and splicing cable and wire
PROJECT: Installing four split or alternating receptacles

TIME TO COMPLETE

EXPERIENCED: 3 hrs.
HANDY: 4 hrs.
NOVICE: 6 hrs.

STUFF YOU'LL NEED

TOOLS: Drill, drywall saw or saber saw, fish tape, screwdriver, lineman's pliers, strippers
MATERIALS: Cable and clamps, receptacles, boxes, wire nuts, electrician's tape, cover plates

Wherever you're likely to plug in more than one high-amp appliance, you run the risk of overloading a circuit. In some cases two appliances or tools plugged into the same receptacle can add up to more than the circuit can handle.

That's why some building departments require kitchen counter receptacles to be split, so that each outlet is on a separate circuit (right). (In this case the receptacles cannot be GFCIs.) Other municipalities prefer alternating the receptacles so that every other one is on the same circuit (below). Either of these configurations may be used in a workshop.

Use 15-amp receptacles and breakers and #14 wire for countertops and shop areas.

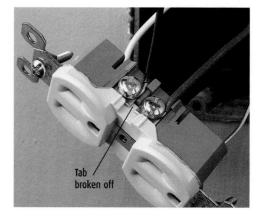

Tab broken off

WIRING SPLIT RECEPTACLES
Run three-wire cable with the black and red wires connected to separate circuit breakers or to the two poles of a double-pole breaker. Break off the connecting tabs on each receptacle (page 143). Using pigtails connect the white wire to a silver terminal, the red wire to a brass terminal, and the black wire to the other brass terminal. Connect the grounds. Wire the other receptacles the same way.

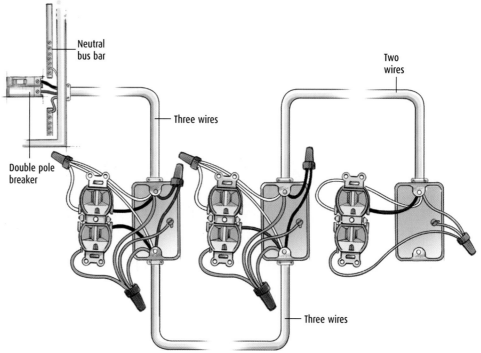

Neutral bus bar

Two wires

Three wires

Double pole breaker

Three wires

ALTERNATING CIRCUITS
Some codes call for a double-pole breaker, as shown, rather than two separate breakers. When one circuit is turned off, the other is off as well. Use three-wire cable. The black wire brings power to every other receptacle, and the red wire energizes the others. All receptacles share the same neutral wire.

Adding a 240-volt receptacle

🏃 PROJECT DETAILS

SKILLS: Running cable, stripping and splicing wire, connecting wires to terminals

PROJECT: Installing a new 240-volt or 120/240-volt receptacle (not including wall patching)

🕐 TIME TO COMPLETE

EXPERIENCED: 3 hrs.
HANDY: 5 hrs.
NOVICE: 7 hrs.

✓ STUFF YOU'LL NEED

TOOLS: Drill, saw, fish tape, screwdriver, lineman's pliers, wire strippers

MATERIALS: 240- or 240/120-volt receptacle, cable, box, wire nuts, electrician's tape

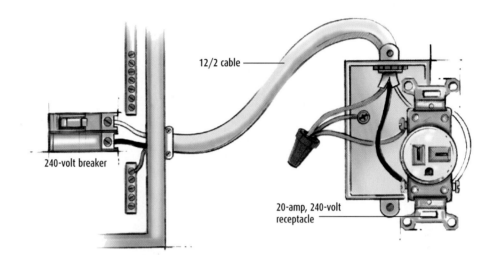

240-VOLT AIR-CONDITIONER RECEPTACLE

A 20-amp, 240-volt receptacle for a window air-conditioner or other appliance requires only 12/2 cable, not the heftier #8 wire most 240-volt receptacles require. Connect the grounds. Mark the white wire black at both ends. Connect the two wires to a 20-amp 240-volt double pole breaker in the service panel and to the receptacle terminals.

High amperage receptacles

iring a high-amperage receptacle is slightly more complicated than wiring a standard 120-volt 15-amp receptacle. Follow safety precautions strictly, however, because this amount of voltage is dangerous.

Choose a receptacle that matches the appliance you will plug into it, both in hole configuration and amperage rating. Recent codes require four-wire receptacles; three-wire receptacles were once acceptable (page 16). Be sure the wires are thick enough. Use #10 wire for a 30-amp receptacle and #8 wire for a 40- or 50-amp receptacle.

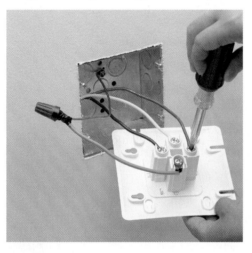

WIRE GAUGE

Always check with your local electrical authority for proper gauges of wire and the type of receptacles when installing any less common circuits, such as 30-amp or higher circuits. Consult with store personnel on the power or amperage required for the appliance you are installing.

INSTALL THE RECEPTACLE

Receptacles are specifically designed for the type of plug coming from the appliance. For instance, dryer plugs will not fit into a receptacle intended for a stove. This ensures that appliances are powered appropriately but not overloaded. If installing a receptacle for an appliance take a look at the plug first so you buy the right receptacle.

9

INSTALLING NEW SERVICES

Adding a fixture with a switch

Power to switch box

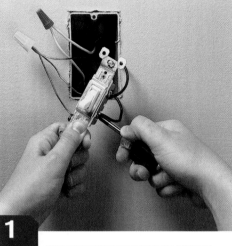

1 **RUN WIRE FROM THE POWER SOURCE TO THE SWITCH BOX**
Run two-wire cable from a power source to a wall switch box, and from there to a ceiling box. Connect the ground. Splice the white wires and connect the black wires to the switch terminals.

2 **WIRE THE FIXTURE**
Connect the ground. Splice the white wire to the white fixture lead, and splice the black wire to the black fixture lead. Restore power and test.

Power to fixture

When planning to install a new light with a switch, decide whether to send power into the switch box (above) or to the fixture box (right). **Shut off power to the box from which you will run power.** See pages 128–131 for instructions on installing boxes and running cable, and page 11 for grounding methods.

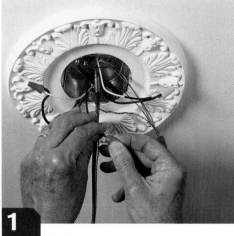

1 **RUN POWER TO THE FIXTURE**
Run two-wire cable from the power source to the fixture box. Run two-wire cable from the fixture box to the switch, and mark the white wire black at both ends. Connect the ground at the fixture box. Splice the black feed wire (from the power source) to the white wire that is marked black. Splice the other black wire to the fixture's black lead, and splice the white wire to the white lead.

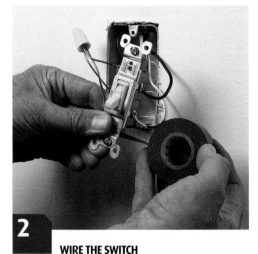

2 **WIRE THE SWITCH**
Connect the ground. Connect the black wire and the white wire (painted black) to the switch terminals. Restore power and test.

Two fixtures with separate switches

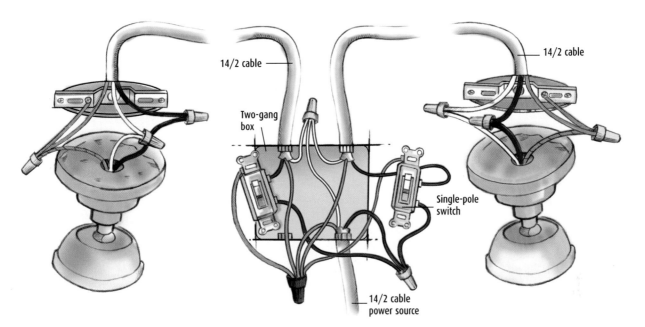

14/2 cable

Two-gang box

Single-pole switch

14/2 cable

14/2 cable power source

WHEN POWER ENTERS THE SWITCH BOX
Shut off power to the circuit. Run one two-wire cable from the power source into a two-gang switch box, and additional two-wire cables from the switch box to each fixture box. At the switch box connect the grounds. Splice all the white wires together and splice two black pigtails to the feed wire. Connect one black pigtail and one black wire to each switch.

At each fixture box connect the grounds. Splice the white lead to the white wire and the black lead to the black wire. Restore power and test.

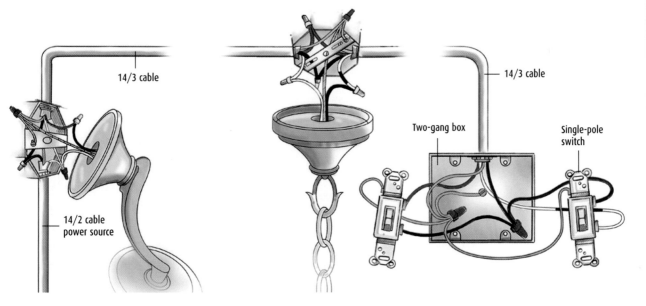

14/3 cable

14/2 cable power source

Two-gang box

Single-pole switch

14/3 cable

WHEN POWER ENTERS THE FIXTURE
Shut off power to the circuit. Run two-wire cable from a power source to one fixture box. Run three-wire cable from there to the second fixture box. Run three-wire cable from the second fixture box to the two-gang switch box and mark the white wire black at both ends. At the fixture box farthest from the switches, connect the grounds. Splice the two white wires to the fixture's white lead and splice the fixture's black lead to the red wire. Splice the remaining black wires. At the second fixture box, connect the grounds. Splice the marked white wire to the fixture's black lead and the unmarked white wire to the fixture's white lead. Splice the red wires together and splice the black wires together. At the switch box splice two pigtails to the black wire. Connect the red wire and one pigtail to one switch and the marked white wire and a pigtail to the other switch. Restore power and test.

Wiring three-way switches

PROJECT DETAILS

SKILLS: Running cable, stripping and splicing wires, following a wiring diagram
PROJECT: Installing a ceiling fixture controlled by a pair of three-way switches (not including wall patching)

TIME TO COMPLETE

EXPERIENCED: 4 hrs.
HANDY: 7 hrs.
NOVICE: 12 hrs.

STUFF YOU'LL NEED

TOOLS: Drill, fish tape, lineman's pliers, screwdriver, wire strippers
MATERIALS: Two three-way switches, ceiling fixture, cable and clamps, wire nuts, staples, electrician's tape

Three-way switches are so named because there are three components: two switches and the light fixture. That means you can turn a stairwell light on or off from the top or bottom of the stairs. In long hallways, three-way switches allow you to conveniently control light fixtures from both ends of the hall. In attics, basements, and garages, they spare you from having to grope in the dark looking for the light switch, and they are particularly useful in households with young children who have a tendency to forget to turn off the lights.

See pages 128–131 for tips on running cable and installing boxes and page 11 for grounding methods.

Three-way switch

Three-way switch

THREE-WAY SWITCHES ON STAIRS
Codes—and common sense—dictate that stairway lighting should be controlled by one switch at the bottom of the stairs and one at the top.

HOW THREE-WAYS WORK

Three-way switches have three terminals. The light they control is turned on when the two switches provide a continuous pathway for power. When either switch creates a gap in that pathway, the light is off.

In a three-way system, a pair of "traveler" wires travel from switch to switch, never to the fixture itself. It is the "common" wire that carries power to the fixture. When you wire a three-way switch, keep in mind that the traveler terminals are interchangeable—it doesn't matter which traveler wire goes to which traveler terminal. Connect either the feed wire (which brings power) or a wire that attaches to the fixture's black lead to a switch's common terminal.

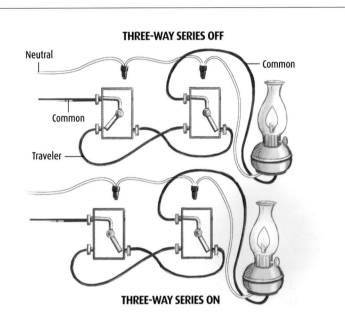

THREE-WAY SERIES OFF

Neutral · Common · Common · Traveler

THREE-WAY SERIES ON

When power runs fixture-switch-switch

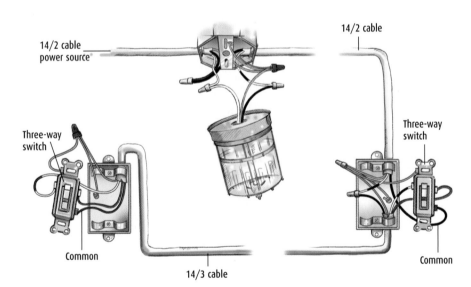

14/2 cable power source · 14/2 cable · Three-way switch · Three-way switch · Common · Common · 14/3 cable

WHEN POWER RUNS TO THE FIXTURE FIRST

Shut off power to the circuit. Run two-wire cable from the power source to the fixture box. Run two-wire cable from the fixture box to the first switch box and mark the white wire black at both ends. Run three-wire cable between the two switch boxes, and mark the white wire black at both ends. Connect the grounds in all three boxes.

At the fixture box splice the black wires together. Splice the unmarked white wire to the fixture's white lead and splice the marked white wire to the black lead. At the first switch box, connect the marked white wire that comes from the other switch and the red wire to the traveler terminals. Connect the black wire that comes from the fixture to the common terminal. Splice together the remaining wires (one black and one white marked black).

At the second switch box, attach the black-marked white wire and the red wire to the traveler terminals. Attach the black wire to the common terminal. Restore power and test.

When power runs switch-switch-fixture

WHEN POWER RUNS TO THE SWITCHES FIRST

This is the simplest way to wire three-ways. **Shut off power to the circuit.** Run two-wire cable from the power source to the first switch box, three-wire cable between the switch boxes, and two-wire cable from the second switch box to the fixture box. Connect the grounds. At the first switch box, splice the white wires. Connect the black feed wire to the common terminal and the other two wires to the traveler terminals. At the second switch box, connect the black wire coming from the fixture to the common terminal (in this case, the lead marked "common" from a three-way dimmer switch). Splice the white wires. Connect the remaining black and red wires to the traveler terminals. At the fixture box, splice the black wire to the black lead and the white wire to the white lead. Restore power and test.

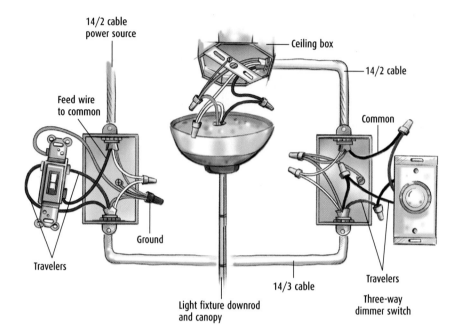

14/2 cable
power source

Feed wire
to common

Ceiling box

14/2 cable

Common

Ground

Travelers

Light fixture downrod
and canopy

14/3 cable

Travelers

Three-way
dimmer switch

When power runs switch-fixture-switch

This is the most complicated three-way wiring configuration, but it is sometimes the easiest way to run the cable. **Shut off power to the circuit.** Run two-wire cable from a power source to the first switch box and three-wire cable from there to the fixture box. Run three-wire cable from the fixture box to the second switch and mark the white wire black at both ends. Connect the grounds in all three boxes. At the first switch box, splice the white wires together. Attach the feed wire to the common terminal and the remaining wires to the traveler terminals. At the fixture box splice the red wires together. Splice the black wire that comes from the first switch to the white wire that is marked black. Splice the remaining black wire to the black lead and the white wire to the white lead. At the second switch box, attach the black wire to the common terminal and the remaining wires to the traveler terminals. Restore power and test.

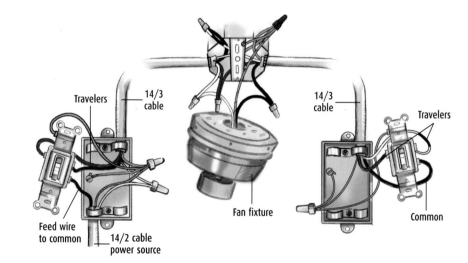

Travelers

14/3
cable

14/3
cable

Travelers

Fan fixture

Common

Feed wire
to common

14/2 cable
power source

Wiring four-way switches

To control a fixture from three or more locations, install a pair of three-way switches at either end and one or more four-way switches in between. The wiring for this setup can get complex, so you may want to hire an electrician. Shown below is a switch-switch-switch fixture; four-way switches also can be wired with power entering the fixture first.

Install as many four-way switches as you like, as long as the first and last switches are three-ways.

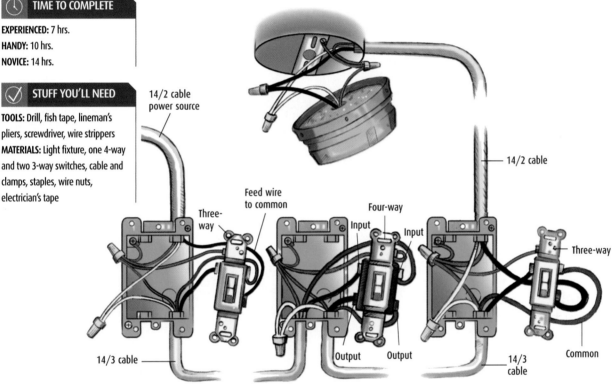

14/2 cable power source

14/2 cable

Feed wire to common

Three-way

Four-way

Input

Input

Three-way

14/3 cable

Output

Output

14/3 cable

Common

WIRING A FOUR-WAY SETUP

Shut off power to the circuit. Run two-wire cable from a power source to the first switch box. Run three-wire cable from the first switch box to the second and from the second to the third switch box. Run two-wire cable from the third switch box to the fixture box. Connect all the grounds.

At the first switch box, connect the black feed wire to the common terminal of a three-way switch.

Splice the white wires and connect the remaining wires to the traveler terminals. At the second switch box, splice the white wires.

Connect the remaining wires to a four-way switch (which has only traveler terminals, no common terminal), as shown. One set of wires should be on the input terminals and the other set on the output terminals.

At the third switch box, splice the white wires. Connect the black wire that comes from the fixture to the common terminal of a three-way switch and the other two wires to the traveler terminals.

At the fixture box splice white wire to white lead and black wire to black lead. Restore power and test.

Adding a wall light

PROJECT DETAILS

SKILLS: Running cable, installing a box, stripping and splicing wires
PROJECT: Installing two wall lights with a wall switch (not including wall patching)

TIME TO COMPLETE

EXPERIENCED: 3 hrs.
HANDY: 6 hrs.
NOVICE: 8 hrs.

STUFF YOU'LL NEED

TOOLS: Drill, saw, fish tape, screwdriver, lineman's pliers, wire strippers, level
MATERIALS: Wall sconces or bathroom wall fixture, boxes, cable with clamps, staples, wire nuts, electrician's tape

The methods for installing wall fixtures are the same as those for wiring ceiling lights (pages 84–85). The difference, of course, is that you're working on a vertical surface.

Wall sconces are ideal for hallways and stairwells. Consider wiring them using three-way switches (pages 148–150).

Most wall fixtures attach to a ceiling box. However, check the hardware to make sure you will be able to install the sconce plumb. Buy a swivel strap (page 85) so you can easily adjust the fixture. A fluorescent fixture (for use over a bathroom mirror, for example) may not require a box (page 102).

REAL WORLD

GETTING THE RIGHT HEIGHT
The height at which light fixtures are hung can be extremely important. Wall sconces in a hallway, if hung too low, may shine in guests' eyes. Installing the sconces at 7 feet provides general illumination—and people can admire them without squinting.

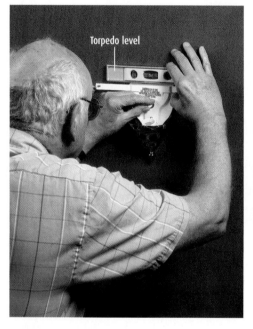

Torpedo level

Support heavy fixtures with a coat hanger

INSTALLING A SCONCE
Run cable from a nearby receptacle or other power source into a switch box and then to a box mounted on the wall. The swivel strap lets you adjust the base until it is level. Depending on the sconce, use either a ceiling fixture box or a switch box. Wire as you would for a ceiling fixture (page 146).

WIRING A VANITY LIGHT
Installing a light over a mirror or medicine cabinet calls for no special wiring techniques. Some fixtures require a box, while others can be wired and attached directly to the wall. If you will be installing a mirror that reaches to the ceiling, give the glass company exact dimensions for cutting a hole to attach the fixture to a box mounted in the wall behind the mirror.

9

INSTALLING NEW SERVICES

Installing a smoke detector

🏷 PROJECT DETAILS

SKILLS: Running cable, stripping and splicing wires

PROJECT: Installing one hardwired smoke detector

🕐 TIME TO COMPLETE

EXPERIENCED: 3 hrs.
HANDY: 5 hrs.
NOVICE: 8 hrs.

✓ STUFF YOU'LL NEED

TOOLS: Drill, fish tape, wire strippers, lineman's pliers, screwdriver

MATERIALS: Smoke detector (hardwired with battery backup), cable with clamps, ceiling box, wire nuts, electrician's tape

Many homes have battery-powered smoke detectors that fail to perform when the batteries die. Other homes have hardwired detectors that don't work if the wiring gets damaged—which often happens in a fire. For the best protection install hardwired detectors that have battery backup.

Most codes allow you to install battery-only detectors. These are fine as long as you test them regularly and immediately replace failing batteries.

Detectors are wired using three-wire cable in a series so that when one is triggered all of them will sound the alarm.s (See pages 128–131 for running cable and pages 132–133 for installing remodeling boxes.)

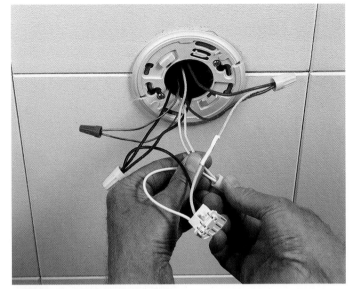

WIRING FOR A SERIES OF DETECTORS
Run three-wire cable to all the detectors so that when one senses smoke, they all screech in unison. (Detectors wired with two-wire cable work independently of one another.) Wire each as shown, following manufacturer's directions.

⊘ SAFETY ALERT

WHERE TO PUT DETECTORS

If your detectors were installed more than 5 years ago, chances are you have too few to satisfy current codes. For instance, detectors are now required both in the hall and inside bedrooms to warn you in case of a bedroom fire. Ask your building or fire department for recommendations.

You should test your smoke detector every month. The electronic sensors last about 10 years in smoke detectors and about 5 years in carbon monoxide detectors. Detectors are inexpensive, are easy to install, and can save your and your family's lives. They are well worth the modest investment.

INSTALLING A DETECTOR
Carefully pack the spliced cables into the ceiling box. Clip the connector onto the back of the detector and install the unit.

Exhaust fans and vents

Chapter 10 highlights

Electric ventilating fans make homes more comfortable by removing fumes, indoor pollutants, and moisture. They also create subtle but refreshing indoor breezes. Today's homes tend to be tightly zipped up with thick insulation and tight-sealing windows and doors . That means that there is a need now more than ever for ventilation that brings in fresh air and blows out stale air. Although primarily used in warm climates, ventilating fans can be an important part of maintaining a comfortable temperature in your home.

This chapter shows how to install the major types of home vent fans. A gable or roof fan keeps an attic from overheating in the summer, thereby reducing cooling costs. A whole-house fan moves air through the lower floors and up out the attic, and may eliminate the need for air-conditioning some of the time. Bathroom vent fans suck out odors and moisture, and may also provide light and heating as well. And a range hood blows cooking odors and smoke out of the kitchen.

Some of these fans pull quite a few amps, so make sure that the circuit you will install them on can handle the extra load (pages 48–49 and 112–113). If the fan contributes to exceeding the load limit of the existing circuit you may need to install a new circuit (see page 192).

Ventilating an attic

To keep your home comfortable and reduce heating and cooling costs, the attic must be able to breathe. To achieve breathability there must be pathways for the air to travel through, so cool air can enter and warm air can exit. The most efficient arrangement includes soffit vents located at the bottom of eaves, and other vents at or near the top of the roof. If you do not have eave vents, then large gable vents, perhaps coupled with roof vents, will do a serviceable job. If you have soffit vents, make sure air can travel freely through them into the attic; if they are blocked with insulation, they will do no good.

What ventilation does: In the summer, good ventilation keeps the attic from overheating. A hot attic forces warmth down through the attic floor into the rooms below—even if the floor is insulated. In cold weather a poorly insulated attic can gather moisture through condensation because of the sharp difference in temperature between inside and outside air. This moisture can damage insulation and even framing. Good ventilation keeps the inside much the same temperature as the outside, so the attic stays dry.

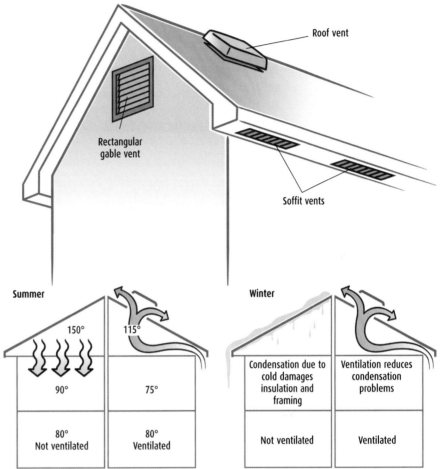

Roof vent

Rectangular gable vent

Soffit vents

Summer

150° 115°

90° 75°

80° / Not ventilated

80° / Ventilated

Winter

Condensation due to cold damages insulation and framing

Ventilation reduces condensation problems

Not ventilated

Ventilated

10

EXHAUST FANS AND VENTS

Wiring options

Vent fans may come with their own switches, but you can use different switches to suit your needs. An attic fan may have a thermostat that turns the fan on and off according to temperature, but you may choose to install a wall switch below to override the thermostat—say, when you want to keep things quiet, or when you anticipate colder weather in the near future. In most cases you will want the switch in a room below. The most common arrangement is to bring power first to the switch, then send a cable up to a junction box in the attic, as shown. If power is already present in a junction box in the attic, you may choose end-line switch wiring instead. See page 143 for the two types of switch wiring.

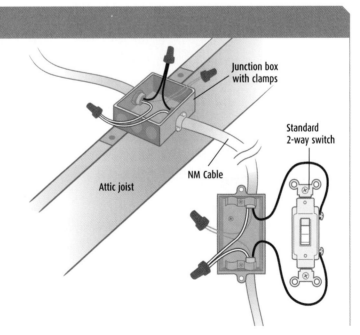

Junction box with clamps

Standard 2-way switch

NM Cable

Attic joist

Installing a gable fan

PROJECT DETAILS

SKILLS: Running cable, making wiring connections, attaching with screws
PROJECT: Installing a fan and attaching electrical wires

TIME TO COMPLETE

EXPERIENCED: 4 hrs.
HANDY: 6 hrs.
NOVICE: 9 hrs.

STUFF YOU'LL NEED

TOOLS: Drill, fish tape, screwdriver, lineman's pliers, combination strippers
MATERIALS: Attic fan, cable with clamps, wire nuts, electrician's tape

O ften the easiest way to cool an attic is to install a fan at one or more gables. If your gable does not already have a louvered section, you will need to cut through the side of the house and install framing.

The manufacturer should provide a chart detailing how powerful a fan you need based on the size of your attic. Depending on the size of your house, you may require more than one fan. If you have no gable, install a roof fan (page 157).

If your attic doesn't have a louvered opening, you will have to install one. They can be purchased at home centers.

Pulling cable through wall cavity

1

BRING POWER INTO THE ATTIC

Before tapping into a receptacle or junction box for power, check the amperage on your attic fan and make sure you will not overload the circuit (pages 112–113). **Shut off power to the circuit.** See pages 128–131 for tips on running cable into the attic. Check with local codes to see whether you need to use armored cable instead of NM cable.

CLOSER LOOK

AN ATTIC MUST BREATHE
An attic fan, whole-house fan, or roof fan moves air efficiently only if the attic is properly ventilated. Usually a house needs vents near the bottom of the attic (usually under the eaves) and vents near the roof peak, such as turbine vents, gable vents, or a continuous vent running along the ridge. Check that eave vents are not clogged with insulation. If you are not sure that your attic is properly vented, have it inspected by a professional roofer.

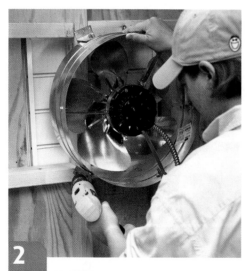

2

MOUNT THE FAN
At a louvered opening in the attic, secure the fan by driving screws through its mounting brackets and into studs. If the studs do not allow you to center the fan in the opening, attach horizontal 2×4s that span between the studs. Attach the fan to the studs. You may choose to install louvers that close when the fan is not operating.

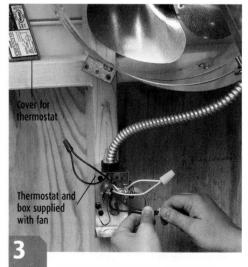

Cover for thermostat

Thermostat and box supplied with fan

3

MAKE THE ELECTRICAL CONNECTIONS
The fan has its own thermostat switch. Mount the thermostat box to a framing member. Follow the manufacturer's instructions for connecting wires. Restore power and adjust the temperature control. Or you can control the fan with a pilot-light switch (page 70) located in the hallway.

Installing a roof fan

PROJECT DETAILS

SKILLS: Running cable, making wiring connections, attaching with screws, basic carpentry skills
PROJECT: Installing a roof fan and wiring a thermostat

TIME TO COMPLETE

EXPERIENCED: 4 hrs.
HANDY: 6 hrs.
NOVICE: 9 hrs.

STUFF YOU'LL NEED

TOOLS: Drill, fish tape, screwdriver, lineman's pliers, wire strippers, reciprocating saw or saber saw, carpentry tools
MATERIALS: Roof fan, cable with clamps, wire nuts, electrician's tape, roofing compound

A roof fan is more efficient at pulling hot air out the top of a roof than a gable fan. Once you figure how to bring power to the attic, the wiring is easy. However, cutting the roofing and installing the fan so that it will not leak can be tricky. Hire a roofer if you have wood shakes, tiles, or any other type of roofing other than asphalt shingles. If the roof already has a non-fan vent, you may be able to remove it and install the roof fan in the same hole.

1 DRILL A LOCATOR HOLE

Near the peak of the roof, but allowing enough room so the fan will not touch the ridge framing, drill a hole in the middle of the space between two joists.

2 CUT THE HOLE AND THE ROOFING

Follow the manufacturer's directions for cutting a hole through the roof and for cutting back shingles from around the hole. You also will need to carefully pry out some hidden nails that would get in the way of the fan's flange.

3 INSTALL THE FAN

This must be done correctly, or the roof will leak. The fan slips under the shingles around the top half of the hole, and rests on top of the bottom-half shingles. Slip the fan in place, attach with roofing nails, and apply roofing cement as directed.

4 WIRE THE THERMOSTAT

Attach the fan's thermostat to a nearby joist. **Shut off power to the circuit.** Run power to the thermostat; you may choose to switch this power (see "Wiring Options," page 155). Wire the grounds, the whites, and the black wires, fold the wires into the thermostat box, and replace the cover. Adjust the thermostat, restore power, and test.

Installing a whole-house fan

PROJECT DETAILS

SKILLS: Basic electrical and carpentry skills

PROJECT: Installing a fan with a thermostat and switch

TIME TO COMPLETE

EXPERIENCED: 6 hrs.
HANDY: 8 hrs.
NOVICE: 12 hrs.

STUFF YOU'LL NEED

TOOLS: Drill, ladder, saw, wire strippers, lineman's pliers, screwdriver

MATERIALS: Whole-house fan, screws, junction box, switch box, cable with clamps, wire nuts, electrician's tape

BUYER'S GUIDE

STRONG, BUT NOT TOO STRONG

The stronger the whole-house fan, the cooler the house will be. However, a fan that's too powerful will waste electricity and make too much noise. Aim for a fan that exchanges the house's air once every four minutes. Determine the total square footage of your home and look at the charts provided by fan manufacturers to find out which size fan you need. To be safe purchase a fan that's a little more than you need, and make sure it has a multispeed switch so you can operate it at lower speeds.

A whole-house fan is ideal for spring and fall cooling in hot climates and it may be the only means of cooling you need in moderate climates. For the fan to work, the attic must have adequate ventilation (page 155) and windows on the first floor must be open. Measure your home's square footage to choose the right size fan to pull air from outside into the house in order to provide a slight but cool breeze.

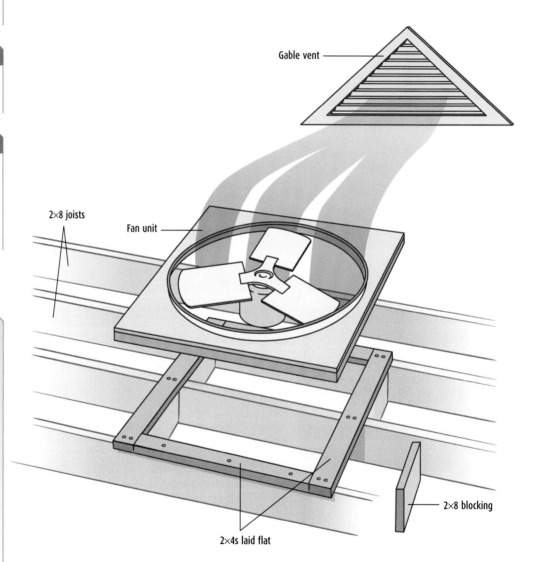

Gable vent

2×8 joists

Fan unit

2×8 blocking

2×4s laid flat

Position a whole-house fan fairly near the middle of an attic. If possible locate it between two joists, with another joist running between, as shown. You will need to cut through the ceiling drywall or plaster, but will not need to cut through any joists. To seal the area below the fan, you may need to install blocking, using 2× material of the same width as the joists. It is important to seal tightly, so dust and insulation do not seep into the room below.

Wiring options

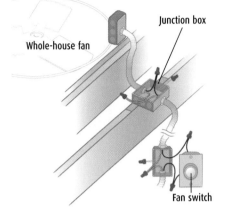

Whole-house fan

Junction box

Fan switch

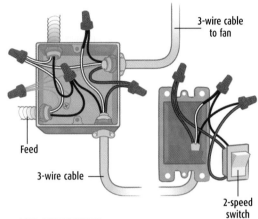

3-wire cable
to fan

Feed

3-wire cable

2-speed
switch

CLOSER LOOK

USING THE FAN
Make sure that the attic is adequately vented, so air will move freely to the outside. Whenever the fan is on, open a couple of windows or doors on the first floor; otherwise, there will be little cooling breeze. See that there is a clear path between the first-floor open windows and the fan.

THROUGH-SWITCH WIRING

Check to be sure that the fan will not overload the circuit (pages 112–113). If the most convenient source of power is in the space below, install a switch box in the hallway below. **Shut off power to the circuit.** Run cable from the power source to the new box, and run cable from the box to a junction box in the attic. Use three-wire cable if you want to wire a multispeed switch. Wire the switch as shown.

END-LINE WIRING

If the most convenient source of power is in the attic, **shut off power to the circuit.** Fish cable from the attic junction box to a new box in the hallway below, and wire it as shown. In the example shown three-wire cable is used in order to wire a 2-speed switch.

Installing the fan

Cutout for
louver

Finder
hole

1

CUT A HOLE

Fans are designed to be positioned over one joist so you don't have to compromise ceiling framing. Cut a 1×2-foot finder hole to confirm that the fan will center on a joist. Mark the cutout for the louver and cut through the drywall or lath and plaster. The fan manufacturer will specify dimensions for the hole.

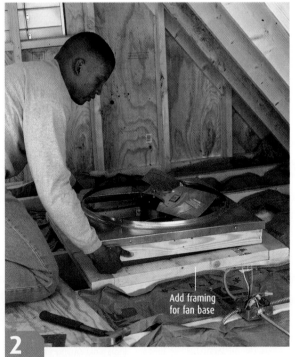

Add framing
for fan base

2

MOUNT THE FAN

With a helper, lift the fan up through the opening and into the attic. Add framing as needed so the fan is securely centered over a joist. Attach brackets to the fan frame and position them so they will slip over the exposed joist. Center the fan over the opening and secure the brackets with bolts.

3

ENCLOSE THE FAN

Pull back the insulation and cut pieces of 2× blocking to fill gaps at either side of the fan. At each side cut two pieces to fit between the joists (shown) or one notched piece that fits over the joist. (Some manufacturers supply blocking.) Attach the wood to the joists by drilling pilot holes and attaching with 3-inch screws or 16-penny nails.

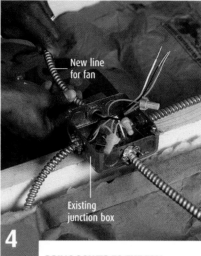

4

BRING POWER TO THE FAN

After making sure that you will not overload a circuit (pages 112–113), **shut off power to the circuit.** Tap into a junction box or run cable up into the attic (see pages 128–131). Local codes may require you to use armored cable instead of NM cable.

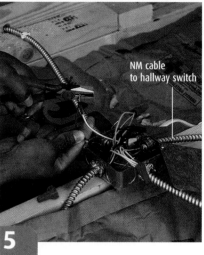

5

CONNECT THE WIRES

A fan-rated rheostat switch lets you vary the fan speed. Bring the two-wire switch cable to the box, marking the white wire black at both ends. Splice it to the black wires in the box. Splice the other switch wire to the fan's black wire and the fan's white to the white wires in the box. Connect the ground.

6

WIRE THE SWITCH

Install a fan-rated switch in the hallway, connecting it to the cable you have run through the wall from the attic junction box. Use the switch manufacturer's directions to wire the switch.

7

ATTACH THE LOUVERS

Hold the louver panel against the ceiling so it covers the hole. Attach the panel by driving screws into the joists and blocking. Restore power and test the fan.

CLOSER LOOK

USING THE FAN

Whole-house fans can do wonders in the hotter months of the year to keep your house cool. However, in winter they can be a source of heat loss unless you insulate them when they are not in use. In the winter close the fan's shutters tightly and cover the fan with insulation, so warm air cannot escape into the attic. Just be sure to remove the insulation before you start using the fan again the following year.

10

EXHAUST FANS AND VENTS

Installing a bathroom vent fan

A vent fan considerably improves the atmosphere in a bathroom by pulling out moisture, odors, and heat. Codes require bathrooms to have vent fans if there is no natural ventilation, such as a window. You may opt for a fan even if you have a window, so you can clear the air in rainy or cold weather. When choosing a fan use these guidelines:

■ Make sure the fan will move the air. Unfortunately, many bathroom fans do little more than make noise. This happens when either the fan is not strong enough or the path through the ductwork is not free and clear. Measure your room and determine how far the ductwork has to travel. Then ask a home center salesperson to help you choose a fan and the ductwork to do the job shown on pages 162–163. Keep in mind that air travels more freely through solid ducts than through flexible hoses.

■ Consider the fan options. Some units have a fan only, while others include a ceiling light, a low-wattage night-light, and even a forced-air heating unit.

■ Consider the wiring options. Some people prefer separate switches for the bathroom fan and light. Keep in mind that some local codes may require that the fan come on whenever the overhead light is turned on.

INSTALLING DUCTWORK

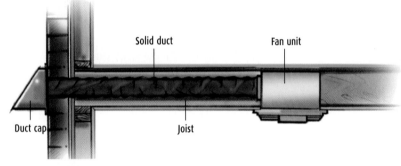

Solid duct · Fan unit · Duct cap · Joist

RUNNING DUCT THROUGH A WALL

Choose the shortest and straightest route. A wall vent is the easiest to install because there is no roofing involved. However, it may be difficult to run ductwork between joists.

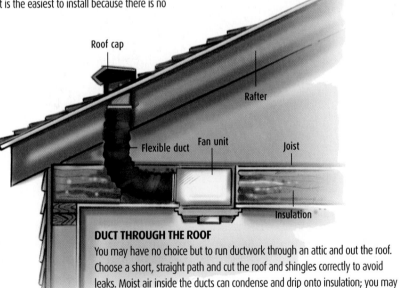

Roof cap · Rafter · Flexible duct · Fan unit · Joist · Insulation

DUCT THROUGH THE ROOF

You may have no choice but to run ductwork through an attic and out the roof. Choose a short, straight path and cut the roof and shingles correctly to avoid leaks. Moist air inside the ducts can condense and drip onto insulation; you may want to cover the duct with pipe insulation.

10

EXHAUST FANS AND VENTS

1 CUT THE HOLE

From the attic above hold the fan against a joist and mark its outline with a pencil. Cut out the opening. If there is no attic above, use a stud sensor to locate a joist and cut the opening from below. **Shut off power to the circuit** and provide power if none is present (page 140).

2 ATTACH THE FAN AND DAM OFF INSULATION

Attach the fan to the joist with screws. Some models require a 6-inch gap between the unit and insulation. Cut or push back the insulation; then cut pieces of 2× lumber to fit between the joists and attach the lumber with screws or nails.

Reciprocating saw

3 CUT A HOLE IN THE ROOF

On the underside of the roof, trace a circle just large enough for the roof cap tailpiece. Drill a hole large enough for the saw blade, then cut with a reciprocating saw, saber saw, or keyhole saw. (If you run the ductwork out the wall, see Work Smarter on the opposite page.)

4 CUT AWAY SHINGLES

Remove shingles from around the cutout without damaging the underlying roofing paper. The lower part of the roof cap flange will rest on top of the shingles, and the top part will slip under the shingles.

5 INSTALL THE ROOF CAP

Smear roofing cement on the underside of the cap flange. Slip the upper flange under the shingles as you insert the cap into the hole. Install the shingles on the side, smearing the undersides with roofing cement. Attach the flange with roofing nails and cover the heads with roofing cement.

BUYER'S GUIDE

FAN EFFICIENCY AND NOISE CONTROL
A label on the fan packaging will indicate how many square feet of bathroom space the fan can successfully clear. If there's any doubt, or if your ductwork will be more than 5 feet long, get a slightly more powerful fan than you need. (However, don't overdo it. Keep the power of the fan appropriate to the size of the room.) The SONE rating on a fan indicates its sound-level rating. A 3 SONE rating is quiet; a 7 will be very noisy.

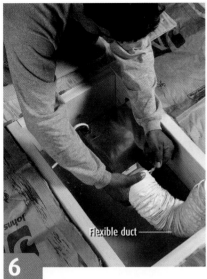

6 CONNECT THE DUCTWORK

Flexible ductwork is the easiest to run, but solid ducts are quieter and more efficient. At both the roof cap and the fan, slide a clamp over the duct and slip the duct over the tailpiece. Slide the clamp back over the tailpiece and tighten the clamp. Wrap the joint with duct tape.

7 WIRE THE FAN

If wiring does not exist, run cable to the fan and to a switch. If you are installing a fan/light, run three-wire cable from the switch to the fan. Connect the wiring according to the manufacturer's directions. Plug the motor into the built-in receptacle.

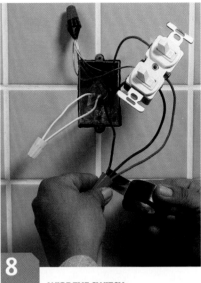

8 WIRE THE SWITCH

For a fan/light switch that has power entering the switch box, splice the white wires and connect the grounds. Connect power to both switches through two pigtails spliced to the feed wire. Connect the red wire to one switch terminal and the black wire to the other terminal.

📖 WORK SMARTER

INSTALLING A WALL VENT

Even if there is an attic above, it is usually easier to run the vent out through a gable wall rather than through the roof. From inside the attic drill a locator hole through to the outside, then cut out the siding with a reciprocating saw, saber saw, or keyhole saw. It often works best to shove in a length of solid ductwork that reaches most of the way to the fan, then run flexible duct the rest of the way.

1 MAKE A TAILPIECE

Press the duct pipe into the cap. Use sheet-metal screws to attach a piece of solid duct to the cap, then caulk the joint or wrap it with duct tape. Apply a bead of caulk to the back of the flange so it will seal against the siding.

2 ATTACH THE VENT

Caulk around the hole and push in the tailpiece. Secure it with four screws. Caulk around the edge of the vent. Complete the connection to the fan indoors using solid or flexible ductwork.

Adding a range hood

PROJECT DETAILS

SKILLS: Advanced electrical skills, carpentry skills
PROJECT: Installing a range hood that vents air from the kitchen through the wall

TIME TO COMPLETE

EXPERIENCED: 6 hrs.
HANDY: 10 hrs.
NOVICE: 14 hrs.

STUFF YOU'LL NEED

TOOLS: Drill, fish tape, saber saw or reciprocating saw, hammer and cold chisel, screwdriver, wire strippers, lineman's pliers
MATERIALS: Range hood, solid duct, wall cap, masonry screws, cable and clamps, wire nuts, electrician's tape, caulk, safety goggles

Most residential range hoods, if correctly installed, remove smoke, odor, and heat from the kitchen. To draw out cooking grease, you need a powerful commercial model.

For the best range hood efficiency, run the duct through the wall directly behind the range hood, in as straight a line as possible. You can run the vents of most hoods out the back or the top of the unit.

If a wall stud is in the way of the ductwork, you could do carpentry work to change the framing (page 165). Or purchase a hood with an extra-strong motor and run the duct around the stud.

Before you purchase a fan, check its "cfm" rating—which indicates the number of cubic feet of air it pulls per minute. Choose a fan with a cfm rating that is double the square footage of your kitchen.

TIME SAVER

DUCTLESS RANGE HOODS

Cutting a hole in the wall and running ductwork is the most time-consuming and difficult part of installing a range hood. Save yourself the hassle by installing a ductless hood, which runs air through a filter and back into the kitchen rather than moving it outside. This unit will not be as effective at removing smoke and odors, however, and you'll need to change filters fairly often.

CLOSER LOOK

POSSIBLE DUCT ARRANGEMENTS

Make sure the range hood comes with all the ductwork you need, as well as a wall cap for the outside. The most common arrangement is to run the duct straight out the back of the hood and through the wall. However, you also can piece together rectangular or round ducting to go up and over and through the wall. Or you can go up through the roof.

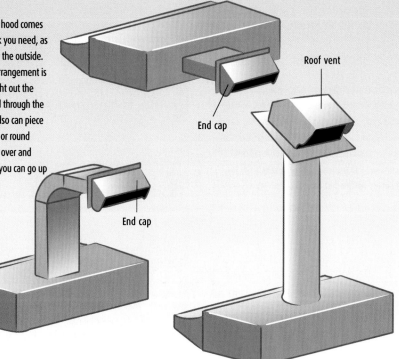

Roof vent

End cap

End cap

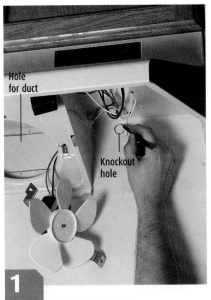
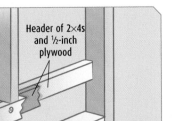

1

MARK FOR HOLES

Remove the filter, fan, and electrical housing cover from the range hood. Use a hammer and screwdriver to remove the knockouts for the electrical cable and the duct. Hold the hood in place and mark the holes for the duct and the cable.

2

CUT THE INSIDE AND DRILL A LOCATOR HOLE

Cut holes through the drywall or plaster. Using a long bit, drill holes at each corner all the way through the outside wall. (If your exterior is brick or block, see page 166.)

3

CUT THE SIDING

Connect the dots between the holes on the outside to mark the outline of the hole. Using a reciprocating saw, saber saw with an extra-long blade, or keyhole saw, cut the outline. Remove insulation or debris that would interfere with installing the duct.

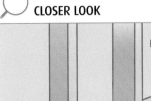

🔍 CLOSER LOOK

FRAMING AROUND A STUD

If a stud is in the way of your duct, you may need to cut the stud and install new framing. Cut an opening in the stud that is the height of the duct, plus 5 inches to accommodate the header above and the plate below. Make a header out of two 2×4s with a strip of ½-inch plywood sandwiched between.

💲 BUYER'S GUIDE

PUT YOUR RANGE HOOD OUT IN THE OPEN

If there is no cabinet above the range hood—or if you want a sleek new look—consider buying an exposed range hood. It can be vented through the roof or the wall. You will likely need to special-order pieces of stainless-steel ductwork to suit your situation.

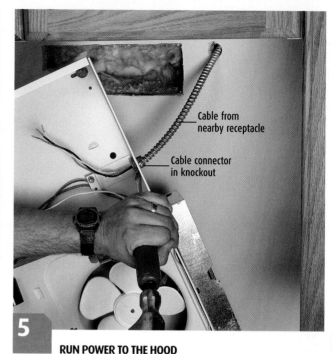

Cable from nearby receptacle

Cable connector in knockout

4 ATTACH THE DUCT CAP

Push the wall cap into the wall to see if the duct is long enough to reach the range hood. If not, purchase an extension and attach it with sheet metal screws and duct tape. Apply caulk to the siding where the cap flange will rest. Push the cap into place and fasten with screws. Caulk the perimeter of the flange.

5 RUN POWER TO THE HOOD

Shut off power to the circuit. Run cable from a nearby receptacle or junction box through the hole in the wall (pages 128–131). Strip the sheathing and clamp the cable to the range hood electrical knockout. Mount the hood securely by driving screws into studs or adjacent cabinets.

🔍 CLOSER LOOK

Masonry bit

Duct cap

VENTING THROUGH A MASONRY WALL

Use a long masonry bit to drill the locator holes (see Step 2, page 165). Draw the outline carefully, double-checking that you can slip in the vent with room to spare. Drill holes about every inch along the outline; then use a hammer and cold chisel to chip between the holes. To attach the duct cap, drill holes and drive masonry screws. Older homes may have double-thick brick walls—a real challenge!

6 CONNECT THE WIRES

Splice the white wire to the white fixture lead, black wire to black lead, and the ground wire to the green lead. Fold the wires into place and replace the electrical cover. Reattach the fan and filter. Restore power and test.

Outdoor wiring projects

Chapter 11 highlights

Outdoor lighting extends the length of an evening patio party, helps you carry in the groceries without tripping, and provides an important measure of security. To install lights and receptacles outdoors, you will use many of the same techniques as for indoor wiring. But be sure to use materials suitable for exterior applications: outdoor light fixtures, watertight boxes, underground feeder (UF) cable, and perhaps watertight conduit.

If you already have an exterior receptacle, you can probably tap into it to provide power for several lights and another receptacle or two. However, first make sure that doing so will not overload the circuit (pages 48–49 and 112–113).

Building codes can vary greatly from town to town, so check to make sure your installation meets requirements. Learn how deep a trench you need for running the cable, what type of cable or conduit to use, and how close the lights can come to the property border. The exception is low-voltage lighting, which can be installed without an inspection.

Low-voltage landscape lights

PROJECT DETAILS

SKILLS: No special skills are required
PROJECT: Installing a series of 6 to 8 low-voltage landscape lights

TIME TO COMPLETE

EXPERIENCED: 1 hr.
HANDY: 2 hrs.
NOVICE: 3 hrs.

STUFF YOU'LL NEED

TOOLS: Screwdriver, drill, tool for trenching, lineman's pliers
MATERIALS: Set of outdoor landscaping lights with a transformer/timer

L ow-voltage landscape lights—those that are 12-volt AC—literally are a snap to install. The lighting parts snap together, and the connectors snap into place. The cable looks like a lamp cord.

Landscape lights are available in a package that contains the transformer, the lights, and the connectors that you'll need. You also can buy the system piece by piece so you get exactly what you want. Talk with the sales staff to make sure you get the right transformer.

If necessary, splice low-voltage wires. Strip the wires, put in a silicone-filled cap (sold as a grease cap), and attach the new wire. Some caps are brand-specific, so make sure you buy a cap designed for your wire.

MOST LOW-VOLTAGE LIGHTING SYSTEMS INCLUDE A TRANSFORMER THAT IS PLUGGED INTO A REGULAR OUTDOOR RECEPTACLE
The size of the transformer varies; most are rated to handle a load of 100 to 300 watts. The higher the rating, the more cable and light fixtures you can connect to the system. A timer in the transformer turns the system on at dusk and off at dawn. One end of the cable connects to the transformer; you can attach lights to the cable anywhere you want.

1

WIRE THE TRANSFORMER
A transformer steps the voltage down from 120 volts to 12 volts. Attaching the cable for the lights is an easy task of screwing the wires in place. Details vary by manufacturer, so follow the directions that come with the transformer.

2

HANG THE TRANSFORMER
Mount the transformer on the wall next to a GFCI outlet. For most types of siding, you can make the attachment with a wood screw. Drive it into the plywood of the sheathing underneath the siding. For masonry drill a hole and drive a masonry screw.

ASSEMBLE THE LIGHTS

Light fixtures usually require assembly. You'll need to snap the socket in place at the very least, and you may need to do some simple wiring. Follow the manufacturer's directions.

PLACE THE LIGHTS

Lay the light fixtures in the approximate spots they will be installed, and run the cable across the ground from light to light.

CONNECT THE LIGHTS

Attach the cable connectors. For this light put half the connecter on each side of the cable and snap it together to connect the lights.

DIG FOR THE CABLE

Dig a shallow trench alongside the cable and place the cable in the trench, but do not bury it yet.

SET THE TIMER

Plug the transformer into the outdoor receptacle and set the timer. Cover the GFCI outlet with a plastic cover, usually sold separately. Test the lights; if they work correctly, bury the cable.

Low-voltage deck lights

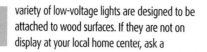

A variety of low-voltage lights are designed to be attached to wood surfaces. If they are not on display at your local home center, ask a salesperson for a catalog, and special-order them. Some mount to the side of a wall, others are inserted into a stair riser, and still others attach to the top of a post.

CONNECT TO A TRANSFORMER

To power these lights plug a transformer into a receptacle and run light-gauge cable from the transformer to the lights, as you would for low-voltage landscaping lights (pages 168-169). Anchor the cable with staples made for the purpose—regular staples may damage the insulation.

POST CAP LIGHT

Choose a post light that will easily attach to your posts. You can simply staple the cable to the side of a post. Or cut a channel (which will later be covered with a piece of trim) and drill a hole through the deck for running a hidden cable.

RISER LIGHT

A riser fixture lights your way as you climb stairs. To install one either remove the tread or work from underneath. Use a drill and saber saw to cut a hole in the riser, insert the light, hook up the wires, and screw the light in place.

Installing motion-sensor lights

PROJECT DETAILS

SKILLS: Stripping and splicing wires
PROJECT: Installing and adjusting a motion-sensor light

TIME TO COMPLETE

EXPERIENCED: 1 hr.
HANDY: 1.5 hrs.
NOVICE: 2 hrs.

STUFF YOU'LL NEED

TOOLS: Wire strippers, screwdriver, drill
MATERIALS: Motion sensor light, wire nuts, electrician's tape, perhaps a mounting strap

1

CONNECT THE LIGHT

Shut off power at the service panel, and remove the existing floodlight. If necessary, install a swivel strap (page 85). Run the wires through the rubber gasket, and splice them with wire nuts. While mounting the light to the box, position the gasket so it will keep the box dry.

2

POSITION THE LIGHT

Restore power. Loosen the locknuts and twist the light until it is directed where you want it. Tighten the locknuts. At night turn the light on permanently by flipping off the wall switch, then on again. Aim the lights, then tighten the nuts to hold them in place.

Motion-sensor lights greet you when you come home at night, and they discourage potential burglars. If you have an existing floodlight, they are easy to install. (To install an exterior box for a new light, see pages 172–173.)

Choose a fixture that lets you control the time and the sensitivity to motion. If the light is connected to a switch inside the house, you can override the motion sensor so the light stays on or off.

3

MAKE ADJUSTMENTS

To activate the motion sensor, manufacturer's instructions will probably tell you to turn off the wall switch, wait a few seconds, and turn it back on. Choose how long you want the light to stay on (ON TIME). There may be a control that keeps the light less bright for the amount of time you choose (DUAL BRIGHT). Set the RANGE to the middle position, and test how sensitive the motion sensor is by walking around near it. Adjust if necessary.

REAL WORLD

BE KIND TO YOUR NEIGHBORS

Installing a floodlight that is activated by movement can provide security when entering a home at night, but if positioned at the wrong angle, it can prove to be annoying to neighbors or people just passing by. Be aware of where the light is installed and positioned.

11

OUTDOOR WIRING PROJECTS

Adding an outdoor receptacle

PROJECT DETAILS

SKILLS: Running cable through walls, stripping and connecting wires
PROJECT: Installing an outdoor GFCI receptacle

TIME TO COMPLETE

EXPERIENCED: 2 hrs.
HANDY: 4 hrs.
NOVICE: 6 hrs.

STUFF YOU'LL NEED

TOOLS: Drill with long bit, saber saw or keyhole saw, wire strippers, screwdriver, lineman's pliers, hammer (for masonry walls, a masonry bit and cold chisel)
MATERIALS: GFCI receptacle, cable with clamps, remodel box, in-use cover, wire nuts, electrician's tape

nless you need an outdoor receptacle in a particular location, plan the easiest path for the cable. One option is to install it nearly (but not exactly) back-to-back with an indoor receptacle. Or run cable through the basement ceiling and out the rim joist.

Even if you install a weatherproof cover, place the receptacle in a dry location and at least 16 inches above the ground. Codes require that an outdoor receptacle be a ground fault circuit interrupter (GFCI).

Ensure that you will not be overloading a circuit when installing the outdoor receptacle (pages 112–113). If you plug in too many Christmas lights or plan to use heavy-duty power tools, you may need to place the receptacle on its own circuit (pages 192–193). Local codes may require that you have a separate circuit for outdoor electrical service. See pages 128–131 for tips on fishing cable through walls.

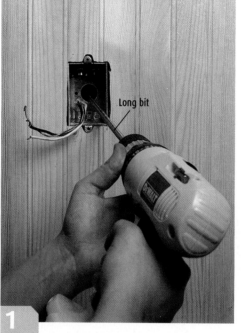

Long bit

1

DRILL A LOCATOR HOLE

Shut off power to the circuit. Pull out an interior receptacle and detach it. Using a hammer and screwdriver, open a knockout hole in the back of the receptacle box. Put a long bit or a bit extension in your drill. (Use a masonry bit if your exterior is brick.) Poke the bit through the hole in the box. The wall may not be thick enough to fit back-to-back receptacles, so aim the drill bit at an angle. Drill through to the outside.

Keyhole saw

2

CUT THE HOLE FOR THE RECEPTACLE

On the outside cut a hole for a receptacle box. Drill a second hole as an entry point and use a saber saw with an extra-long blade, a reciprocating saw, or a keyhole saw. If the exterior is masonry, see page 166 for tips on cutting the hole.

3 RUN THE CABLE

Cut cable about 2 feet longer than you need, and strip the sheathing from both ends. Have a helper push the cable from indoors as you pull it out through the hole. Clamp the cable to the remodel box and mount the box (pages 132–133). Install a new GFCI receptacle outside (page 74). Connect to power in the interior box.

4 INSTALL AN IN-USE COVER

In-use cover

This kind of cover will keep the receptacle dry even when it has a cord plugged into it and it can be locked shut. In addition to the plastic cover, install the rubber gasket behind the plate. Restore the power and test the receptacle.

WORK SMARTER

RUNNING CABLE THROUGH A BASEMENT WALL

If your basement ceiling is unfinished, this is probably the easiest method. **Shut off power to the circuit** and tap into a receptacle or junction box. Cut a hole through the rim joist and siding, and staple the cable to the joist.

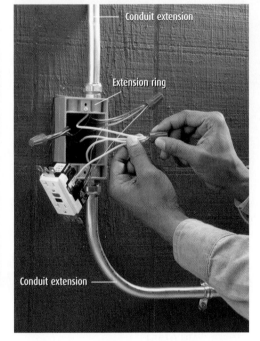

Conduit extension

Extension ring

Conduit extension

EXTENDING SERVICE FROM AN OUTDOOR RECEPTACLE

Adding an extension ring to the receptacle box allows you to run cable or conduit from the receptacle to supply outdoor lights and other receptacles. Two screws attach the extension ring to the box. Remove one or more knockouts in the ring to extend the circuit.

Running conduit and cable

T hough you can run cable to an outdoor light or outlet several ways, the easiest is with UF cable, which is waterproof and can be buried directly in the ground. Code requires that you protect the cable above ground, so you'll have to do some basic conduit work where the cable enters and exits the ground.

Other methods require you to enclose wiring in conduit for the entire length of the trench. You won't have to bury the cable quite as deeply, but you will have to fish wires and cut conduit. It's best to stick with UF.

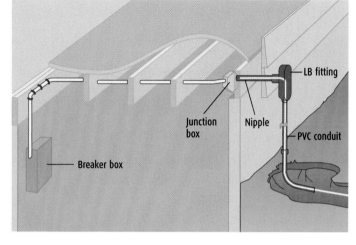

INSIDE THE HOUSE, CABLE RUNS FROM THE BREAKER BOX TO A JUNCTION BOX NEAR THE FOUNDATION WALL

Inside the junction box each wire in the cable is attached to a corresponding wire in a UF (underground feeder) cable. A length of conduit, called a nipple, protects the cable's run through the wall. Outside, attach the nipple to an LB fitting—an L-shape fitting with a removable plate that turns the cable toward the ground. The fitting attaches to conduit that goes down the house wall into a 24-inch-deep trench. The conduit then stops and the cable continues along the bottom of the trench. At the end of the trench it reenters conduit and is routed up to the fixture it will power.

Installing PVC conduit

1

DRILL A HOLE

Drill where you want the wire to enter the house, at a point just above the foundation. Measure and make sure the hole will go through the rim joist and not into the foundation or first floor. Make the hole wide enough to accommodate the short section of conduit that protects the cable.

2

INSTALL AN LB FITTING

Cut a PVC nipple to length so it extends 1 inch into the basement, and test the fit. Glue it to the LB fitting and push the assembly into the hole until the fitting is against the wall of the house.

3

DIG A TRENCH

Dig a trench for the cable below the LB fitting. Make the trench about the width of a shovel and 24 inches deep. Code requires this depth for UF cables buried without conduit.

4

ATTACH A PIECE OF CONDUIT TO THE LB FITTING

Cut a piece of conduit to reach from the fitting to an elbow at the bottom of the trench. Spread PVC solvent cement onto the conduit and push it into the fitting.

5

ATTACH THE ELBOW

Glue the elbow in place. The lower end should be at the bottom of the trench. UF cable will come out the opening and travel directly along the bottom of the trench until it reaches the other end.

Using metal conduit above grade

ALTHOUGH PVC IS FLEXIBLE, RUSTPROOF, AND EASY TO WORK WITH, SOME LOCAL CODES WON'T ALLOW PVC MORE THAN 6 INCHES ABOVE GROUND

Metal conduit, which is more durable and less likely to be damaged accidentally, is required instead. With metal conduit all connections must be made with compression fittings, which have a compression ring (like plumbing fittings do) to keep out water. Thin-walled tubing, called EMT (electrical metallic tubing), is the easiest conduit to use. A nipple connects an interior junction box to an exterior metal LB fitting. Metal conduit extends down from the fitting to 6 inches above grade, where a compression fitting is screwed to a plastic transition fitting. An elbow is added at the bottom and then the cable runs along the bottom of the trench to the area requiring power.

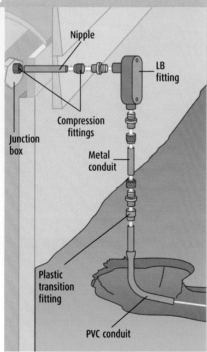

Nipple

LB fitting

Compression fittings

Junction box

Metal conduit

Plastic transition fitting

PVC conduit

BUYER'S GUIDE

USING CONDUIT

Code lets you bury NMWU cable directly in the ground, which is the easiest method of running a circuit, but you also can run conduit the length of the trench. If you do, you won't have to bury the cable quite as deep—18 inches instead of 24 inches. You will, however, have to fish cable through the conduit. Running UF or other cable through conduit meets code, but cable adds expense and the sheathing may make it difficult to fish. Most electricians feed three single wires, known as TW wires, through the conduit instead. If you do this, run the conduit first, and glue the sections together. Once the conduit is in place, fish all three wires at once.

Cutting conduit

Running lengths of conduit often requires a fair amount of cutting. Begin by clamping the conduit in a vise. Cut PVC conduit with a hacksaw that has a blade with 32 teeth per inch. Then remove any burrs with a utility knife and bevel the outside edges to fit the couplings. For metal conduit use a pipe cutter or hacksaw that has a blade with 18 teeth per inch. Wrap a piece of masking tape around the area that is to be cut to prevent the blade from slipping. Remove any burrs with a half-round file.

6

ATTACH THE CONDUIT
Fasten the conduit to the house wall with plastic straps. Drill holes in the foundation and use masonry screws to screw the straps in place.

7

APPLY CAULK
Caulk the gaps between the siding and the conduit to create a watertight seal.

Running the cable

1

LAY CABLE
Remove the cover from the LB fitting. Install the fixture at the other end of the trench and uncoil enough UF cable to reach up from the trench to the fixture—plus approximately 2 feet—and leave it at the end of the trench. Then work your way back toward the house, laying cable in the trench as you go.

2

FISH THE TAPE THROUGH THE CONDUIT
Pushing wire through a conduit by itself is next to impossible, so use fish tape—a flat, springy length of metal in a roll. Insert the end into the fitting and push the tape until it reaches the end of the conduit.

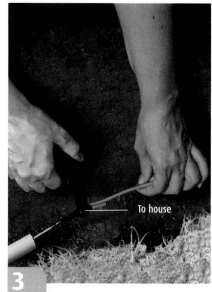

To house

3

TAPE THE CABLE TO THE FISH TAPE
To hook the cable onto the fish tape, bend the cable to form a hook and interlock it to the fish tape. Use black electrical tape to bind the fish tape and the cable together. Then pull the tape and the cable through the conduit elbow. Use conduit lubricant to make pulling easier and to prevent damage to the cable.

11

OUTDOOR WIRING PROJECTS

Installing a lamppost

A lamppost and light fixture are usually sold as a unit. The majority of the work is in digging a trench and running cable from the house to the spot where the lamp will be installed. The depth of the trench depends on whether you use conduit in the trench (see pages 174–176). In this case UF cable is buried 24 inches deep.

Anchor the post in a footing made of quick-setting concrete poured in a fiber tube form. Keep the post vertical while the concrete sets using 2×4s staked to the ground and clamped to the post.

Lampposts may differ in fixture styles or in material used for the posts. However, the electrical connections are the same for all types of posts.

When working with electricity, **always turn off the power** by shutting off the appropriate breaker at the service panel.

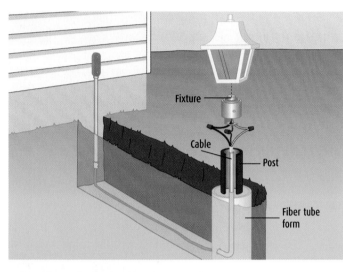

Fixture

Cable

Post

Fiber tube form

WHAT YOU DON'T SEE WHEN YOU LOOK AT A LAMPPOST IS THE WORK THAT WENT INTO IT

Here waterproof UF (underground feed) cable is buried in a trench 24 inches deep and runs from the house to the location of the post. (If you run conduit, you can dig a shallower trench. See pages 174–176.) A concrete footing made with a fiber tube form provides support for the lamppost. The wire connections are a simple matter of joining three pairs of wires with wire nuts.

⊘ **SAFETY ALERT**

HOT TO THE TOUCH

Halogen and mercury-vapor lights are extremely hot when they are on.

📖 **WORK SMARTER**

RUNNING WIRING UNDER A SIDEWALK

Use this method whether running cable or conduit. Cut a piece of metal conduit 2 feet longer than the sidewalk width and flatten one end with a hammer to make a sharp point. Drive the pipe under the sidewalk with a hammer and a block of wood. Cut off the sharp end with a hacksaw. Install a plastic bushing at each end so the cable won't get nicked as it is pulled through the conduit.

1 DIG THE TRENCH

Dig a trench 24 inches deep and a hole deep enough for the lamppost and wide enough for a fiber tube form. Cut the form to reach the bottom and cut a slot in the bottom for the conduit elbow. Fish cable from the trench through the conduit, and lower the post into the form. Fill the form with concrete per manufacturer's instructions. Brace the post until the concrete is set.

2 WIRE THE LIGHT

Strip the cable wires and connect them to wires in the light. Twist and connect the black wire to the black wire, the white to the white, and the ground to the ground. Tuck the wires into the post.

3 ATTACH THE LIGHT

Screw the cap to the top of the post, then mount the light socket in the cap. The mounting method depends on the type of fixture. Check the instructions that came with the lamppost.

Home networking

Chapter 12 highlights

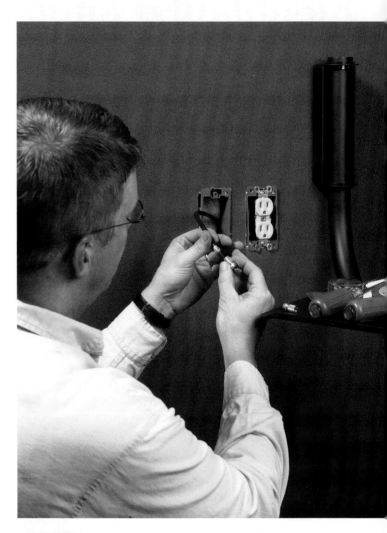

 **REAL WORLD**

DRILL NEW HOLES

TV cables and phone cables require separate holes. Threading the cable through the same hole will result in static and buzzing on the phone line. Always keep phone and TV cable 2 inches apart from electrical cable when running parallel, and 1 inch apart wherever they cross.

I n addition to having miles of standard-voltage wiring, your home likely has hundreds of yards of thin wires that carry little or no power. These wires lead to telephones, thermostats, door chimes, VCRs, and TVs.

These wires and cables carry voltage that is so low it cannot harm you. Still, you should respect low-voltage wiring. Once the wiring is damaged, it can be difficult to diagnose and repair the problem. Hide low-voltage wiring inside walls or behind moldings when possible. If wires must be exposed, pull them taut and staple them firmly.

Planning for a home network

If your household has two or more computers, several television sets, Internet access, a couple of telephone lines, and maybe a fax machine, it may be time to consider installing a home network. Or perhaps you are yet again adding to the tangle of cables running along the baseboard—and are getting more than a little confused about what cable goes where. The devices strung together with low-voltage lines are with us to stay; it makes sense to install a permanent system to accommodate them.

Consider your network needs

A home network lends order to the devices you have and has built-in flexibility so it is ready to make room for the new innovations in communication and entertainment that are yet to come. Consider the potential networking needs for each room in the house. For example, a basic setup for each bedroom might be an outlet that has a video jack, a phone jack or two, and a data jack for a computer. A living room, family room, or great-room could benefit from an outlet that could serve an entertainment center, including a couple of video jacks, two phone or data jacks, and two pairs of speaker wire connectors. A home office needs voice and data ports; even a shop area might benefit from Internet access. And don't forget the kitchen. In addition to outlets for a television and a phone, it needs Internet access. And if you someday expect to own a stove or refrigerator with "smart" technology that allows you to launch meal preparation remotely, even your appliances may need nearby data jacks.

Home network cabling

The workhorse cable for home networking is CAT 5e cable. This eight-wire cable is designed for high-speed data transmission, but it can also be used in place of 4- or 6-wire CAT 3 telephone cable. CAT 5e is available in several colors, which is useful when you are "bundling" several cables (see page 187). For video and Internet cable access, use RG6/U coaxial cable. Both CAT 5e and RG6/U coaxial cable can be bought in a variety of lengths up to 100 feet, with connectors factory-attached. These connectors are a bit tricky to attach, so ready-made cables are an advantage. However, you can buy bulk amounts of cable and, with special tools, attach connectors yourself (see pages 184–185 and 188).

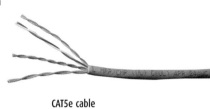

CAT5e cable

RG6/U coaxial cable

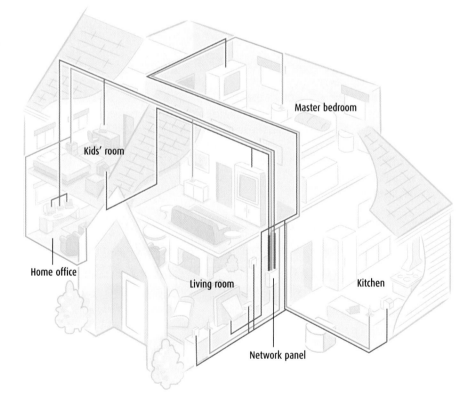

Master bedroom

Kids' room

Home office

Living room

Kitchen

Network panel

MULTIPURPOSE OUTLETS
At the user end of the network, outlets like this combine voice, data, and video jacks. Snap-in jacks allow you to customize the outlet to meet your needs.

12

HOME NETWORKING

CABLE BEHIND THE WALLS
This is an example of how a home network can link various communication and entertainment devices. The network panel located in a downstairs closet makes it easy to alter services and add new cable.

Drawing a plan

Even if your immediate goal is only to add a video outlet or telephone extension, making a master plan for a whole-house network still makes sense. You may find that while pulling one cable, you can add another for future use. At the very least you'll have a plan you can build upon. A home network doesn't require a highly precise plan; all that is necessary is a drawing roughly to scale (helpful in estimating how much cable you'll need) with the location of each outlet and the types of jack you want in each outlet.

Give each outlet a code that you'll use for labeling cable. The first outlet in a master bedroom might be "MB1." The third of three outlets in the family room might be "FR3." As you label each cable (see page 187), indicate its specific use—"MB1-V" for a voice line or "MB1-D" for a data line, for example.

In making your plan be aware that your modem should always be next to a computer so you can troubleshoot any Internet service problems. To let other computers share Internet access, you'll need a router. It can be located next to the modem or in the network panel.

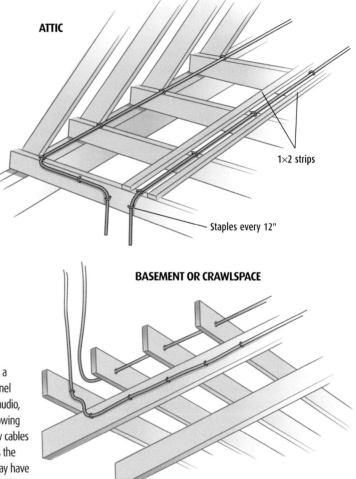

ATTIC

1×2 strips

Staples every 12"

CLOSER LOOK

HANDLE WITH CARE

Network cabling is more delicate than standard electrical wiring. RG6/U cable should not be bent to more than a 2½-inch radius; CAT 5e no more than a 1-inch radius. Both can be pulled using a fish tape, but always have a helper unkink and feed the cables into the wall cavity as you pull. (For tips on preparing pathways and pulling cable, see pages 131–131).

Routing cable

The ideal setup for a home network has a centrally located network panel. This panel neatly puts all the primary voice, data, audio, and video connections in one place, allowing you to alter existing services or add new cables as needs change. For making cable runs the attic is ideal. In two-story homes you may have to use the crawlspace or basement as well. A 2- or 3-inch PVC pipe located near the network panel is a convenient way to route cables in a two-story house. Such a pipe also makes it easy to pull additional cable at a later date. A single run of CAT 5e can be up to 300 feet long—far more than most homes would require. RG6/U can run as far, but if you split it to more than three outlets, you'll need to add an amplifier (see page 189).

BASEMENT OR CRAWLSPACE

CABLE DEFENSE

Protect your cable runs by running them through or along the sides of framing members—wherever they are least likely to get snagged or stepped on. Use protective strips when running cable perpendicular to attic joists where items might be stored.

Securing network wiring

Unlike standard electrical boxes, boxes and brackets for network wiring are open at the back. Their main function is to provide a means of fastening the outlet faceplate and its various snap-in jacks to the wall. Both "old-work" and "new-work" brackets are available. Use plastic, not metal, cable staples. Make a neat installation, with the cable well out of the way of possible damage. Install a staple every foot or so. Attach cable along the sides of attic joists so it will not be be crushed by someone stepping on it. In basements or crawlspaces bore access holes through the floor joists if the cable runs perpendicular to the joists. If you must cross over AC wiring, do so at a 90-degree angle and make sure the two cables do not touch.

Installing telephone wiring

PROJECT DETAILS

SKILLS: Attaching with screws; stapling, stripping, and connecting thin wires

PROJECT: Running about 50 feet of phone cable and installing two jacks

TIME TO COMPLETE

EXPERIENCED: 2 hrs.
HANDY: 4 hrs.
NOVICE: 6 hrs.

STUFF YOU'LL NEED

TOOLS: Drill, screwdriver, lineman's pliers, wire strippers
MATERIALS: Solid-core telephone cable, phone jacks, staples

Adding a new telephone jack is straightforward work. Just run cable and connect wires to terminals labeled with their colors. The most difficult part is hiding the cable.

Depending on your service arrangement, it may be less expensive to have the phone company install new service for you. The lines they install will be under warranty—all future repairs will be free.

Not all telephone wires are made to the same specifications. It is worth paying the slightly higher cost for solid-core wires within the cable because they are less likely to result in faulty connections.

Make all connections in a jack or junction box. Plan cable paths so as little of the cable as possible can be seen. For instance, going through a wall (page 182) saves you from running unsightly cable around door moldings. Use these same techniques to run speaker wire.

$ BUYER'S GUIDE

WIRE FOR THE FUTURE

As long as you're running phone lines, spend a little more for Category 5e cable, which can handle connections for Internet and high-speed data networks as well as standard telephone connections.

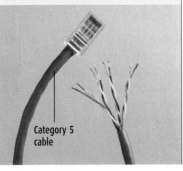

Category 5 cable

WORK SMARTER

FRAGILE WIRES

The wires withing Category 5e cable are telephone wires and are fragile. Don't bend, flatten, or otherwise compromise these wires. A damaged wire can result in a distorted connection, especially for computers.

1

OPTION A: TAP INTO A PHONE JACK

Unscrew the cover from a phone jack or a phone junction box. Strip about 2 inches of sheathing and ½ inch insulation from each wire. (Standard phones use only two of the wires, but it doesn't hurt to connect all the wires.) Loosen each terminal screw. Bend the wire end in a clockwise loop, slip it under the screw head, and tighten the screw.

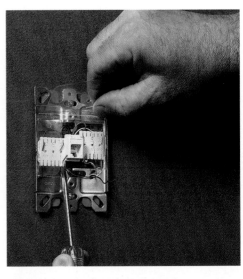

OPTION B: USE PUSH-ON CONNECTORS

Some jacks have terminals that clamp onto the wire so you don't have to strip it. Just push the wire down into the slot until it snaps into place.

12

HOME NETWORKING

2 HIDE CABLE

Use any trick you can think of to tuck away unsightly cable. Pry moldings away from the wall, slip the cable in behind, and renail the molding. Or pull carpeting back one short section at a time, run cable along the floor behind the tack strip, and push the carpet back into place.

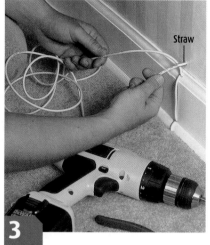

3 RUN CABLE THROUGH A WALL

To go through a wall, drill a hole using a long, ¼-inch drill bit, then insert a large drinking straw. Fish the cable through the straw. When you're finished, split and remove the straw.

Straw

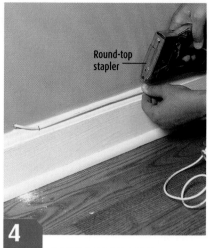

4 STAPLE EXPOSED CABLE

When there is no choice but to leave cable exposed, staple it in place every foot or so along the top of the baseboard. Use a round-top stapler or plastic-shielded staples that hammer into place. (Square-cornered staples damage the cable sheathing.)

Round-top stapler

Installing a wall jack

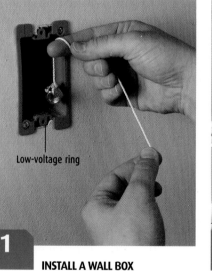

Low-voltage ring

1 INSTALL A WALL BOX

A wall jack can attach to a low-voltage ring (as shown) or to an electrical remodel box. Cut a hole in the wall and install the ring. Tie a small weight to a string and lower it through the hole until you feel it hit the floor.

2 PULL THE CABLE

Drill a ⅜-inch hole at the bottom of the wall where you want the wire to go. Bend a piece of wire into a hook, slip it into the hole, and pull out a loop of the string. Tape the string to the cable and pull the cable up through the remodel box.

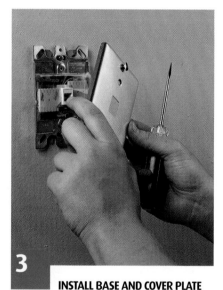

3 INSTALL BASE AND COVER PLATE

Attach the base of the jack and make the connections. Install the cover plate.

12

HOME NETWORKING

Distributing telephone lines

PROJECT DETAILS

SKILLS: Stripping cable, following logic of circuits
PROJECT: Connecting low-voltage phone lines

TIME TO COMPLETE

EXPERIENCED: 2 hrs.
HANDY: 3 hrs.
NOVICE: 4 hrs.

STUFF YOU'LL NEED

TOOLS: Drill, screwdriver bits, longnose pliers, cutting pliers
MATERIALS: 66 block, CAT 5e cable, bridging clips, cable clips

A split 66 block is used to "distribute" incoming lines to the various extensions throughout the house. The block has four columns of punch-down terminals. The first two columns (think of them as A and B) are connected as are the last two (C and D). However, columns B and C are not connected unless you press into place a metal bridging clip (see step 3). While not as versatile as the voice and data modules used in network panels (see pages 186–189), a 66 block is a great way to organize your phone lines. Here's how to install three incoming "trunk" lines to several extensions.

TOOL SAVVY

SPEED THE JOB WITH A PUNCH-DOWN TOOL
A spring-mounted punch-down tool not only pushes a wire into a punch-down terminal or jack, it automatically trims off excess wire. Ideal if you'll be making a lot of connections, it uses reversible multipurpose tips. The 66 block tip must be bought separately.

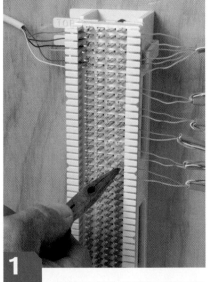

1
CONNECT THE INCOMING LINE AND ALL EXTENSIONS
Using a longnose pliers or punch-down tool, push the incoming wires in place. No stripping is required (the terminals bite through the insulation when you push the wire in), but you'll need to nip off excess wire. The green and red lines are line one, black and yellow line two, and blue and white line three. The first extension cable on the right side of the block carries all three lines to one outlet (personal, business, and fax lines); the other extensions go to outlets with only one line. Fold back unused lines.

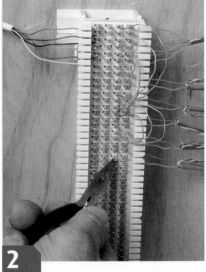

2
INSTALL JUMPERS
Strip a foot or so of cable of its outer jacket. Separate the wires and use them as jumpers to connect each extension wire to its incoming line. One wire can jump to several extensions—punch the jumper in where needed and trim it off at the final connection.

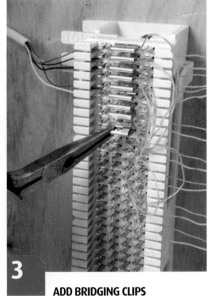

3
ADD BRIDGING CLIPS
To complete the connection across the columns of the block, purchase bridging clips. Push them into place between the incoming lines and the six wires of the first three extension lines.

12

HOME NETWORKING

Running coaxial cable

Cable TV companies will run new lines and install jacks. Some do simple installations for free; for longer runs they may charge and may not hide as much of the cable as you like. They also may increase your monthly fee after installing a second or third jack. Still it's worth checking out the service options before doing your own installations.

Purchase RG6 coaxial cable for all runs through the house. Don't use RG59, which has less-substantial wire wrapping. Coaxial cable is thick and ugly, so fish it through walls when possible (pages 128–131).

If your cable signal is weak after adding new lines, install a signal booster to solve the problem. The booster attaches to the coaxial cable and plugs into a receptacle.

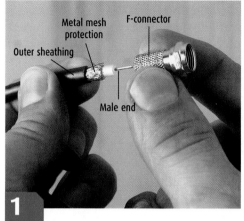

1

MAKE A MALE END
Use wire strippers to strip ¾ inch of insulation, exposing the bare wire. Do not bend the exposed wire. With a knife carefully strip and additional ⅜ inch of the thin outer sheathing only—do not cut through the metal mesh wrapping. Firmly twist a screw-on F-connector according to the instructions on its package. Some connectors require you to peel back a portion of the metal mesh wrapping.

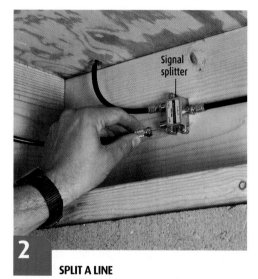

2

SPLIT A LINE
Cut the line you want to tap into. Install male ends on both ends of the cut line and the end of the new line. Insert and twist all three male connectors onto a signal splitter. Anchor the splitter with screws.

3

INSTALL A JACK
Cut a hole in the wall and run cable to it using the technique shown on page 182. (A regular electrical box can be used, though a low-voltage ring is preferable. See page 182.) Strip the insulation to make a male end in the cable. Clamp the mounting brackets in the hole. Attach the cable end to the back of the jack by twisting on the F-connector. Tighten the connection with pliers or a wrench. Attach the jack to the wall by driving screws into the mounting brackets.

Coaxial connection options

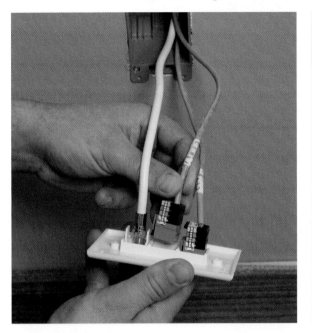

MULTI-JACK CONNECTION

An F-connector, whether a crimp-on type (see opposite page) or non-strip (shown), is used to attach coaxial cable to multi-jack outlets. The video jacks snap into the outlet plate.

RIGHT-ANGLE ADAPTER

Coaxial cable can be damaged if it is bent to more than a 2½-inch radius. Add the F-connector to that and you need about 4 inches of clearance to connect to an outlet. A right-angle video adapter makes the best of tight quarters without compromising the cable.

Keeping water out

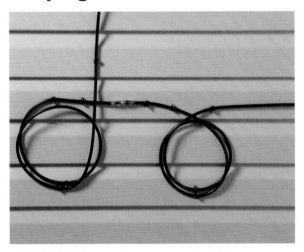

USING DRIP LOOPS

Where your coaxial cable meets that of the cable provider, the cable from the satellite, or antenna, coil two drip loops and fasten them in place with cable staples. The loops direct moisture away from the connector.

 TOOL SAVVY

ONE-STEP STRIPPING

If your network calls for numerous coaxial connections, consider investing in this one-step coaxial cable stripper. With one squeeze and a pull, you can cleanly strip the jacket from the metallic shield (always tricky) and the insulation from the center copper pin (otherwise tough to do without nicking).

Installing a network panel

PROJECT DETAILS

SKILLS: Stripping cable, following logic of circuits

PROJECT: Organize cables and devices by installing a network panel and component modules

TIME TO COMPLETE

EXPERIENCED: 4 hrs.
HANDY: 6 hrs.
NOVICE: 8 hrs.

STUFF YOU'LL NEED

TOOLS: Drill, screwdriver bits, combination strippers, longnose and cutting pliers, punch-down tool, torpedo level

MATERIALS: Panel, panel door, bushings, telephone distribution panel, voice and data module, coaxial distribution panel, video amplifier, power module, patch cords, 2-inch general-purpose screws, wire wraps

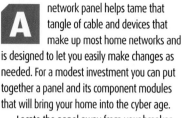

network panel helps tame that tangle of cable and devices that make up most home networks and is designed to let you easily make changes as needed. For a modest investment you can put together a panel and its component modules that will bring your home into the cyber age.

Locate the panel away from your breaker box or subpanel. Avoid areas like basements, garages, and attics where there is wide temperature variation or high humidity. A centrally located closet or utility room is the best location. A panel needs a 120-volt receptacle nearby to plug in power module adapters. More elaborate panels have a power source module that will require running a new 120-volt line.

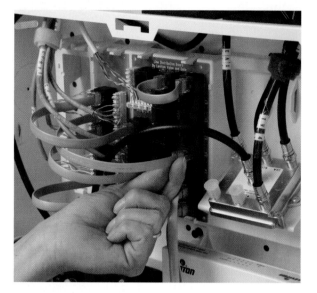

QUICK CHANGE

Change is the one constant in home networking. A network panel allows you to easily upgrade and alter your system. Should you need to add a new phone extension, change a voice line to a data line, or add a new video line, a network panel helps ease the transition.

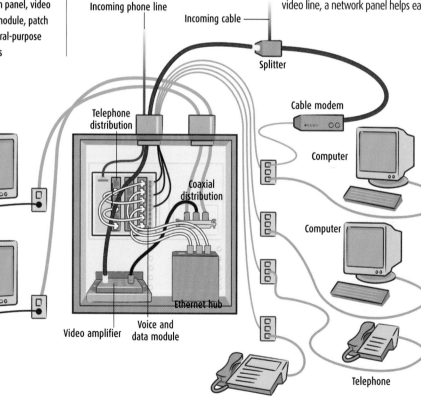

HOME NETWORK PANEL

This example of a home network shows how various modules link devices throughout your house. Patch cords allow you to quickly change the distribution of voice and data lines. Modules ease the addition of new lines.

1

INSTALL THE PANEL

Remove the number of knockouts you think you'll need for your cable runs. Insert plastic bushings to protect the cable jackets as they are pulled into the panel. If surface mounting the panel (shown), use 2-inch general purpose screws to fasten it to framing members. If you choose to set the panel into the wall, cut the opening and pull the cable bundles into the panel before installing it.

2

PULL THE CABLE

Label each of the cables and pull them to the outlet location. By "bundling" multiple cables as shown, you can pull them all through at once. As you pull the cables, have a helper guide them into the wall cavity to avoid kinks and abrasions.

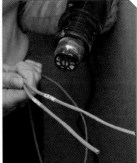

CLOSER LOOK

LABELING THAT HANGS TIGHT
Label each cable using self-adhesive alphabetical and numerical labels available from the electrical department of your home center. Cover the label with clear tape, or best of all, wrap it with transparent heat-shrink tubing. When pulling cable permanently attach one label about 4 inches from the end to leave room for stripping. Stick the label for the other end of the cable to the box or spool and apply it after the cable has been pulled. Pull enough cable so there is adequate extra length at both ends; 2 feet at a network panel and 12 inches at a box.

3

STRIP THE JACKET

Remove the fish tape and install the bracket. Strip about 2 inches of the jacket from the cable. A cable stripper made to handle CAT 5e cable (shown) does the best job.

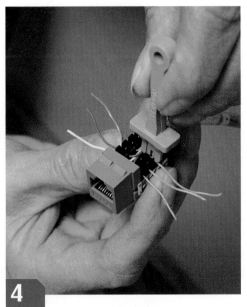

4

MAKE THE CONNECTIONS

Separate the four pairs of wires. Using the "B" color code (technically known as T568B wiring), punch the wires into place. Make sure the wires stay wound to within ½ inch of their punch-down connection.

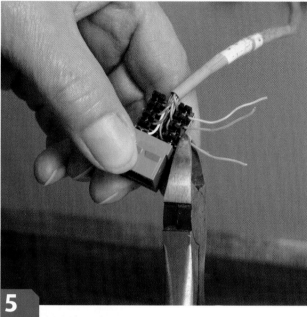

5

TRIM THE WIRES

Use a pair of wire nippers to trim the wires even with sides of the connector. Check that the cable jacket extends into the connector. Place the cover over the connections and press it in place.

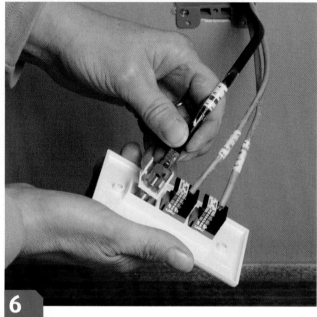

6

INSTALL JACKS

Add an F-connector (see pages 184–185) to the coaxial cable and attach the cable to the back of the jack. Clip the jacks in the mounting plate and attach the mounting plate to the wall.

7

INSTALL THE MODULE

Install the telephone and video module. Locate this and each module so cables can be attached without crowding. Most panels come with prepunched holes for mounting modules with push pins. Some panels are backed with plywood to which modules can be fastened with screws.

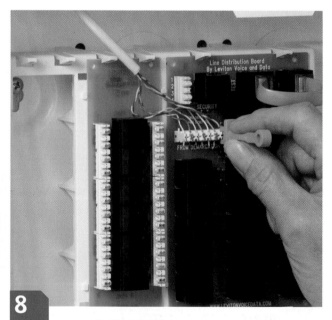

8

WIRE THE VOICE MODULE

Follow manufacturer's directions for attaching the wires of the incoming telephone line. Strip off 3 inches of the outer jacket and match the wires to the color coding of the connector strip marked "From Demarcation." Use the plastic punch-down tool provided with the module to attach the wires.

9

WIRE THE DATA MODULE

Following manufacturer's instructions punch in wires from voice, fax, modem, and computer cables to the voice and data module. Strip away 3 inches of jacket, matching the color code on the connector strip, and punch each wire in.

10

INSTALL ETHERNET HUB

Attach the Ethernet hub. Follow manufacturer's instructions for installing the patch cords between the hub and the data module to link the incoming line from the modem and the outgoing lines to other computers in the network.

11

INSTALL THE VIDEO AMPLIFIER

Fasten in place the video amplifier module. Hook up the coaxial line from the cable source. Use a coaxial patch cord to link the amplifier to the video splitter.

12

CONNECT CABLES TO THE VIDEO SPLITTER

Connect your video cables to the video splitter. Plug the power adapters into the video amplifier and Ethernet hub and run the adapter power cords to a nearby 120-volt receptacle.

13

SECURE THE CABLES

Connections will be protected and the panel easier to work in if you tidy up the cables. Use Velcro wire wraps; that way you can readily remove them should you choose to pull in additional cables. Secure the cables to the wall near the box with bundle clips.

14

ATTACH THE COVER

After giving the connections a final check and testing the system, install the cover on the network panel using the fasteners provided by the manufacturer.

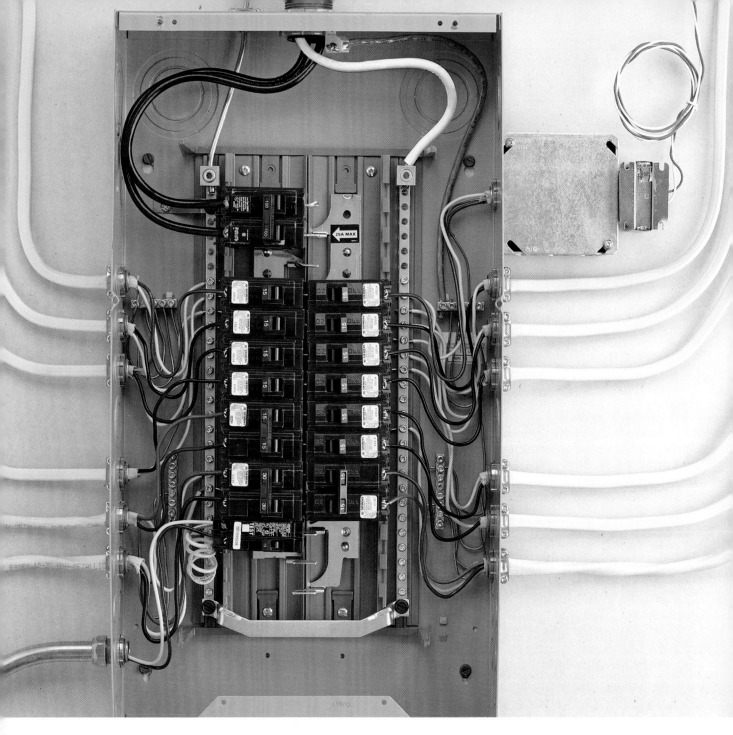

Chapter 13 highlights

Major projects

The installations described in this chapter involve adding new circuits. Once you have learned how electricity works and how to calculate loads, and have successfully completed several electrical installations, you are ready for the serious business of installing new circuits. However, proceed with caution, and never begin any project that involves running cable without first consulting a building inspector.

Your local building department may not allow unlicensed homeowners to run new circuits, install panels or subpanels, or wire entire rooms. If you hire out the work, use this chapter to understand what is involved and how to judge the quality of the work being done.

Before attempting any of the projects in this chapter, be sure you have a thorough understanding of the wiring principles presented in Chapter 1.

Replacing a service panel

Although homeowners sometimes install new service panels themselves, many building departments insist that the job be done only by licensed and bonded electricians. Because the job is complex and potentially dangerous, tackle it only if you have an excellent source of professional advice.

When to install a new panel

If your service panel is an old-fashioned fuse box, you may want to update it by installing a breaker panel. However, if your circuits rarely blow fuses, the box is not damaged, and you do not plan to add new circuits, there is no compelling reason to upgrade it.

If you need to add new circuits and the service panel cannot accept additional breakers, the easiest solution is to add a subpanel (pages 194–195). A professional electrician—who is accustomed to working with live electricity and sorting out tangles of wires—may prefer to replace the old service panel with a larger one.

If your existing electrical service is insufficient—for example, if you have 60-amp service and need 100 amps or if you have 100-amp service and need 200 amps—you need a new service panel. You also may need to have the utility company change the wires that enter your home. See page 194 for more information.

What's involved

An electrician or the utility company must first disconnect the power coming to the house—often by cutting live wires near the service entrance. The electrician can then provide temporary electrical service by tapping the live wires. Obviously, all this is too dangerous for a homeowner.

If your service amperage needs to be increased, the utility company may need to install thicker wires. If you have very old electrical service with only two wires, the utility company must run three wires to your home.

Replacing the service panel is primarily a matter of managing a tangle of wires. All the wires running to the panel must be disconnected, tagged, and pulled out of the panel. Then the panel must be removed and another one mounted. It's important to position the new panel so that all the wires can reach the breakers and bus bars. When the wires are attached, power can be reconnected.

It's a tangle

Sorting out the incoming circuits and hooking them up properly is a job best left to the pros. It's not a highly technical job, but it does require clear thinking and the skills that come with practice. Hire a professional electrician to do this.

MAJOR PROJECTS

Adding a new circuit

PROJECT DETAILS

SKILLS: Understanding circuits, stripping and splicing wire
PROJECT: Hooking up a new circuit after cable has been run

TIME TO COMPLETE

EXPERIENCED: ½ hr.
HANDY: 1 hr.
NOVICE: 2 hrs.

STUFF YOU'LL NEED

TOOLS: Hammer, screwdriver, lineman's pliers, wire strippers
MATERIALS: Cable and clamp, new circuit breaker

T he physical work of installing a new electrical circuit is simple and calls for no special skills. Most of the work is completed outside the service panel. To get a breaker that will fit in your panel, jot down the brand and model number, or bring a sample breaker to the store.

First, determine whether your service panel can accommodate a new breaker, and then plan a circuit that will not be overloaded (pages 112–113). Install the new boxes. Run cable from the boxes back to the service panel (pages 128–131). (Electricians call this practice a "home run.") Hook up the devices and fixtures. Now you're ready to energize the new circuit by installing a new breaker and connecting the wires to it.

Main circuit breaker

1 SHUT OFF MAIN POWER

Work during the daytime and have a reliable flashlight on hand. Turn off the main circuit breaker. All the wires and circuit breakers in the panel are now de-energized except for the thick wires that come from the outside and connect to the main breaker. **Do not touch the thick wires.**

SAFETY ALERT

FIRE PROTECTION
Some codes now require the use of arc fault circuit interrupters (AFCI) for bedroom circuits. AFCIs provide greater fire protection than a regular breaker. Regular breakers trip for overloads and short circuits. AFCIs offer protection when arcing occurs because of frayed and overheated cords, and impaired wire insulation. See page 76 for more information.

CLOSER LOOK

Half-size

Double-pole

Tandem

Quad

Single-pole

BREAKER OPTIONS
If the service panel has room, install full-size, single-pole breakers. If you're out of space, see if your panel can accommodate half-size or "skinny" breakers, or tandem breakers. In some panels these breakers only fit in slots near the bottom. Your building department limits the number of breakers that can be installed. If you add too many, they will require you to put in a new panel or a subpanel (pages 194–195). You'll need double-pole breakers for 240-volt circuits. A quad breaker supplies one 240-volt circuit and usually two 15-amp 120-volt circuits in the same space of a double pole breaker.

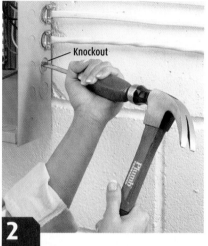

2 **REMOVE A KNOCKOUT**

Remove the service panel cover (page 46). To remove a knockout slug from the side of the service panel, first tap it with a hammer and screwdriver, then twist it off with pliers. Install a cable clamp. Also remove a knockout tab from the panel cover.

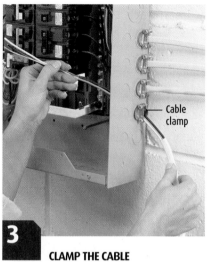

3 **CLAMP THE CABLE**

Determine how far the wires must travel to reach the breaker and the neutral bus bar. To avoid tangles plan a path around the box perimeter. Strip about a foot more sheathing than you think you need. Thread the wires through the clamp and secure the cable. Don't overtighten.

4 **CONNECT THE NEUTRAL AND GROUND WIRES**

Run the neutral wire toward an open terminal in the neutral bus bar, bending the wire carefully so it will easily fit behind the panel cover. Cut the wire to length and strip off about ½ inch of insulation. Poke the end into the terminal and tighten the setscrew. Connect the ground wire to the ground bar (or neutral bar if there is no ground bar).

5 **WIRE THE NEW BREAKER**

Run the hot wire, bending it carefully so it will easily fit behind the panel cover. Cut the wire to length. Strip off ½ inch of insulation. Poke the wire into the new breaker terminal. If bare wire is visible, remove the wire, snip it a little shorter, and reinsert it. Tighten the setscrew.

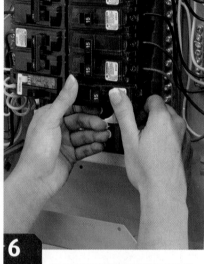

6 **SNAP THE BREAKER INTO PLACE**

Slip one side of the breaker under a tab to the right or left of the hot bus bar. Push the other side onto the bus bar until the new breaker is flush with the other breakers. (Some brands of breakers may require a slightly different installation method. Check the instructions.) Restore power and test.

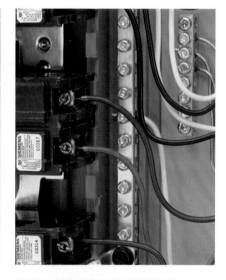

INSTALLING DOUBLE-POLE BREAKERS

Shut off the power. Wire a 240/120-volt circuit with the black and red wires connected to the breaker terminals. Connect the white wire to the neutral bus bar. Wire split circuits the same way (page 144). To wire a straight 240-volt circuit (page 145), connect the two hot wires to the breaker and the ground wire to the ground bar (or neutral bar if there is no ground bar).

Installing a subpanel

PROJECT DETAILS

SKILLS: Attaching with screws, running cable, stripping and splicing wires

PROJECT: Installing a subpanel with several new circuits after the circuit cable has been run

⏱ TIME TO COMPLETE

EXPERIENCED: 3 hrs.
HANDY: 5 hrs.
NOVICE: 8 hrs.

✓ STUFF YOU'LL NEED

TOOLS: Drill, hammer, screwdriver, wire strippers, lineman's pliers
MATERIALS: Subpanel, screws, cable with clamps, staples

A n experienced homeowner can tackle a subpanel, but hire a pro if a new service panel is needed.

When to add a subpanel

Install a subpanel to handle new circuits if the existing service panel does not have open breaker slots and you cannot use half-size breakers (page 192).

A subpanel doesn't add to the total amount of power entering the home. If you have 100-amp service and the new circuits you are installing will require more than that (see pages 112–113 for how to add up your requirements), call an electrician. Electricians working with the utility company can bring 200-amp service to your service head and can install a new service panel.

Getting ready

Purchase a subpanel. Unlike some main service panels, it has separate bus bars for neutral and ground wires. Figuring the size of the subpanel, feeder cable, and feeder breaker can be complicated, so consult an electrician or your building department.

In most cases, to add up to six new circuits with a total of 6,000 watts or less (pages 112–113), you'll need a 30-amp, 240-volt subpanel. Open two spaces in the main panel and install a 30-amp double-pole feeder breaker. Run 10/3 feeder cable between the main panel and the subpanel. Or install a 40-amp subpanel and feeder breaker, and use #8 wire. Once your plan is approved, you may receive a permit to do the work.

1
MOUNT THE SUBPANEL
Position the subpanel for easy access but out of reach of small children. Anchor it firmly by driving screws into studs. On a masonry wall drill holes and drive masonry screws. Remove the brass screw in the neutral bus bar when using the box as a subpanel.

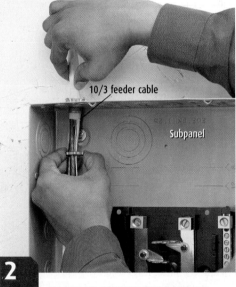

2
CLAMP THE CABLE TO THE SUBPANEL
Ask the building department what kind of feeder cable or conduit to use. Punch out the slug from a knockout. Install a cable clamp in the hole. Strip plenty of sheathing so that the wires can run around the perimeter of the subpanel. Clamp the cable to the box.

Subpanel

3
CONNECT THE WIRES IN THE SUBPANEL

Carefully bend the feeder wires so they run around the perimeter of the subpanel. Run the white wire to the main terminal on the neutral bar and run the ground wire to the ground bar. Run the red and black wires to each of the main terminals on the hot bars. Snip each wire to length and strip off ½ inch of insulation. Poke the wires into the terminals and tighten the setscrews.

Main panel

4
MAKE ROOM FOR THE FEEDER BREAKER IN THE MAIN PANEL

Shut off the main breaker in the main service panel. If you do not have two open slots for the feeder breaker, replace two full-size 15-amp breakers with one quad breaker using the double pole breaker to feed the subpanel. Attach the two circuits that used the replaced breakers to the two single pole breakers in the quad breaker.

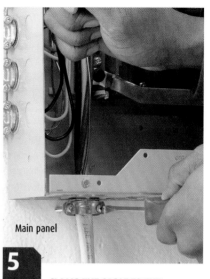

Main panel

5
CLAMP THE CABLE TO THE MAIN PANEL

Run the feeder cable to the service panel. Strip plenty of sheathing, punch out a knockout slug, and clamp the cable.

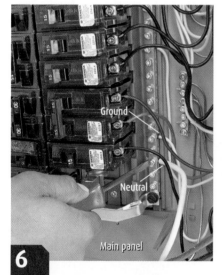

Ground

Neutral

Main panel

6
CONNECT THE GROUND AND NEUTRAL WIRES AT THE MAIN PANEL

Bend the ground wire and the neutral wire around the perimeter of the service panel to open terminals on the neutral bar, and snip them to length. Strip ½ inch of insulation from the neutral wire. Poke the wires into the terminals and tighten the setscrews.

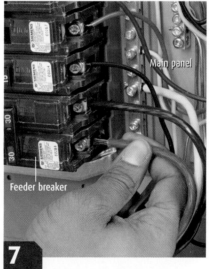

Main panel

Feeder breaker

7
CONNECT THE WIRES TO THE FEEDER BREAKER AT THE MAIN PANEL

Cut the red and black wires to length. Strip ½ inch of insulation from each and connect them to the two setscrew terminals of a double-pole feeder breaker. Snap the feeder breaker into place. Turn off the feeder breaker and turn on the main breaker.

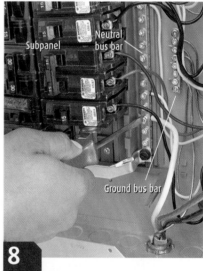

Subpanel

Neutral bus bar

Ground bus bar

8
WIRE NEW BREAKERS TO THE SUBPANEL

Run cable for new circuits into the subpanel. Connect the wires to new circuit breakers as you would in a main service panel (pages 192–193), but connect the neutral and ground wires to separate bus bars. Turn on the feeder breaker in the main panel to energize the subpanel.

13

MAJOR PROJECTS

Wiring a bathroom

Bathrooms are usually small, with only a few electrical fixtures and devices. Because they are damp places, specific code requirements apply. You'll need at least two circuits—one for the lights and one for the receptacles.

A bathroom must have at least one ground fault circuit interrupter (GFCI) receptacle on a 15-amp circuit. The receptacle must not be above the sink, but within 12 inches of it. If the sink has two bowls, place a single receptacle between the bowls or put one receptacle on each side of the sink. Some codes allow bathroom receptacles to share a circuit with another receptacle elsewhere in the house.

Codes usually require a vent fan. Usually a vent fan supplies light as well as ventilation. Unless the fan is very powerful or has a heating unit, a vent fan can share a circuit with other bathroom lights.

All overhead lights must be approved for moist rooms. Install lights over the sink, in the main area, and over the tub/shower. Canadian codes require all bathroom outlets to be GFCI protected. Check your local codes specifying types of lights and installation of them in bathrooms, especially those lights over tubs and showers.

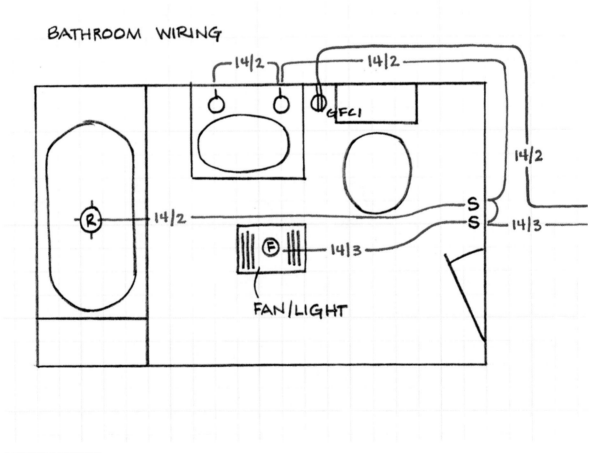

BATHROOM WIRING

A TYPICAL BATHROOM

Only one receptacle is usually needed in a bathroom. Here a single GFCI is on its own 20-amp circuit. One 15-amp circuit supplies waterproof can lights over the tub/shower, the lights beside the mirror, and the fan/light.

If you install a fan/light with a heating unit, it may pull as much as 1,500 watts and will require a separate 20-amp circuit depending on your local codes. Switches are conveniently positioned beside the door.

Wiring a kitchen

A kitchen is the room that has the most electrical devices and fixtures. It's not unusual to have eight or more circuits in a large kitchen, an organizational challenge. Listed below are only a few considerations. If you've taken on creating your own wiring diagram always have it reviewed by your local electrical regulatory authority to confirm that it meets your local codes.

- **Receptacles**: Position small-appliance receptacles over the counter no more than 4 feet apart and a couple of inches above the countertop backsplash. One reason kitchens have many receptacles is to avoid tangles of cords for small appliances. Plan the placement of the toaster, mixer, and other appliances before wiring a kitchen. Islands and peninsulas also need appliance receptacles, which can be mounted on the sides of cabinets. Older microwaves are heavy users of electricity. Many kitchens have a dedicated 20-amp circuit supplying the microwave receptacle. But most new microwaves use far less power

and can be safely plugged into any small-appliance receptacle.

A refrigerator receptacle needs its own 15-amp circuit. Wire a split and switched receptacle (pages 143–144) for the garbage disposer, and place the switch on the wall above the countertop or on a base cabinet. This receptacle has an always-hot outlet that can be used for another appliance.

- **Appliances**: A dishwasher is hardwired, meaning you run cable directly into it. Hardwire a range hood as well (pages 164–166). An electric range needs a 240/120-volt receptacle; however, a gas range needs only a 120-volt receptacle.
- **Lights**: A kitchen with many lights might need more than one 15-amp circuit; add up the kitchen's total wattage to find out. Position switches for maximum convenience. A large kitchen may need three-way switches. Codes in some areas require at least one fluorescent fixture for ambient lighting.

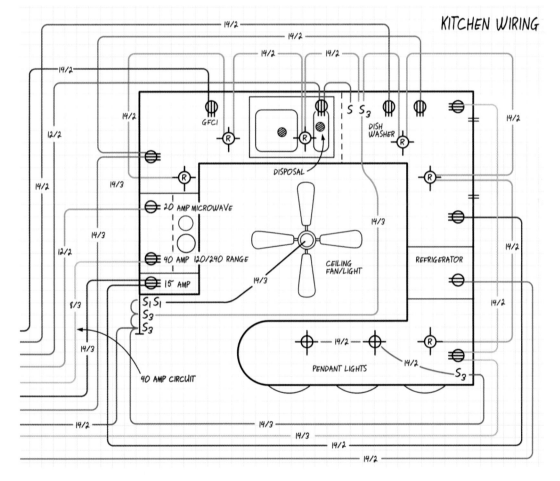

KITCHEN WIRING

13

MAJOR PROJECTS

A MODEST-SIZE KITCHEN

A 15-amp lighting circuit supplies a single ceiling fan/light, pendent lights, and recessed can lights; many lights are controlled by 3-way switches. The dishwasher and disposer share a circuit; the microwave and refrigerator each have their own circuit. Receptacles next to the sink are GFCI

protected. If they're split (page 144), as required in some areas, none could use a GFCI receptacle. The electric range has its own 50-amp, 240-volt circuit. (For a larger kitchen, see pages 110–111.)

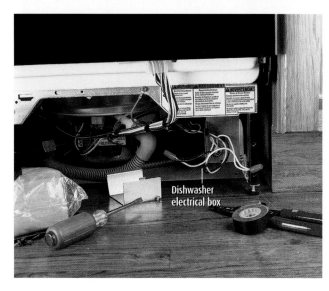

Dishwasher electrical box

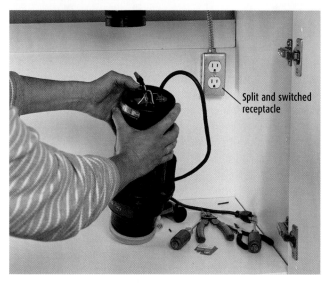

Split and switched receptacle

WIRING A DISHWASHER

Run two-wire cable into the space, leaving plenty of slack. Slide in the dishwasher and connect the plumbing. Remove the electrical cover and clamp the cable to the dishwasher electrical box. Splice white to white, black to black, and connect the ground. Fold back the wires and snap on the cover.

WIRING A GARBAGE DISPOSER

Install a receptacle box in the wall under the sink and a switch box in an easy-to-reach place above the countertop. Wire for a split and switched receptacle (pages 143–144). Remove the electrical cover from the disposer, strip the ends of an appliance cord, and wire the cord to the disposer. After completing plumbing connections, plug the disposer into the switched outlet.

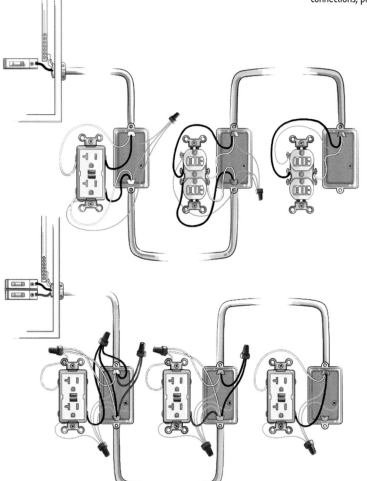

ADDING SMALL-APPLIANCE RECEPTACLES (GFCI TO STANDARD RECEPTACLES)

Depending on your local inspector, you may need to add GFCI protection with a GFCI breaker for receptacles next to kitchen sinks. Some codes allow you to protect a circuit with one GFCI receptacle at the start of the circuit. A GFCI installed at the first box in the run will protect the standard receptacles that follow it as long as the power and neutral wires run "through" the GFCI. Run 12/2 cable from a single-pole 20-amp breaker into the first receptacle box and then on to the other boxes, and install the receptacles as shown. Keep in mind that if local codes require split receptacles, you can't install GFCIs. You may also be limited to how many receptacles you can have on a circuit.

ADDING SMALL-APPLIANCE GFCI RECEPTACLES

If you can, run separate power and neutral wires for alternating circuits. If you have only 12/3 cable, use the pigtails and GFCIs at each outlet as shown so that you don't have to run new cable. Here the receptacles are wired from a double-pole breaker in an alternating pattern (page 144), with every other receptacle on the red wire and the others on the black wire. The white wire connects to all the receptacles. This arrangement allows you to install GFCIs. Keep in mind that if local codes require split receptacles, you can't install GFCIs. Your local codes may also limit the number of receptacles you can have on a circuit for appliances.

Wiring a bedroom

Most bedrooms have either an overhead switched light or one switched receptacle, plus a receptacle or two on each wall. You can go beyond the basic necessities and supply your bedroom with electrical service to outfit a small office or to add a few creature comforts. **NOTE: AFCIs (Arc Fault circuit Interrupters, page 76) have been required since January 2002 to be installed for each bedroom receptacle circuit.**

■ **Receptacles:** Codes typically allow bedroom receptacles to be up to 12 feet apart. If you cut this distance in half, you'll improve receptacle accessibility and give yourself more options for arranging bedroom furniture. To provide a computer with maximum protection against power surges, wire an isolated-ground receptacle. For comfortable TV viewing while in bed, install a wall bracket for a TV with a nearby receptacle, about 6½ feet above the floor.

Avoid placing a receptacle directly below a window: It may get wet if the window is open during a rainstorm. If you use a window air-conditioner, install a receptacle near the window. An average window unit does not pull heavy amperage, so you can use a 15-amp receptacle but it must have its own circuit. A heavy-duty air-conditioner may need a dedicated 20-amp receptacle.

■ **Lights:** To control an overhead fan/light, run three-wire cable from the ceiling box to the switch box and install a fan/light switch (page 95). Consider installing three-way switches at the door and by the bed for convenience. Or install a remote-control switch (page 95). Place a reading lamp at both sides of the bed, each with its own switch.

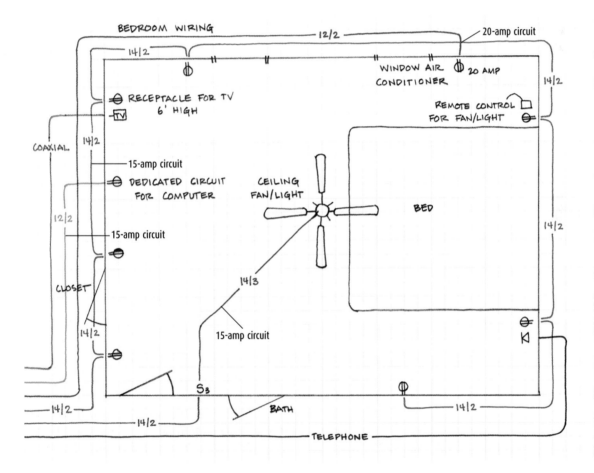

A MULTIUSE BEDROOM

Separate reading lights on each side of the bed each have conveniently placed switches. A receptacle with its own dedicated circuit guards a computer against damage caused by power surges (page 82). A receptacle 6 feet from the floor supplies power to a wall-mounted TV and VCR, and eliminates unsightly dangling cords. The fan/light is controlled by a wall switch and a remote control. (Wire the fan and light separately, using the three-way wiring described on pages 148–150.) A receptacle placed higher than usual near the window accommodates a window air-conditioner.

Wiring a laundry room

I n a laundry room receptacles that feed the washing machine, gas dryer, and other appliances must be on 20-amp circuits that are not used by any other room. The receptacles must be ground fault circuit interrupter (GFCI) protected.

If the dryer is electric, you also will need a 30-amp, 120/240-volt receptacle. Use 10-gauge wire and connect the dryer directly to a 30-amp, 240-volt breaker or fuse (page 145). In this example the washer is on its own circuit.

Because these machines vibrate, fasten the wiring securely. Local codes may allow NM or armored cable, but conduit is more secure. See pages 122–124 for conduit installation instructions.

Laundry room lights don't need their own circuits. But you shouldn't put them on circuits other than receptacle circuits so you won't be without light if a faulty appliance causes a circuit overload.

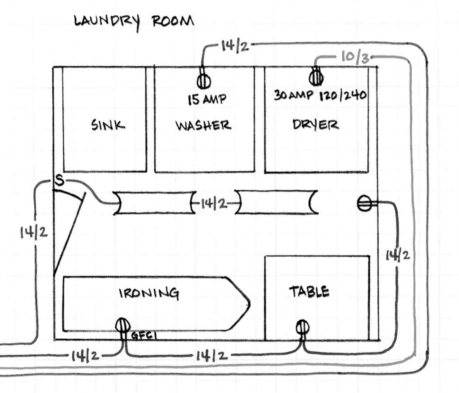

CLOSER LOOK

LIGHTING CLOSETS AND STORAGE SPACES
The days of exposed lightbulbs on pull-chain switches are past. Lights in closets, attics, crawlspaces, and other storage areas must now be recessed or enclosed, controlled by wall switches, and positioned at least 18 inches away from flammable materials. Wherever there is equipment that must be serviced—such as a sump pump or a water heater—there must be a light controlled by a wall switch.

A HARDWORKING LAUNDRY AREA
The dryer has a dedicated 30-amp, 240-volt circuit, and the washer has its own 20-amp, 120-volt circuit. Because this area could become damp, use ground fault circuit interrupter (GFCI) receptacles throughout (page 74). Fluorescent lights are on a 15-amp circuit, which they may share with lights in other rooms.

Electric baseboard heaters

A n electric baseboard heater can get heat into a cold part of the house. But head for the breaker box first because a new heater requires a new circuit, and you want to make sure you have room for it. You will need at least one empty spot on the panel. Two are better. If there's no room for an extra circuit, find another way to heat the cold spot. Code requires an electric heater to have its own circuit, and even if it didn't, combining it with an existing circuit would overload the breakers every time the heat came on.

You can attach an electric heater against plaster, drywall, wallpaper, or wood paneling. If you want to attach to another surface, consult the manufacturer's instructions.

Use the gauge wire recommended for the amount of power the heater requires. The directions here are for a 240-volt heater, which is both the most efficient and the most common. Regardless of the amount of electricity the heater will draw, consult the manufacturer's recommendations for installation and check with your local electrical regulatory authority to ensure your following proper safety and installation procedures.

Be sure that you have room in the breaker box for a new circuit before you decide to install a new heater.

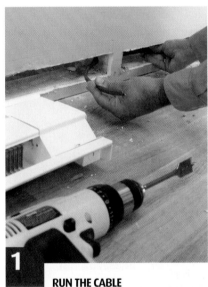

1 RUN THE CABLE
If you're using a heater with a built-in thermostat, run 12/2 cable from the heater to the service panel. See page 129 for running cable behind a baseboard. Leave about 2 extra feet of cable at the heater. Run the cable to the panel, leaving the cable long enough to run around the perimeter to the breaker and the bus bars.

IF YOU'RE USING A WALL-MOUNTED THERMOSTAT, THE CABLE FROM THE BREAKER PANEL WON'T RUN DIRECTLY TO THE HEATER.
Run the cable to where the thermostat will be and run a second length of cable from there to the heater. Feed both through a junction box and install it, marking the wires so that you know which is which.

2 WIRE THE HEATER
Remove the knockout in the back of the heater by giving it a sharp blow with the blade of a screwdriver. Put in a connector—a type of clamp required by code to prevent the edge of the box from accidentally shorting out the cable. Strip about 12 inches of sheathing. Fish it through the connector and tighten the clamp around the end of the outer insulation.

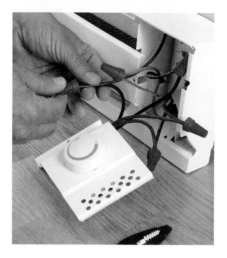

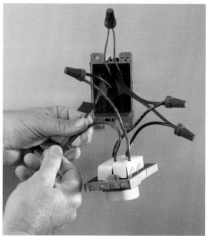

3

MOUNT THE HEATER

Line up the holes in the back of the heater with the studs. Push any extra cable inside the wall, then screw the heater in place as directed by the manufacturer. (Accessing the screw holes sometimes involves removing a part or two.)

OPTION A: IF YOU'RE USING A BUILT-IN THERMOSTAT

Usually the incoming black and white supply wires connect to two red wires on the thermostat. The two black wires on the thermostat connect to the two black heater wires that were twisted together. On a 240-volt circuit like the one shown here, the white wire is hot, and code requires you to mark it with a piece of black tape as a reminder.

OPTION B: IF YOU ARE USING A WALL-MOUNTED THERMOSTAT

Use a double-pole, 240-volt thermostat designed for baseboard heaters; a standard low-voltage thermostat will burn up. The double-pole switch in the thermostat shuts off power to both 120-volt lines that make up the 240 volts going to the heater. Use a larger capacity box to hold the bigger thermostat. Wire the thermostat as directed by the manufacturers instructions. Connect the grounds.

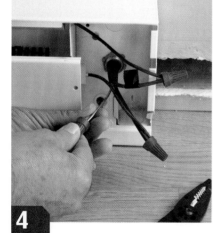

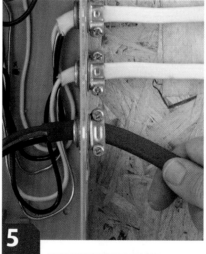

4

WIRE THE HEATER

The bare wire coming into the heater is connected to a green ground screw in the heater. If you have cable that has white and black wires as opposed to red and black, mark the white wire with black tape to show anyone working on it in the future that the wire is hot.

5

RUN CABLE TO THE PANEL

See pages 192–193 for instructions on installing a new breaker. Punch out a new knockout in the side of the service panel, and install a cable clamp. Run the ground wire to the ground bar (or the neutral bar if there is no ground bar). Attach the black and white wires to the breakers, or to the two terminals of a double breaker. Wrap black tape around the insulation of the white wire to show that it's hot.

6

ATTACH TO THE BREAKER

A 240-volt circuit requires a double pole breaker. Screw the black wire into one of the breakers; screw the white wire into the other and mark it with a piece of black tape. To install a breaker, put the tab on one end of the breakers under the notch for it. Bring the other end down onto the other tab and press until it snaps into place. Screw the bare ground wire to the ground bus bar. Restore power and test.

13

MAJOR PROJECTS

Electrical repairs

When electrical devices and fixtures no longer work, often the logical solution is to replace rather than repair them. Switches, receptacles, lamps, and overhead lights may not cost enough to warrant the time it takes to diagnose and repair them.

Some repairs, however, take only minutes. You may be able to get your lamp to work again just by pulling up the tab on the light socket (see page 204). If you have a valuable antique lamp or overhead light—a treasured part of your home—you certainly have a vested interest in getting it back into working order.

Fixing lamp sockets

PROJECT DETAILS

SKILLS: Testing for continuity, attaching wires to terminals
PROJECT: Testing and replacing a table lamp socket

TIME TO COMPLETE

EXPERIENCED: 15 min.
HANDY: 30 min.
NOVICE: 1 hr.

STUFF YOU'LL NEED

TOOLS: Screwdriver and a continuity tester or multitester
MATERIALS: New socket if needed, electrician's tape

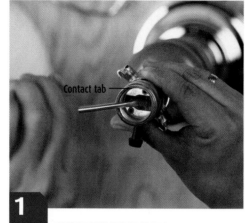

1 PRY UP THE CONTACT TAB

Unplug the lamp and remove the bulb. If the contact tab is corroded or rusty, scrape it with a screwdriver. If the tab lies flat, it may not be making solid contact with the base of the bulb. Gently pry up the tab about ⅛ inch and retest. If the lamp still doesn't work, go to the next step.

Contact tab

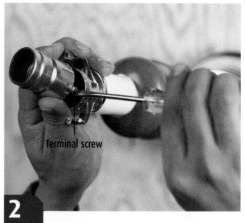

2 REMOVE THE SOCKET

Look for the word PRESS on the socket shell. Push there with your thumb as you squeeze the shell and wiggle it up and out. If there is a cardboard sleeve, remove it too. Loosen the two terminal screws and pull out the socket.

Terminal screw

Connect the ridged (neutral) wire to the silver terminal and the smooth (hot) wire to the brass terminal.

I f a lamp doesn't work, eliminate the obvious causes first. Make sure the lamp is plugged in. Make sure the bulb is OK. A burned-out bulb usually makes a tinkling sound when you shake it. Screw in a fresh bulb if necessary.

Check that the receptacle's circuit hasn't blown a fuse or popped a breaker. If the lamp still doesn't work, test by plugging in a lamp that you know is in working order. If it lights up you've isolated the problem to the lamp itself. Before replacing the cord or switch, take a look at the socket.

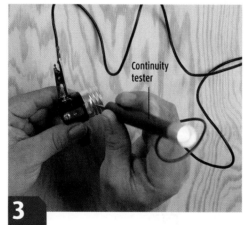

3 TEST THE SOCKET AND SWITCH

Test the socket with a continuity tester (shown) or a multitester (pages 30–31). Touch one probe to the neutral (silver) screw and the other to the threaded metal of the socket. If the tester bulb doesn't light, replace the socket. If the socket has a switch, touch the clips to the brass terminal and to the contact tab. If the switch is defective, replace it. If it is not test the cord and plug (page 206–207).

Continuity tester

4 REPLACE THE SOCKET

You may need to loosen a small setscrew in order to unscrew the old socket base. Install the new base, threading the cord carefully so you don't nick the insulation. Tie the wires with an underwriters knot as shown. Twist the strands together with your fingers, and form a partial loop. Wrap each wire clockwise around a terminal, and tighten its terminal screw. Slip on the cardboard sleeve, and snap down the socket shell into position.

Underwriters knot

14

ELECTRICAL REPAIRS

Replacing lamp switches

PROJECT DETAILS

SKILLS: Testing for power, splicing wires

PROJECT: Replacing and wiring a lamp or fixture switch

TIME TO COMPLETE

EXPERIENCED: 15 min.
HANDY: 30 min.
NOVICE: 45 min.

STUFF YOU'LL NEED

TOOLS: Voltage tester, wire strippers, pliers
MATERIALS: New switch, electrician's tape, wire nuts

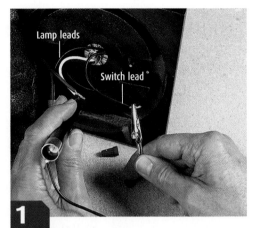

1

TEST THE SWITCH

Unplug the lamp. Remove the bottom of the lamp to access the wiring. Remove one of the wire nuts that connects a lead from the switch to the lamp wires. Clip one probe of a continuity tester to the switch lead and the other to the lamp wires. Try the switch several times. If the continuity detector doesn't light, the switch is defective.

2

REPLACE THE SWITCH

Unscrew the switch retaining nut—you may need to use pliers. Unravel the wires, then pull out the switch. If the wires on the lamp are damaged, snip off the stripped portion and restrip the insulation. Insert the switch into the hole, and tightly screw in the retaining nut. Splice the switch leads to the lamp, and twist on the wire nuts.

A toggle, pull-chain, or twist switch is not an integral part of the lamp or the fixture on which it's mounted. It's an inexpensive switch that can be easily replaced—and may need to be replaced yearly, if heavily used.

There's one universal hole size, so you can interchange twist switches with toggles or pull-chains.

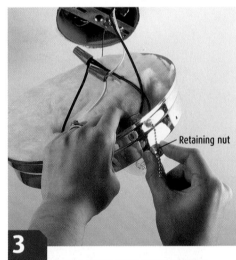

3

REPLACING A PULL-CHAIN SWITCH

Test a switch like this (common on ceiling lights and fans) in the same way as a toggle or twist switch. It mounts with a retaining nut. Some porcelain ceiling fixtures have built-in switches; these can't be repaired.

WORK SMARTER

WIRING A THREE-LEVEL SWITCH
If a fixture-mounted switch powers a light or fan at more than one level, the wiring is more complicated. If the switch has more than two leads, **carefully tag the lamp or fixture wires with pieces of marked tape** so you know which wire goes where when you install the replacement. **Take the old switch with you** to the hardware store or home center to buy an exact replacement.

14

ELECTRICAL REPAIRS

Rewiring lamps

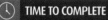
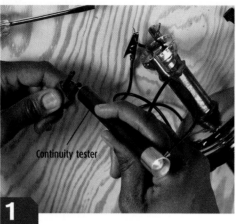

Continuity tester

1

TEST WIRES FOR CONTINUITY

With the socket removed (page 204), touch the probes of a continuity tester or multitester (pages 30–31) to the end of the ridged (neutral) wire and the wide prong of the plug. Then touch the probes to the smooth (hot) wire and the narrow prong. If either test fails to show continuity, replace the cord and plug. If the prongs are the same size, test each wire with both prongs. The meter should show continuity on one prong only.

Wiring lamps is easy work. Electricity travels up through the lamp body through a cord until it reaches the socket. If the tests show that the socket works OK (page 204), the problem is probably with the cord. Don't repair a section of a cord: Cord splices never look good and they unravel easily. Install a new replacement lamp cord, which has a molded plug.

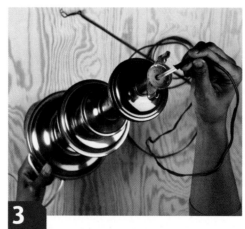

3

PULL THE NEW CORD THROUGH

This step is easier with a helper. While pulling up on the old cord at the top of the lamp, feed the new cord into the hole at the base. If the tape gets stuck, pull the cord out and wrap the tape more tightly. Keep pulling until the new cord emerges from the top. Unwrap the tape. Tie an underwriters knot and connect the new cord to the socket (page 204).

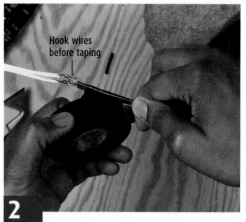

Hook wires before taping

2

TO PULL THE NEW CORD THROUGH THE LAMP, HOOK THE NEW CORD TO THE OLD

Cut the old cord about 8 inches past the lamp base. Strip the ends of the old and new cords. Twist all the strands clockwise with your fingers so that no strands are loose. Bend the old wires and the new wires. Hook them together as shown. Wrap the joint tightly with electrician's tape.

SAFETY ALERT

EXTRACTING A BROKEN BULB

If a bulb is broken and stuck in the socket, don't try to unscrew it by hand. **Unplug the lamp. Press a potato onto the broken glass and then twist.** Or insert the end of a wooden broom handle into the middle of the socket and twist.

14

ELECTRICAL REPAIRS

Repairing a two-socket lamp

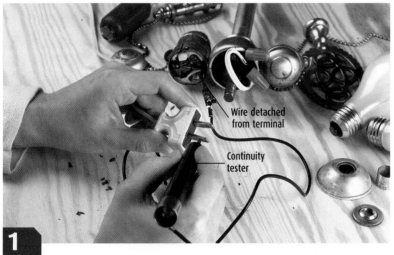

Wire detached from terminal

Continuity tester

1 REMOVE THE COVER AND TEST THE LAMP

If a lamp has two or more sockets and only one doesn't operate, test and replace the defective one as you would a one-socket lamp (page 204). Remove the cover plate and make sure the wire connections are tight. With the lamp switch on, use a multitester or continuity tester to check for continuity (pages 30–31). If only one socket fails to light, the wire between the splice and the socket is probably the culprit. If all the sockets fail to work, then the cord between the plug and the splice is bad.

Two leads of one cord

2 REWIRE THE LAMP

Replace one cord at a time. For the sockets cut and strip pieces of cord to the length of the old pieces. Connect the ridged (neutral) wire to the silver socket terminal and the smooth (hot) wire to the brass terminal. When splicing always connect ridged wire to ridged and smooth to smooth.

Dividing and stripping lamp cord

1 DIVIDING THE LAMP CORD

Separate part of a lamp cord into two wires before making connections. Stick the tip of a knife blade into the little valley between the two cords, and push down until it jabs firmly into the work surface below.

Wire strippers

2 STRIPPING THE LAMP CORD

Pull the cord—not the knife—to separate the wires. Once you have made this cut, pull the wires farther apart if needed. Use wire strippers to remove insulation. Work carefully so that you don't pull off more than a couple of wire strands with the insulation.

 **WORK SMARTER**

A LAMP REWIRE KIT

Some lamps have special components—such as washers or plastic stoppers. Replace them while you are rewiring. A lamp rewire kit contains the cord with plug and the little parts unique to that kind of lamp. The kit shown is for a bottle-type lamp.

Repairing pendent fixtures

Regular flush-mounted ceiling fixtures rarely need repair, and when they do, the wiring is straightforward. Pendent fixtures or chandeliers, however, often have a tangle of wires running through narrow tubes. When old insulation cracks, pendent lights start to fail and sparks may fly.

If one wire has brittle insulation, replace all the wires; the others are just as old.

If only one light malfunctions, turn off the switch and test its socket. Replace the socket if it is defective (page 204).

To get ready, **shut off power to the circuit at the service panel.** Have a helper hold the fixture, or bend the ends of a coat hanger to support it. Loosen the screws holding the canopy in place.

1

OPEN THE FIXTURE
Slide down the canopy. Pull out and separate the wires. Carefully remove the wire nuts. **Test for the presence of power in the box (pages 30–31). If any wires are live, shut off the correct circuit.** Disconnect the wires and take down the fixture. Remove the cover near the bottom of the fixture to expose the connections.

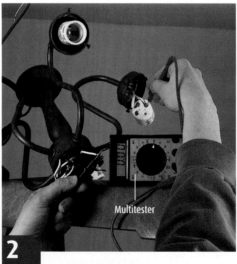

2

TEST THE SOCKET WIRES
If some of the sockets do not light, test each wire for continuity. To find out which cord goes where, tug on the cord at the socket end while holding the wires at the base. Unscrew the wire nuts at the base, and test both the ridged (neutral) wire and the smooth wire for continuity. If you do not get a positive reading for both wires, replace the cord. Test and repair all malfunctioning light sockets.

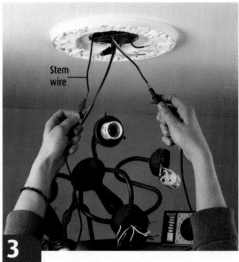

3

TEST THE STEM WIRES
If all the lights fail to come on, the stem wires probably need replacing. To make sure twist the stem wires together at the base. Touch tester probes to both wires at the top of the fixture. If no continuity is indicated, replace the stem wires as shown on page 206. If light still fails to come on, test the wires from the ceiling box as shown above.

Replacing plugs and switches

PROJECT DETAILS

SKILLS: Stripping wire, dividing cord, attaching wire to terminals
PROJECT: Replacing one plug or adding one cord switch

TIME TO COMPLETE

EXPERIENCED: 5 min.
HANDY: 15 min.
NOVICE: 30 min.

STUFF YOU'LL NEED

TOOLS: Wire strippers, utility knife, screwdriver
MATERIALS: Replacement plug or cord switch

Installing flat replacement plugs

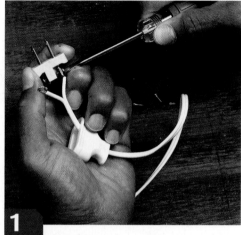

1 JOIN THE WIRES TO A FLAT REPLACEMENT PLUG

Cut the cord near the old plug. Slide the cord through the replacement plug body. Separate and strip the cord wires (page 207). Twist the wire strands tightly with your fingers, and wrap the strands clockwise around the core terminals connecting the side of the wire with ridges to the wider prong. Tighten the screws.

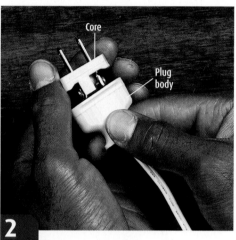

Core

Plug body

2 SNAP ON THE BODY

Make sure the connections to the terminals are tight. Hold the core with one hand and push the body onto it with the other hand until the two pieces snap together.

A plug with loose prongs or a cracked body is dangerous and should be replaced. If the cord and the plug are damaged, rewire the lamp or appliance with a one-piece cord and plug (page 206). If only the plug is damaged, save yourself the chore of rewiring the entire device by using one of the replacement plugs shown here.

Note that lamp cords have ridges on one wire. These ridges allow you to preserve the polarity of the existing wiring. Rewire the new cord with the ridged side attached to the same wire in the lamp or appliance.

A cord switch (see page 210), which is almost as easy to install, is ideal for lamps that have hard-to-reach switches. You can add a cord switch in minutes.

Installing a quick-connect plug

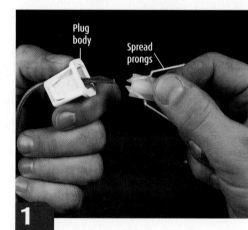

Plug body

Spread prongs

1 INSERT THE WIRES

With this type of plug, you do not have to divide or strip the cord. Cut off the old plug. Thread the cord through the plug body. Spread the prongs apart, and push the cord into the core. Connect the ridged (neutral) wire to the wider prong.

2 SQUEEZE AND SLIDE TOGETHER

Squeeze the prongs together so they bite down on the cord. While still squeezing slip the body onto the core until it snaps into place.

14

ELECTRICAL REPAIRS

Installing a grounded round plug

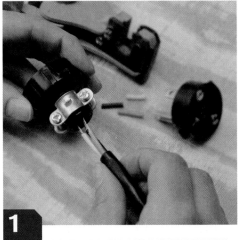

1 **STRIP THE CABLE AND INSERT THE WIRES INTO THE PLUG BODY**

If you are replacing an old plug, cut the old cord near the plug. Separate the replacement plug core and body. Use a wire stripper or a utility knife to strip 1½ inches of sheathing, being careful not to nick the insulation of the three wires inside. Strip about ½ inch of insulation from each of the wires. Thread the cord through the new plug body.

2 **MAKE THE CONNECTIONS**

Twist the wires together with your fingers so there are no loose strands. Wrap each wire clockwise around a terminal on the core: black wire to the brass terminal, white wire to the silver terminal, and green wire to the round green grounding terminal. Tighten the screws, snap the body onto the core, and tighten the clamp screws to the cord to secure the plug to the cable.

SAFETY ALERT

RATE THE WIDTH OF YOUR APPLIANCE CORDS

Most lamp cords are a standard thickness, but appliance cords vary. **When you buy an appliance cord, make sure it is rated to handle the appliance amperage (page 49).** A cord that's too thin will dangerously overheat. To see whether a cord needs to be replaced, bend it at several points. If the insulation cracks or feels like it's about to crack, replace the cord.

$ BUYER'S GUIDE

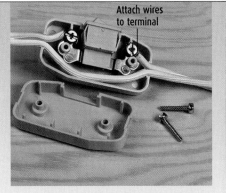

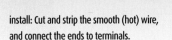

Push uncut wire into channel

Clip one wire

Attach wires to terminal

QUICK-INSTALL CORD SWITCHES

Choose the location of the switch carefully: You won't be able to move it after it is installed. An inexpensive **rotating switch** will not last long if the switch is used daily but **is fine for occasional use.** To install one, use a utility knife to cut a 1-inch-long slit to divide the cord; then snip the smooth (hot) wire,

but do not strip it. Insert the wire into the switch, and screw the two halves of the switch together.

A **rocker switch is more solidly built** and will last longer. It will fit with a flat lamp cord or a round appliance cord. It takes a few minutes longer to

install: Cut and strip the smooth (hot) wire, and connect the ends to terminals.

A **toe-button switch is ideal for torchiers** and plant lights that are otherwise hard to reach. It installs like on-cord rotating and rocker switches.

14

ELECTRICAL REPAIRS

Repairing fluorescents

Fluorescent lights use less energy and last longer than incandescent lights, but they can be finicky to repair. The greatest challenge can be finding the right replacement parts. Starters will need replacing on older fixtures (newer fixtures don't need them). Consider replacing starters when you replace tubes. Sockets can loosen or crack; ballasts are particularly troublesome and expensive to replace. Save yourself time and trouble by taking down the fixture to repair it on a bench.

Troubleshooting

A flickering or partially lighted tube is the most common problem. Take these steps to troubleshoot:
■ Rotate the tube for a better connection.
■ Replace the starter.
■ Replace the ballast or the fixture.

If a tube has very dark spots at either end:
■ Replace it, even if it works. It may cause the ballast to wear out.

If the tube does not light at all:
■ Rotate the tube to get a better connection.
■ Check the ballast for a temperature rating. Some fixtures will not start in cold or hot temperatures.
■ Make sure the circuit is getting power. Test, then replace the wall switch (pages 66–67) if necessary.
■ Replace the tube, especially if it's dark at the ends or if a pin is bent.
■ Replace the socket if it is cracked or if the tube does not seat tightly.
■ Replace the ballast or the fixture.

If the ballast hums:
■ Try turning off a nearby radio or heavy-use electrical appliance.
■ Tighten the ballast-mounting screws.
■ Replace the ballast.

If the ballast is oozing a thick black substance:
■ Replace the fixture or, wearing protective gloves, replace the ballast.

BUYER'S GUIDE

FIX OR REPLACE?
New fluorescent light fixtures are fairly inexpensive and will likely last longer than a new ballast or starter. If the old fixture is easy to remove and a new fixture will easily install in the same location, you may choose to replace rather than repair the fixture.

CLOSER LOOK

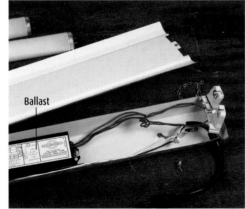

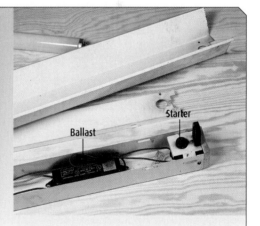

KNOW YOUR FIXTURE
It takes an initial burst of high voltage to light a fluorescent tube. Once it's lit, the voltage is cut back because the tube can "coast" on very little current. The ballast, a transformer, initially steps up the voltage and then reduces it after the tube is lit. In older models the ballast is a bulky and heavy rectangular object. Newer models have electronic ballasts. In a rapid-start fixture (above left), the ballast performs this two-level delivery of power. In a starter-type fixture (above), a small cylindrical starter acts as a switch, sending a greater amount of current to the tube until it lights.

14

ELECTRICAL REPAIRS

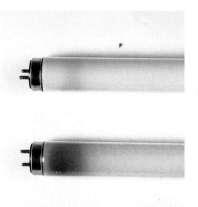

SIGNS OF TUBE WEAR

If a tube suddenly stops lighting and is not blackened at the ends, gently rotate it while the fixture is turned on and see whether that brings it back to life. Gray spots near the ends of a tube (top) are signs of normal aging. If the ends are black or dark gray (bottom), you should replace the tube. If a fixture has two tubes, always replace both at the same time.

REPLACING A TUBE

To remove a tube hold it at each end and twist carefully until you feel it loosen. Remove it, being careful not to damage the tube pins or the sockets. Replace it with a tube of the same size and wattage. With dual lamps replace both tubes at the same time to so the fixture emits even light.

REPLACING A STARTER

If it takes more than a few seconds for a starter-type fixture to light up, remove the tube and twist the starter to see whether you can seat the starter more firmly. If the ends of a tube light up but the center doesn't, replace the starter. Press in the starter and twist counterclockwise to remove it. Buy a starter with the same part number as the old one. Push in and twist clockwise to install it.

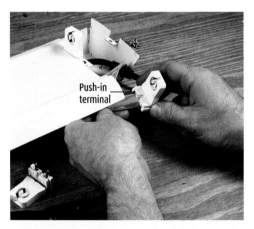

REAL WORLD

EASY DOES IT
When installing a replacement socket for a fixture, do not be too aggressive when poking the wires into the push-in terminals. If the wires are pushed in too hard, it may cause the insulated part (rather than the stripped part) of the wire to connect to the terminal. No connection. No light. Push until it can be felt that the socket grabs the stripped wire.

REPLACING A SOCKET

These crack easily, especially if you are not careful when removing or installing a tube. Unscrew the bracket holding the socket in place, or slide the socket out of the groove. If the socket has push-in terminals, poke the slot to release the wire. If the socket has attached wires, cut the wires and strip off about ½ inch of insulation. Install a new socket with push-in terminals or screw terminals.

REPLACING A BALLAST

Shut off power to the circuit supplying the light, and check for the presence of power. Disconnect the wires if possible. If it's not possible, cut them close to the ballast. Either way tag the remaining wires so you'll remember which wire goes where. Unscrew the ballast and take it to a home center or electrical supply store for a replacement. Install the new ballast in just the same way as the old one was installed. You may prefer to replace the fixture entirely.

Repairing wires in boxes

PROJECT DETAILS

SKILLS: Wrapping tape around wires in tight spots
PROJECT: Taking measures to safeguard several wires in a box

TIME TO COMPLETE

EXPERIENCED: 10 min.
HANDY: 30 min.
NOVICE: 45 min.

STUFF YOU'LL NEED

TOOLS: Screwdriver
MATERIALS: Electrician's tape, BX bushings

You open a box in your older home and find old wiring with insulation that is cracked and frayed. Very likely, all the hidden wires in the house are in equally bad shape. What can you do?

Rewiring is the safest solution. It is not too big a job if all the wires run through conduit or Greenfield flexible conduit (pages 122–124), but many homes are wired with cable. Replacing cable means making holes in walls, followed by time-consuming, expensive patching and redecorating.

Wires wrapped tightly in cable are likely to be in better condition than wires exposed to air. Insert a plastic bushing and tape the wires to protect the circuit until you rewire. Better yet protect the wire with a hot-shrink sleeve (right).

While the box is open, take the following precautions as well. A box recessed behind the wall surface poses a fire danger and is out of code. Slip in a box extender (below right), and add the cover plate. Debris that collects in an electrical box, especially sawdust, poses a fire hazard; vacuum it out immediately.

Hot-shrink sleeve

Heat gun

SHRINK ON NEW INSULATION

If a wire has cracked, brittle, or otherwise damaged insulation, buy a small bag of plastic sleeves made to protect wires. **Shut off power to the circuit.** Disconnect the damaged wire and slip a sleeve down over it. Point a hair dryer or heat gun at the sleeve until it shrinks, forming a long-lasting protective coating.

🔍 CLOSER LOOK

LEAKY WIRES

Wiring with cracked insulation can leak small amounts of electricity. Known as a high-resistance short circuit, this power loss won't blow a fuse or trip a breaker, but it can overheat wires. To test for this problem, completely shut down the house. Remove all lightbulbs, unplug all lamps and appliances, and disconnect hardwired appliances such as electric water heaters and whole-house fans. **Turn on all the switches. Then watch your electric meter.** If it shows power usage, then you have a high-resistance short.

Test circuits one by one to narrow down the source of the leak. It may be a bad connection or damaged wire insulation in an electrical box. If you can't find the source, call in a professional.

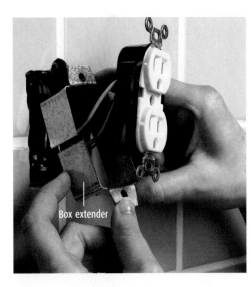

Box extender

EXTEND A RECESSED BOX

If a box is recessed from a wall surface, there is a danger of fire—especially if the wall surface is wood paneling. However, even tile edges or drywall should be covered. Purchase a box extender sized to fit your box, and slip it on.

14

ELECTRICAL REPAIRS

Troubleshooting a door chime

A doorbell or chime system is supplied with low-voltage power—between 8 and 24 volts—by a transformer. When the button is pressed, the circuit closes and sends power to the chime or bell.

Fixing common problems

Because the voltage associated with doorbells and chimes is low, there is no need to shut off power unless you are working on the transformer. Here's how to troubleshoot most problems.

■ **If a bell or chime develops a fuzzy sound,** remove the chime cover and vacuum out any dust and debris and brush off the bell or chimes.

■ **If you get only one tone** when the front (or only) button is pushed, check the wiring in the chime to see that the button is connected to the "front." On many two-button systems, the chime is supposed to "ding dong" when the front button is pushed, and only "ding" when the rear button is pushed.

■ **If the chime suddenly stops working** at the same time you blow a fuse or trip a breaker, restore power to the circuit supplying the transformer.

■ **If the chime stops working altogether,** conduct a systematic investigation, moving from the simplest to the most complex repairs. First check out the button(s), then the chime, and then the transformer. If none of these reveals a problem, the wiring may be damaged.

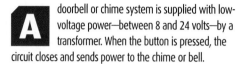

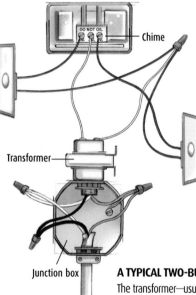

Chime

Transformer

Junction box

1

EXAMINE THE BUTTON
Remove the screws holding the button in place, and gently pull out the button. (Make sure the wires do not slide back into the hole.) Clean away any debris, cocoons, or corrosion, and tighten the terminal screws. If either wire is broken, restrip it then reconnect it. Retest the button.

A TYPICAL TWO-BUTTON SETUP
The transformer—usually located in an out-of-the-way spot such as the basement, crawlspace, or cabinet interior—sends low-voltage power to the chime. There one wire is connected to the chime. Another wire is spliced to two different wires, each of which travels through a button and back to the chime. When either button is pressed, the circuit is completed, power travels to the chime, and the chime rings.

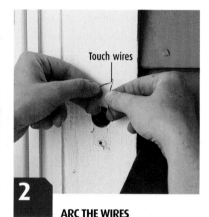

Touch wires

2

ARC THE WIRES
If the button still doesn't work, loosen the terminal screws and remove the wires. Holding each wire by its insulation, touch the bare ends together. If the chime sounds, the button is faulty and needs to be replaced. If you see or hear a tiny spark but the chime does not sound, the chime may be faulty (Step 3). If there is no sound and no spark, check the transformer (Step 4).

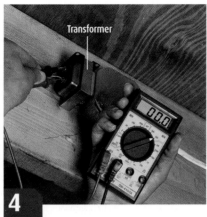

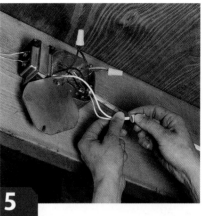

3

TEST THE CHIME

Remove the chime cover and ensure that all the wires are securely connected to the terminals. Vacuum out any dust and scrape away any corrosion near the terminals. When you pull back a plunger and release it, the chime should sound. If not, clean any greasy buildup that may gum up the springs. If the chime still does not work, touch the probes of a multitester to the "front" and "trans" terminals, and to the "rear" and "trans" terminals. If power is present within two volts of the chime's printed voltage rating, then the chime is faulty and should be replaced.

4

TEST THE TRANSFORMER

Follow the bell wires and look for an exposed electrical box with the transformer attached. Touch the probes of a multitester to both transformer terminals. If you get a reading of more than 2 volts below the transformer rating, the transformer is faulty and should be replaced.

5

REPLACING A TRANSFORMER

Purchase a transformer with the same voltage rating as the old one. Shut off power to the circuit and open the adjacent junction box. Label the bell wires and disconnect them. Disconnect the transformer leads inside the junction box and disconnect the transformer. Thread the new transformer leads into the junction box, fasten the transformer to the box, and splice the leads to the wires. Connect the bell wires, restore power, and test.

Installing wireless chimes

INSTALLING THE CHIME

Rather than going through the trouble of replacing defective bell wire, buy a wireless chime system. Installation is easy: Plug the chime into a standard receptacle, power the button with a battery, and attach the button to the house.

ADDING A WIRELESS CHIME TO AN EXISTING CHIME SYSTEM

If you can't hear your door chime everywhere in your home, add a wireless chime to your wired system. Remove the cover from the existing chime and loosen the terminal screws. Take the leads of the wireless chime's sending unit and insert them under the screws. Tighten the screws. Using its double-sided tape, stick the sending unit to the chime housing. Plug the wireless chime into a receptacle.

$ BUYER'S GUIDE

REPLACING A CHIME

Purchase a chime with the same voltage rating as your transformer. It should be at least as large as the old chime so that you don't have to paint the wall around it. Label the wires with pieces of tape, unscrew the terminal screws, and remove the wires. Remove the screws holding the chime to the wall and pull it away. Thread the wires through the new chime and fasten the chime to the wall. Connect the wires to the terminals.

14

ELECTRICAL REPAIRS

Troubleshooting a thermostat

The round, low-voltage unit featured in most of these pictures is the most common type of thermostat in use. Yours may be rectangular, but its functions are the same.

If your furnace or air-conditioner fails to operate, check the thermostat for mechanical problems. The cover may be jammed in too far, disrupting the mechanism. A wire may have broken or come loose. Or the parts may be covered with dust, inhibiting electrical contact.

If cleaning and adjusting do not solve the problem, replacing a thermostat is an easy job. Consider installing a programmable unit for more control options. Remember that a thermostat contains mercury, so dispose of it properly.

CHECKING A LINE-VOLTAGE THERMOSTAT

If your thermostat uses household current, **always shut off power to the circuit before pulling it out.** If it fails, disconnect it and take it to a dealer for service or replacement.

REVIEWING THE ANATOMY OF A LOW-VOLTAGE THERMOSTAT

Thin wires come from a transformer and connect to the thermostat base. You'll probably find one wire for the transformer, one for heat, one for air-conditioning, and one for a fan. (A heat pump uses six or more wires and has a special thermostat. Contact a dealer for repairs.) **To protect circuitry shut off power before you start to work.**

WORK SMARTER

SEAL OFF DRAFTS

Even if your thermostat is on an interior wall, air coming through a hole behind it may throw its temperature readings out of whack, resulting in erratic heating. Remove the thermostat base from the wall and fill the hole with insulation or caulk.

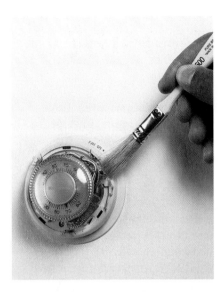

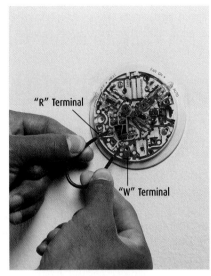

CLEANING THE CONTACTS WITH A BRUSH
Pull off the outer cover and use a soft, clean, dry brush to remove dust from the bimetal coil. Turn the dial to get at all the nooks and crannies.

CLEANING THE SWITCH CONTACTS
Remove the screws holding the thermostat body and pull out the body. Gently pull back on the fan control lever, slip a piece of white bond paper behind it, and slide the paper back and forth to clean the contact behind it. Do the same for the mode control lever, if there is one.

CONDUCTING A HOT-WIRE TEST
If heat does not come on, test to see if power is getting to the thermostat. Cut a short length of wire and strip both ends. Holding only the insulated portion, touch the bare ends to the terminals marked W and R. If the heating system starts to run, replace the thermostat. If nothing happens, troubleshoot or replace the transformer (page 215).

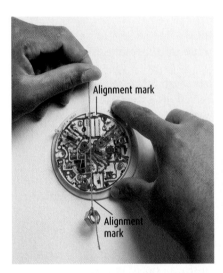

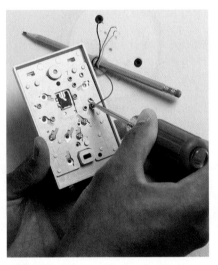

LEVELING A THERMOSTAT
If the temperature is always warmer or cooler than the thermostat setting, the thermostat may be out of level. Hold a level or a weighted string in front of the thermostat to see if the two alignment marks line up. If not, remove the mounting screws, realign the thermostat, and drive new screws.

REPLACING A LOW-VOLTAGE THERMOSTAT
Loosen the terminal screws and pull out the wires. Remove the mounting screws and pull out the plate. Clip the wires so they cannot slide back through the hole. Thread the wires through the new thermostat and hook the wires to the terminals. Check for leveling and attach the base to the wall with screws.

INVESTING IN A PROGRAMMABLE THERMOSTAT
Spend a little more and save money in the long run with a thermostat that adjusts heating or cooling several times a day.

14

ELECTRICAL REPAIRS

GLOSSARY

Amp. A measurement of the amount of electrical current in a circuit at any moment. *See also* Volt and Watt.

Antioxidant. A paste applied to aluminum wires to inhibit corrosion and maintain safe connections.

Armored cable. Two or more insulated wires wrapped in a protective metal sheathing.

Ballast. A transformer that regulates the voltage in a fluorescent lamp.

Bell wire. A thin, typically 18-gauge wire used for doorbells.

Box. A metal or plastic enclosure within which electrical connections are made.

Bus bar. A main power terminal to which circuits are attached in a fuse or breaker box. One bus bar serves the circuit's hot side; the other, the neutral side. Some service panels and all subpanels have separate neutral and ground bus bars.

BX. Armored cable containing insulated wires but no ground wire.

Cable. Two or more insulated wires wrapped in metal or plastic sheathing.

Canadian Standards Association (CSA). An independent testing agency that examines electrical components for safety hazards.

Circuit. The path of electrical flow from a power source through an outlet and back to ground.

Circuit breaker. A switch that automatically interrupts electrical flow in a circuit in case of an overload or short.

Codes, electrical. Laws and regulations governing safe wiring practices.

Common. A terminal on a three-way switch, usually with a dark-colored screw and marked COM.

Conductor. A wire or anything else that carries electricity.

Conduit. Rigid (metal or PVC) or flexible plastic tubing through which wires are run.

Continuity tester. An instrument that tells whether a device is capable of carrying electricity.

Dimmer. A rotary or sliding switch that lets you vary the intensity of a light.

Duplex receptacle. A device that includes two plug outlets. Most receptacles in homes are duplexes.

Electrical metallic tubing (EMT). Thin-walled, rigid conduit suitable for indoor use.

End-of-the-run. An adjective describing devices located at the end of a circuit. No wires continue from an end-of-the-run device's box to other receptacles, switches, or devices.

Feed wire. A wire that brings household current to a device.

Fishing. Pulling cables through finished walls, ceilings and conduit.

Fish tape. A hooked strip of spring steel used for fishing cables through walls and for pulling wires through conduit.

Fixture. Any light or other electrical device permanently attached to a home's wiring.

Flexible metal conduit. Tubing that can be easily bent by hand. *See also* Greenfield.

Fluorescent tube. A light source that uses an ionization process to produce ultraviolet radiation. This radiation becomes visible light when it hits the coated inner surface of the tube.

Four-way switch. A type of switch used to control a light from three or more locations.

Fuse. A safety device designed to stop electrical flow if a circuit shorts or is overloaded. Like a circuit breaker, a fuse protects against fire from overheated wiring.

Ganging. Assembling two or more electrical components into a single unit. Boxes, switches, and receptacles are often ganged.

Greenfield. Flexible metal conduit through which wires are pulled.

Ground. Refers to the fact that electricity always seeks the shortest possible path to the earth. Neutral wires carry electricity to ground in all circuits. An additional grounding wire, or the sheathing of metal-clad cable or conduit, protects against shock from a malfunctioning device.

Ground fault circuit interrupter (GFCI). A safety device that senses any shock hazard and shuts off a circuit or receptacle.

High-intensity discharge (HID). A type of lighting, including lamps such as halogen, mercury vapor, metal halide, and sodium. All HIDs produce a bright, economical light.

Hot wire. The conductor of current to a receptacle or other outlet. *See also* Neutral wire and Ground.

Incandescent bulb. A light source with an electrically charged metal filament that burns at white heat.

Insulation. A nonconductive covering that protects wires and other electricity carriers.

Junction box. An enclosure used for splitting circuits into different branches. In a junction box, wires connect only to each other, never to a switch, receptacle, or fixture.

Kilowatt (kW). One thousand watts. A kilowatt hour is the standard measure of electrical consumption.

Knockouts. Tabs that can be removed to make openings in a box for cable or conduit connectors.

LB connector or fitting. An elbow for conduit with access for pulling wires. Connections cannot be made within this fitting.

Lead. A short wire coming from a fixture, typically stranded, to which a household wire is spliced. It is used instead of a terminal.

MC cable. Armored cable containing at least two insulated wires and an insulated ground wire.

Middle-of-the-run. An adjective used to describe devices located between two other devices on a circuit. Wires continue from its box to other switches, receptacles or devices.

Multitester. A device that measures voltage in a circuit and performs other tests.

Neutral wire. A conductor that carries current from an outlet back to ground, clad in white insulation. *See also* Hot wire and Ground.

New-work box. A metal or plastic box attached to framing members before the wall material is installed.

Nonmetallic (NM) sheathed cable. Two or more insulated wires and a bare ground wire clad in a plastic covering.

Old-work box. *See* Remodel box.

Outlet. Any potential point of use in a circuit, including receptacles, switches, and light fixtures.

Overload. A condition that exists when a circuit is carrying more amperage than it was designed to handle. Overloading causes wires to heat up, which in turn blows fuses or trips circuit breakers.

Pigtail. A length of wire, stripped at both ends, spliced with one or more other wires. It is used instead of attaching two or more wires to a terminal, an unsafe connection.

Polarized plugs. Plugs designed so the hot and neutral sides of a circuit can't be accidentally reversed. One prong of the plug is a different shape than the other.

Raceway wiring. Surface-mounted channels for extending circuits.

Receptacle. An outlet that supplies power for lamps and other plug-in devices.

Recessed can light. A light fixture set into a wall cavity so the lens and trim are flush with the ceiling.

Remodel box. A metal or plastic box, sometimes called an "old-work" box, designed for a hole cut in drywall or plaster and lath.

Rigid conduit. Wire-carrying metal tubing that can be bent only with a special tool.

Romex. A trade name for nonmetallic sheathed cable. *See* Nonmetallic sheathed cable.

Service entrance. The point where power enters a home.

Service panel. The main fuse box or breaker box in a home.

Short circuit. A condition that occurs when hot and neutral wires contact each other. Fuses and breakers protect against fire, which can result from a short.

Stripping. Removing insulation from wire or sheathing from cable.

Subpanel. A subsidiary fuse box or breaker box linked to a service panel that has no room for additional circuits.

System ground. A wire connecting a service panel to the earth. It may be attached to a main water pipe, to a rod driven into the ground, or to a plate embedded along a footing.

Three-way switch. Operates a light from two locations.

Time-delay fuse. A fuse that does not break the circuit during the momentary overload that can happen when an electric motor starts up. If the overload continues, the fuse blows, shutting off the circuit.

Transformer. A device that reduces or increases voltage. In home wiring, transformers step down current for use with low-voltage equipment such as thermostats and doorbell systems.

Travelers. Two of the three conductors that run between switches in a 3-way installation.

Underwriters knot. A knot used as a strain relief for wires in a lamp socket.

Volt. A measure of electrical pressure. Volts x amps = watts.

Watt. A measure of the power an electrical device consumes. *See also* Volt, Amp, and Kilowatt.

Wire nut. A screw-on device used to splice two or more wires.

INDEX

INDEX

Bryan Verhulp
Ottawa, ON

John O'Reilly
Ottawa, ON

Mark Geertsema
Ottawa, ON

Andrew Yull
Whitby, ON

John L. Lane
San Mateo, CA

Guy Dixon
Folsom, CA

Gerald Morrow
Whitby, ON

Rudolph Kos
Plano, TX

Larry Cuttrell
McKinney, TX

John Tsigas
Scarborough, ON

Michael Bier
San Leandro, CA

**Many thanks to
the employees of
Home Depot® whose
"wisdom of the aisles"
has made Wiring 1-2-3®
the most useful
book of its kind.**

Victor Swaga
Scarborough, ON

Micheal Knish
Toronto, ON

H. Louis Topel
Richardson, TX

Barbara Fargo
Atlanta, GA

Kenneth Alley
Fort Worth, TX

Jeff Potts
Rockwall, TX

Keith Keller
San Ramon, CA

Sidney T. Smith
Plano, TX

Anne Reissing
Atlanta, GA

R. Keith Stanley
Cleburne, TX

Tom Sattler
Atlanta, GA

John Angle
Ancaster, ON

Ian Cleghorn
Scarborough, ON

Nathan D. Ehrlich
Atlanta, GA

John DeSantis
Ancaster, ON

Denis Woods
St. Catharines, ON

Jim McFarland
Ancaster, ON

Toolbox essentials: nuts-and-bolts books for do-it-yourself success.

Save money, get great results, and take the guesswork out of home improvement projects with a growing library of step-by-step books from the experts at The Home Depot®.

Packed with lots of projects and practical tips, these books help you design, remodel, decorate, and repair your home or garden. Easy-to-follow, step-by-step instructions and colorful photographs ensure success. Projects even estimate time, skills, materials, and tools required.

You can do it.
We can help.℠

Look for the books that help you say "I can do that!"
at The Home Depot,® www.meredithbooks.com,
or wherever quality books are sold.